Capitalizing on Language Learners' Individuality

MIX
Paper from
responsible sources
FSC
www.fsc.org   FSC® C013604

SECOND LANGUAGE ACQUISITION
Series Editor: Professor David Singleton, *Trinity College, Dublin, Ireland*

This series brings together titles dealing with a variety of aspects of language acquisition and processing in situations where a language or languages other than the native language is involved. Second language is thus interpreted in its broadest possible sense. The volumes included in the series all offer in their different ways, on the one hand, exposition and discussion of empirical findings and, on the other, some degree of theoretical reflection. In this latter connection, no particular theoretical stance is privileged in the series; nor is any relevant perspective – sociolinguistic, psycholinguistic, neurolinguistic etc. – deemed out of place. The intended readership of the series includes final-year undergraduates working on second language acquisition projects, postgraduate students involved in second language acquisition research, and researchers and teachers in general whose interests include a second language acquisition component.

Full details of all the books in this series and of all our other publications can be found on http://www.multilingual-matters.com, or by writing to Multilingual Matters, St Nicholas House, 31–34 High Street, Bristol BS1 2AW, UK.

Capitalizing on Language Learners' Individuality

From Premise to Practice

Tammy Gregersen and Peter D. MacIntyre

MULTILINGUAL MATTERS
Bristol • Buffalo • Toronto

Library of Congress Cataloging in Publication Data
Gregersen, Tammy, author.
Capitalizing on Language Learners' Individuality: From Premise to Practice/Tammy Gregersen and Peter D. MacIntyre.
Second Language Acquisition: 72
Includes bibliographical references and index.
1. Language and languages—Study and teaching. 2. Second language acquisition.
3. Individualized education programs. 4. Individualized instruction. I. MacIntyre, Peter D. – author. II. Title. III. Series: Second language acquisition; 72.
P53.G678 2013
418.0071–dc23 2013032426

British Library Cataloguing in Publication Data
A catalogue entry for this book is available from the British Library.

ISBN-13: 978-1-78309-120-1 (hbk)
ISBN-13: 978-1-78309-119-5 (pbk)

Multilingual Matters
UK: St Nicholas House, 31–34 High Street, Bristol BS1 2AW, UK.
USA: UTP, 2250 Military Road, Tonawanda, NY 14150, USA.
Canada: UTP, 5201 Dufferin Street, North York, Ontario M3H 5T8, Canada.

The policy of Multilingual Matters/Channel View Publications is to use papers that are natural, renewable and recyclable products, made from wood grown in sustainable forests. In the manufacturing process of our books, and to further support our policy, preference is given to printers that have FSC and PEFC Chain of Custody certification. The FSC and/or PEFC logos will appear on those books where full certification has been granted to the printer concerned.

Typeset by Techset Composition India (P) Ltd., Bangalore and Chennai, India.
Printed and bound in Great Britain by the CPI Group Ltd.

To Mi Vida, Mario:

Gracias a la vida...

Gracias a la Vida que me ha dado tanto
me ha dado el sonido y el abedecedario
Con el las palabras que pienso y declaro
madre amigo hermano y luz alumbrando,
La ruta del alma del que estoy amando.

Gracias a la Vida que me ha dado tanto
me ha dado la marcha de mis pies cansados
con ellos anduve ciudades y charcos,
playas y desiertos montañas y llanos
y la casa tuya, tu calle y tu patio.

And to my children, Reycito, Margie and the Abinator:

Gracias a la Vida que me ha dado tanto
me ha dado la risa y me ha dado el llanto,
así yo distingo dicha de quebranto
los dos materiales que forman mi canto
y el canto de ustedes que es el mismo canto
y el canto de todos que es mi propio canto.

I'd like to dedicate this work to my wife Anne,

Woman I can hardly express
My mixed emotions at my thoughtlessness
After all I'm forever in your debt
And woman I will try to express
My inner feelings and thankfulness
For showing me the meaning of success

– John Lennon, Woman

Also to my children Valerie and Robert

When the waves roll on over the waters
And the ocean cries
We look to our sons and daughters
To explain our lives
As if a child could tell us why

That as sure as the sunrise
As sure as the sea
As sure as the wind in the trees
We rise again in the faces
of our children
We rise again in the voices of our song
We rise again in the waves out on the ocean
And then we rise again

– Leon Dubinsky, Rise Again

Contents

Foreword

This volume offers a double-barrelled approach to understanding individuality in language learning by focusing on both the 'premise' and the 'practice' of individual differences as related to language learners. The premise section of each chapter offers theory and research about a given individual difference variable, such as learning strategies or motivation, and explains that area's importance or utility for language learning and teaching. In contrast, the practice section of each chapter provides hands-on activities related to that particular individual difference. We might think of these two sections of each chapter as the parts of a tree. The premise section comprises the roots and the trunk of the tree. The practice section constitutes the tree's crown, which, in turn, is made up of leaves and branches that reach out into the surrounding environment. Figure 1 shows the parts of a tree and indicates how the premise and the practice sections relate to those parts.

If one part is missing, the tree is not complete. A full-grown tree or even a tree on its way to full maturity cannot live and thrive without all of its parts. Similarly, any discussion of an individual difference variable is likely to have insufficient health and liveliness if the premise (i.e. the theory and research combined with comments about importance) is considered by itself, without any *practical* aspects, implications or outreach into the classroom.

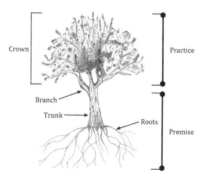

Figure 1 Premise to practice tree metaphor

Moreover, the practical aspects cannot stand on their own without a sufficient base of theory and research. These statements are reminiscent of the old saying, 'Theory without practice is futile, and practice without theory is fatal.' But as the title of this volume suggests, we must also consider the tree as a whole. Language learners are individuals and their 'differences' or characteristics permeate their experience and approaches in learning a second language. Individual difference research originated from the interest of researchers and teachers to explain why some learners were more successful than others. Contemporary research in individual differences, as this volume maintains, seeks to understand the individual experience of each language learner.

This book systematically looks at the premise and the practice within seven individual difference areas – anxiety, beliefs, cognitive abilities, motivation, learning strategies, learning styles, and willingness to communicate – that are of tremendous importance to language learning and teaching. In this way, the tree of individuality not only survives but thrives.

Let us pursue the tree metaphor still further. In the psychology of language learning, individual differences are typically understood as contrasts between or among people with respect to phenomena such as motivation, anxiety and learning styles. However, to understand how people differ in terms of psychological variables, it is essential to understand the 'inner workings' of these variables *within* a given person. In other words, we need to grasp not only interpersonal differences (differences among a group of people) but also intrapersonal dynamics (how the phenomena actually operate inside someone). Looking only at the differences between or among people is like observing just the outer aspects of the tree. Examining the inner workings or intrapersonal dynamics of a given phenomenon within a person goes further, like moving beneath the bark of the tree trunk or peering inside the leaves. Both of these views are important. Please keep the tree metaphor in the back of your mind as you read and cherish this valuable book.

Rather than reiterating the information in the books' introduction, we would like to share some of the most notable aspects of the book. One of these is the creative, story-based way that the premise sections open themselves to the reader. For instance, the premise of the anxiety chapter opens with a short paragraph about debilitating anxiety but then immediately moves to a story – a parable – about a water bearer and his load. The premise of the beliefs chapter contains a story about a wealthy father taking his son on a trip to see how the poor live, but the son interprets the findings entirely differently from the father because of differences in their beliefs. In the cognitive abilities chapter, the opening of the premise sparkles with the stories of Charles Darwin, Albert Einstein and August Rodin, all of whom were considered cognitively deficient by those around them. The premise of the motivation chapter touches on the story of Sir Edmund Hillary, the first person to reach the summit of Mount Everest; consider how strong his motivation must have been. The parable of the donkey falling into a well introduces the premise section of the learning strategies chapter. A boy and a butterfly populate a story that highlights the premise of the learning styles chapter. Two paradoxes, one about Taeko and the other about John, both students, open the premise of the chapter on willingness to communicate. These stories, while very different in content, have some general characteristics in common. First, they are intriguing. Second, they are accessible and relevant, bringing us face to face with the phenomenon being discussed. Third, they offer a painless way to enter a particular area of individual differences. Finally, and perhaps most importantly, they demonstrate that individual differences and learning are not isolated phenomena but aspects of a total human being and his or her life history.

Another notable aspect of the book is the richness of the activities in the practice section of any given chapter. Let us take, for example, the chapter on willingness to communicate (Chapter 7). The practice activities in Chapter 7 include the focused essay technique. A modification mentioned by the authors is to put the essay into a Wiki document to which learners can contribute. A second activity concerns exploring driving and restraining forces that influence willingness to communicate (WTC). This is done through a beautiful sequence of events for students: keeping a daily list in language diaries, analyzing the data in a table, summarizing main driving and restraining forces in sentences, randomly receiving summary sentences of others and giving feedback, receiving one's own sentences with feedback from others, and then having a debriefing. Modifications are given for emergent learners and for the uses of different technologies, such as mobile hand-held electronic recording devices for oral practice, electronic journals for written practice, and discussion boards. A third WTC activity focuses on past experiences to increase perceived competence. That activity contains seven steps from purposing to debriefing, with two technology-related modifications. The fourth WTC activity concerns 'if-then' scenarios that can convert intentions into actions. Not only are there seven useful steps, but there are also modifications for emergent learners, large groups, and different types of technology. These are just four of the ten activities for this chapter. Imagine the richness and plentitude of activities such as these, which are found not only in this chapter but are spread across all seven individual-difference chapters in the volume. In our experience, language teachers value the concept of meeting the needs of all learners, but the realities of modern classrooms make that objective truly challenging. This volume offers teachers concrete and realistic ideas to help them embrace their students' individuality.

A remarkable feature of this book has already been intimated: the intentional way that the book caters to a wide range of learners and their teachers. The activities can be used by emergent learners (pre-beginners), as well as by beginning, intermediate, and advanced learners. They can also be employed by those who have access to high-level technology and those who do not.

Moreover, the chapters can be approached in any order, meaning that teachers can 'redesign' the book in any way they wish. All of these features make the book extraordinarily accessible.

An additionally useful characteristic is that the book does not become muddied or muddled by theoretical arguments by experts in the field of individual differences. For instance, the area of learning strategies has been marked by great differences of opinion about how to define, categorize, and explain these strategies. The chapter on learning strategies in the present book refuses to sink itself (literally) into these weighty arguments but instead finds value in multiple theoretical perspectives on learning strategies. Similar things can be said about the chapter on motivation. In other words, the authors are open to the best ideas in a given area, without feeling the need to adjudicate differences among theorists.

To return to the initial metaphor, this book captures the vibrancy of the tree's roots and trunk (the premise), with its crowning branches and leaves (the practice) that reach outward into language classrooms and into the hearts of learners and their teachers. The premises and the practice activities embodied in this volume constitute a great resource to language instructors and students alike.

Rebecca Oxford and Elaine K. Horwitz

Introduction

Teachers who effectively capitalize on their learners' individuality view their language classrooms as a kaleidoscope. When they pan across the room moving from learner to learner, savvy teachers see unique and colorful designs. The patterns are in constant motion even when looking at one particular learner. Not only are language learners different one from another, but learners change – and sometimes it's because teachers change them. The way that a learner feels, thinks and acts in one moment is different from the feelings, thoughts and actions that he or she experienced a moment ago or from what will be experienced in the next.

A learner's behavior, thoughts and emotions are interwoven into a dynamic system. We can and do discuss individual differences among learners as if they are relatively stable traits: Johnny is extroverted, Santana is conscientious, Reiko is a nice person. But even as we see the stability in learners' actions and reactions, they are changing – sometimes in subtle ways and sometimes in substantial ways. The various attributes of a learner are interconnected – like a fishing net. If we tug on one end of the net, the shape of the entire net changes. Teachers are continuously tugging on the learner's net by their activity choices, their instruction, their feedback, and their mentorship.

Even as teachers create lesson plans with learning goals and objectives, they are continuously (maybe unconsciously) engaging learners' individuality in powerful and personal ways. At times, language learning can be a difficult chore but language is the most powerful tool humans have to connect with one another. In every case, languages are learned by a person who has thoughts and feelings. Both positive and negative emotions figure prominently in the learning process. On the one hand, studies of the psychology of negative emotions reveal that they have a specific role to play in our experience. Negative emotions tend to focus attention on specific events and predispose people to certain types of actions. For example, anger tends to be associated with an obstacle or obstruction, disposing us to act to eliminate or destroy the obstacle. This is not a bad thing at all – successful learners overcome obstacles. But the negative emotion has additional effects that can be less facilitating. On the other hand, recent theory in positive emotion points to its power to broaden our field of attention and build resources for the future. For example, when we are happy, we are more likely to notice pleasant things that might have escaped our attention otherwise. Positive emotions help us to build relationships, personal strength, and tolerances for the moments when things become difficult.

Our book seeks to close the gap between theory and classroom application concerning individual differences in second or foreign language (FL) learning. Through an exploration of the existing literature and theoretical underpinnings of each of the most prominent learner characteristics – anxiety, beliefs, cognitive abilities, motivation, learning strategies, learning styles, and willingness to communicate – teachers expand their knowledge and become better equipped to meet the challenges created by negative-narrowing affect and capitalize on the positive-broadening power of facilitative emotions as they guide their learners through the research-based activities specifically created to inspire learners' self-discovery in an affectively nurturing environment while learning a target language (TL). Until now, teachers' access to books on the psychology of the language learner and what makes each one unique has been limited to those which take a predominantly theoretical perspective with few practical classroom activities offered. Although innovative language learning activity books also have been available, few provide the research contexts that would inform the intellectually curious reader about reasons why certain techniques are more effective than others. This book is our attempt to wed pioneering research premises with innovative practices.

From Premise...

Readers can pick and choose from among the chapters in any order. Each chapter concentrates on a psychological/cognitive variable or a combination of closely related ones and begins with answers to the questions: 'What is it?' 'Where does it come from?' and 'Why is this important?' Once definitions, origins and significance for the given variable are established, readers explore pedagogical implications that include research applications that directly impact classroom practices. Although individual differences (ID) researchers in the past have rarely outlined specific step-by-step classroom activities, many have often proposed valuable guiding principles meant to steer teachers in the direction of more effective and affective classroom techniques. These principles directly inspired the activities in each chapter and provide the order for their sequence.

Language anxiety, as characterized in the Premise Section of our chapter, concerns the negative-narrowing worry experienced by learners as they use their TL, arising in part from a learner's cognizance that the authenticity of self and its expression cannot be communicated as readily in his or her second language as in the first. Debilitating anxiety engenders undesirable consequences in a variety of domains, including the physical, emotional/affective, cognitive/linguistic and interactional/social. The activities in the Practice Section target actions that teachers and learners can take to create positive-broadening comfort zones characterized by mutual encouragement and community building. For teachers, we offer opportunities to review instructional choices, classroom procedures and assessment practices. For learners, we provide tasks that focus attention on previous achievement and progress rather than past failure and expectations of perfection. For teachers and learners working together, we present activities that promote the community-building and social networks necessary for positive interaction.

The Premise Section of our chapter on 'Beliefs' recognizes that students and teachers hold countless notions about language learning that influence their behavior and impact the choices they make. Formed through a variety of sources – such as previous experience, observation and imitation, or through listening to others – teachers' and learners' beliefs cover an assortment of issues ranging from the nature and difficulty of language learning to individually defined expectations and motivations. These preconceived ideas fall on a wide array of continuums that range from harmful to helpful; from erroneous to accurate; and from destructive to productive. Through the activities in the Practice Section, we hope to shift learners' negative-narrowing beliefs to positive-broadening ones through processes that clarify teachers' and learners' beliefs, increase self-awareness, address any mismatches between what learners and teachers believe, and directly confront specific ill-advised and counter-productive beliefs.

Our chapter on cognitive abilities brings together premises and practices for capitalizing on aptitude, working memory and multiple intelligences. We characterize them as interrelated dynamic variables as well as notions deserving of consideration as separate domains as learners process information and obtain new knowledge. In the Practice Section, our aptitude activities provide opportunities for learners to increase their skills with the four macro-components of noticing, patterning, controlling and lexicalizing language forms; our working memory activities encourage learners to maximize their storage and processing capacities through repetition and rehearsal of input, visualization, invoking schema, and experimenting with working memory strategies; and our activities that target multiple intelligences offer thematically organized interdisciplinary tasks that promote cooperative learning and provide learners with choices to awaken and amplify a variety of intelligences.

Rather than highlighting differences among motivational theories, our chapter on motivation emphasizes the congruencies among several, including those grounded in social and cognitive psychology. We introduce the importance of a process orientation to account for dynamic moment-to-moment changes that occur in the classroom with particular consideration to the role of tasks. Looking at motivation in this way draws out the social and emotional nature of learning, where identity, self, and the imagination figure prominently. The motivational qualities of integrativeness and imagination are interwoven among many of our activities as learners: explore their social identity by understanding their own investment and imagined communities; develop their international posture and bi-cultural identity; and create, strengthen, substantiate, activate, operationalize, and balance their possible selves.

While acknowledging the complicated task of finding a consensual definition for language learning strategies, we propose in our Premise Section that they are consciously or semi-consciously chosen by learners. Strategies operate on a continuum between being intentionally deliberate and fully automatic, are purposeful and goal-directed and can be enhanced through instruction. We contend that the self-regulatory function of strategies is optimized when learners make choices that consider the specific learning context, including the individual learner, the task, and the environment and that the effectiveness of strategies is not measured by the frequency of their use, but rather their appropriate exploitation within a given context. To meet the primary goal of increasing learners' self-regulation, our Practice Section contains activities that take learners through a series of sequential tasks that raise and deepen learners' strategy awareness and provide opportunities for presenting, modeling, practicing, transferring and evaluating strategies.

We cast a broad net in our Premise Section on Learning Styles by characterizing them as 'comfort zones' – those 'go-to places' where both teachers and learners can approach learning by drawing upon their preferences and habits – which can include personality and/or sensory preferences as well as cognitive styles. As value-neutral preferences, there are no 'end-all' learning styles to which all learners must cater to find success. With this in mind, throughout our Practice Section we capitalize on the diversity of learning styles found in language classrooms by advocating a 'mixed and many' approach that provides balance and choice. Presented in pairs that allow teachers and learners to experiment with matching AND stretching their comfort zones, our activities promote teachers' discovery of their own instructional preferences, encourage learners' exploration and definition of their favored learning approaches, foster teacher-learner teamwork in the pursuit of balance, juxtapose tasks that expose learners to both style matching and stretching, and provide opportunities for learners to reflect and gain insight into their strategies, linguistic progress and affective responses under matching and stretching conditions.

Willingness to Communicate (WTC) is described in our Premise Section as a conglomeration of dynamic antecedents – both enduring and situational – to TL communication that potentially facilitates or inhibits language learners' in-the-moment decisions to speak. Our activities in the Practice

Section seek to increase learners' volition to use their TL by turning the tide of learners' ambivalence, reducing learners' restraining forces and energizing their driving ones, increasing learners' perceived competence, converting learners' intentions into actions, limiting learners' hesitations, balancing temperament, reflecting on future uses of the TL, intensifying classroom excitement and security and exploring the multi-componential nature of self-esteem.

To Practice...

Each activity guides learners through a series of steps aimed at improving language proficiency by increasing learners' self-awareness, autonomy and emotional well-being in a comfortable and supportive environment. Intuitive teachers recognize the dynamic relationship among a learner's language skill, emotional/psychological state, and classroom atmosphere. Often, to improve one is to advance all three. In attempting to meet this three-part objective, we interweave several fundamental principles that transform traditional classroom practices and alter teacher roles. We advocate simple classroom procedures such as:

- asking for volunteers rather than calling on individuals;
- integrating the four skills by exposing learners to large amounts of varied, authentic input and providing opportunities for extended genuine output;
- utilizing dyads and small groups rather than whole or large group venues;
- using out-of-class naturalistic interactions as a basis for in-class tasks;
- setting wide task parameters to allow for greater learner choice; and
- allowing learners to use their first language when it facilitates communication in the TL or when the affective benefits outweigh the linguistic costs.

We also revise teachers' job descriptions. Because our activities incite learners to generate considerable written and spoken authentic output while interacting in small groups and dyads on both sides of the classroom door, teachers move from center-stage to back-stage, intermingling and working together with students while still maintaining their directing and facilitating roles. Simultaneously, the activities spur learners on to develop their receptive skills through reading and listening to naturalistic input in a variety of interactional venues – thus transforming the teacher from orator of course book dictations to purveyor of interesting opportunities.

The activities are described in an easy-to-implement format with limited previous teacher preparation time, sophisticated materials or technology necessary. (However, for teachers whose classrooms are well-equipped technologically or who have tech-savvy learners, we have included ideas for modifying the tasks.) Each activity includes:

(1) targeted language proficiency level;
(2) an inspirational quote;
(3) before class preparations, when necessary;
(4) step-by-step procedures including a preface and an opportunity for debriefing; and
(5) modifications for emergent learners, large classes, and technology, where appropriate.

The language proficiency ratings are roughly based on the broad categories of beginning, intermediate, and advanced. Some 'intermediate/advanced' activities contain adjustments for emergent learners in the 'modifications' section following the procedures. We have created the majority of our activities for multiple-level proficiencies. Adjustments can be made by teachers in situ through strategic scaffolding and instruction, changing the difficulty of language forms targeted, altering the complexity of the teacher-provided authentic materials, and/or varying the teacher-defined levels of fluency and/or accuracy of the students' work. Our modifications for emergent learners include precise ways of carrying out those alterations. In addition, we provide specific modifications for large classes, and because pedagogically sound strategies for sizeable groups often intersect with best practices for all, many 'large group' strategies are interwoven throughout our 'mainstream' procedures, such as:

• breaking into small groups or dyads for discussion, role play, or exchanging feedback;
• using language diaries for reflections and responses;
• integrating peer and self-assessment;
• asking volunteers at intervals to summarize or paraphrase whole group discussions; and
• incorporating peer tutoring.

Explicit modifications for large groups include among other things, adjustments to interaction strategies, de-briefing suggestions and different feedback and assessment approaches. Technology modifications, described later in the introduction, also mitigate many of the problems posed when teachers must accommodate instruction to many learners, each with their own unique individuality.

We share an inspirational quote at the beginning of each activity that is directly connected to our affective aim and is meant to create an emotional vibe. Use them as activity openers, triggers for small group discussions, prompts for journal entries, or as any other creative stimulus to focus learners' attention on the positive and to frame their minds for the ensuing tasks.

Instructions for the few activities that need preparation are found in the 'In Preparation' segment. Extending from the minimal preparations of arranging the physical classroom for enhanced learner interaction, to the more moderately time-consuming preparations of writing on and hanging newsprint or poster paper on walls, to the rare occasions when teachers compose artifacts to account for the idiosyncrasies of their specific learners, we attempted to limit the amount of time and planning teachers need to prepare by supplying as much background information as possible.

All activities begin with a 'preface,' end with a 'de-briefing' and contain step-by-step procedures that often culminate in oral or written authentic artifacts that can be used along with the de-briefing feedback as alternative assessments to informally and formatively measure the attainment of the activities' objective(s). The preface defines and focuses on the specific linguistic and/or affective objectives that undergird the entire activity, and when teachers share those objectives, it allows learners to appreciate the tasks' purpose(s), and more importantly, it informs learners as to *why* they are doing it. Every objective, firmly grounded in research, is directly connected to information in the chapter's preceding 'Premise' section. This information keeps learners abreast of SLA processes and how languages are learned – an important contributing factor that applied linguists suggest is pivotal to the positive affect that accompanies a learner's metalinguistic and self-awareness. The objective found in the premise also clearly articulates a goal to guide teachers' post-activity reflection and appraisal of the objective's attainment, ideas that we will return to later in the introduction when we discuss assessment.

The 'de-briefing prompt' at the conclusion of each activity allows students to digest what they learned experientially and to reflect upon implications for their future autonomous language learning endeavors. The learners' linguistic and affective feedback informs teachers' subsequent instructional decisions and provides a basis for whether specific activities are worth repeating. Although we often suggest that prefacing is done in a whole group venue in order to address learners' questions and provide activity instructions, we recommend teachers of large groups to use alternatives to whole class de-briefings as this format frequently becomes unwieldy and denies some learners the opportunity to respond. Furthermore, reticent learners may choose to forfeit participation in spontaneous unrehearsed speech in front of sizeable groups. In these instances, we recommend that post-activity feedback discussions occur in small groups with an appointed recorder, through written responses to the de-briefing prompts in learners' language diaries, or through other creative means that guarantee that all learners have the opportunity to be heard, that venues are provided for tentative speakers, and that whenever possible teachers have access to the feedback.

In between the objective-defining preface and the feedback-producing de-briefing is a series of tasks that guide learners to increased language proficiency by capitalizing on greater affective/emotional self-awareness in a comfortable and supportive classroom environment. These tasks produce an artifact – taking any myriad of authentic forms like dyadic conversations, group role plays, or lists of brainstormed ideas, among other possibilities – that can be assessed to measure learners' growth and provide data for teachers' instructional decision-making.

Assessment

Effective teachers understand that successful instruction is not the mere execution of language tasks, but that it begins with learner-centered measurable and explicitly communicated objectives and does not end until those objectives are assessed with alternative tools whose criteria for evaluation were provided to learners from the outset. Hence, the practices outlined in this book are optimized by strategic teachers who complete the following assessment cycle for each activity:

1. Define purpose and/or objectives and clearly communicate them

Each activity contains a series of tasks that targets a single objective or focuses on several different but related ones. By carefully reading the preface for each activity, teachers extract the objective and use it to complete the sentence, 'Through these tasks, learners will...' From these objectives, teachers formulate a question ('Did the learner...?') that will be answered by the data gathered through the artifact.

2. Identify the artifact(s) produced from the tasks

Every activity generates one or more artifacts that need to be plainly distinguished (e.g. oral/written, group/individual) in order to create the appropriate instruments.

3. Create and implement informal formative assessment tools with criteria clearly established and communicated

Because naturalistic authentic tasks generate the majority of the artifacts, somewhat unconventional assessment tools and techniques are necessary to assess them. Couple this with the need for teacher access to the results for reflection and future action, and quite a complex set of assessment requirements is created. Concerning which tools to use, rubrics and observation checklists containing simple language, well-defined observable criteria, and categories ranging simply from one (1) to three (3) will suffice. We believe that these tools are sufficient to meet the formative purposes of providing feedback on goal achievement without over-burdening teachers and learners with formal summative instruments. Formal evaluation can come with the baggage of negative-narrowing emotion that defeats the original purpose of using fun alternative language learning techniques to improve learner affect and create a supportive environment. In reference to techniques, peer and self-evaluations guided by well-designed tools provide an effective alternative style of evaluation because they develop learners' autonomy and self-direction, making learners responsible for their own learning and assessment. Informal teacher observation conducted with rubric or checklist in hand while mingling among interacting dyads or small groups also provides a solution to supplying evidence of progress and goal compliance in an affective, non-threatening way. These alternative tools and techniques create the positive-broadening effect of seamlessly transitioning from instruction to assessment, leaving learners wondering where language practice ended and testing began.

3. Use results from the artifact assessments coupled with learner feedback from de-briefing to decide on the next action plan

Reflective teachers understand the necessity of triangulating assessment (artifact) data with learners' own (de-briefing) interpretations to assemble an ample perspective of learners' linguistic progress and affective states. Action plans are continually modified, data-driven, works-in-progress that consider the degree to which learners attained the language/affective objectives of an activity and teachers' appraisal of how to most effectively move forward from that point onward.

We have provided an example of how to complete our four-step assessment cycle by applying it to the first activity of the Anxiety chapter (p. 14).

A few final words on assessment... Formal summative testing is often a negative-narrowing stimulus for many learners in traditional language classrooms. Throughout the premise sections of most of our chapters, readers discover that it frequently wreaks havoc on learners' motivation and self-confidence and induces debilitating anxiety. Rather than being an impetus to celebrate language learning progress, testing is repeatedly used punitively to show learners what they failed to accomplish. Furthermore, traditional evaluative procedures provide limited evidence of a learner's linguistic ability in naturalistic out-of-class communicative interactions – skills which most learners undoubtedly value over the ability to correctly conjugate present tense verbs on a written fill-in-the-blank grammar test. Thus, for the language and affective objectives we define in our activities to be fully met, they must be assessed in positive-broadening ways, continually informing learners of task objectives and assessment criteria.

Technology

Although we recommend specific technology modifications for many of our activities, creative language teachers will easily find a myriad of other ways to implement technology to meet activities' objectives. The abundance of fun and engaging opportunities available with technology make it easy to get distracted from core instructional objectives, thus making it imperative that teachers ponder several variables before deciding on which technologies to use. For example, sometimes affective objectives like maintaining learner anonymity to stimulate the nonjudgmental flow of ideas during electronic brainstorming will take priority over the interaction that could be stimulated if the same exercise is done on the electronic class discussion board where contributors are identified. Consider the affective implications of synchronous communication technologies like chats (where learners have little time to plan and revise) versus asynchronous communication like blogs (where learners can plan, write, and revise before posting). Think about language objectives for speaking and listening. Their attainment may be facilitated when the nonverbal cues that accompany social conversation are visualized through learner-posted videotaped exchanges. However, reading and writing objectives are targeted more accurately with the use of blogs, discussion boards and wikis. Blogs and electronic diaries catalogue learners' written contributions in one place, allowing learners to access the continuity of their thoughts and their language progress, but makes commenting from others cumbersome; class discussion boards, on the other hand, are designed for learners to interact and exchange ideas with ease. When weighing the benefits of the continuity afforded by blogs or the interaction provided by discussion boards, which best meets learner goals? Is the collaborative easy-to-modify wiki more efficient for writing group compositions than exchanging email attachments? Does the succinct nature of learners tweeting feedback trump the more inclusive detailed responses that learners could provide through blogs or discussion boards? It is imperative that teachers not lose sight of their objectives in pursuit of the glitz, so before pursuing the bells and whistles of some incredibly enticing innovative technology, pause and reflect upon:

- Are learner objectives focused on receptive (listening and reading) or productive (reading and speaking) skills?
- Are learner objectives best attained through responder anonymity? Should input be available for comment?
- How important is it that learners see and have access to a running account of their own work?
- How much visualization is necessary to optimize understanding?
- Does asynchronous or synchronous communication best meet learner objectives?

- How much collaboration is desired?
- How synthesized should the end product be?

We provide short descriptions of some of the most popular electronic classroom tools available – all of which are mentioned as alternatives at some point in our activities. After the descriptions, Table 1 offers an at-a-glance summary of the characterizing features of each option for teachers to consider in answering the above questions. Keep in mind that our technology suggestions are only a starting point to spark teachers to further creativity.

(1) **Mobile hand-held devices** capture on-the-spot language data in electronic format through using text or voice input, thus making the language learning diary 'electronic'. Many of today's cellular telephones are not limited to the mere recording of audio data but are also capable of capturing video images. Although the audio technology is ideal for learners to record language in naturalistic settings to be used and processed later in class activities, the video capacity allows learners to videotape one another in role plays and other speaking exchanges for later viewing.

(2) **Blogs** (**Web + Log**) are personal websites 'owned' by individuals (or groups) that allow them to share a running narrative of events and/or reflections with an online audience. Although blogs are often considered 'online journals,' conversation is facilitated by comments that readers (not anonymously) add to the 'owner's' posts, but content is considered static in the sense that once posted, the posting does not change. Although not the most ideal technology for collaboration and interaction, it does provide learners with a more personal space to reflect and store a *written* running account of their thoughts and serve as a medium to view their language progress.

(3) **Wikis**, invaluable as a collaborative composition tool, are web pages that permit learners to create and modify pages easily and quickly. Unlike blogs, content is effortlessly revised and comments are not expected. Content can be displayed in nodes or in a tree structure, which provides even greater potential for language classroom application.

(4) **Discussion boards** are ideal for soliciting learner responses through posting or answering questions to idea 'threads' created by either the teacher or the learners. As a collaborative tool, they effectively provide a forum for brainstorming and decision-making. Although the fact that learners are identified when they post is beneficial for teachers who desire to monitor learner progress and feedback, it may not be the most advantageous for brainstorming where anonymity is often desired.

(5) **Electronic brainstorming** can be done electronically through EMS (electronic meeting systems), via email, or with peer-to-peer software. With an electronic meeting system, learners independently share their

Table 1 At-a-glance technology use summary

	Reading/ writing	Speaking/ listening	Anonymous	Input for comment	Collaborative	Visualization (still images)	Visualization (video)	Synchronous	Asynchronous	Readily available artiface	Eloborated learner feedback	Succinct feedback
Hand-held devices	X	X					X	X	X			X
Blogs	X			X	X				X	X	X	X
Wikis	X			X	X				X	X	X	X
Discussion board	X			X	X				X	X	X	
Electronic brainstorm	X		X	X	X			X	X	X		X
Chat	X			X				X			X	
Voicethread	X	X		X	X	X	X		X	X	X	X
YouTube		X					X		X			
Twitter	X			X	X				X	X		X
Tumblr	X	X		X	X	X	X		X	X		X
Skype	X	X			X	X	X	X	X	X	X	
Powerpoint/Prezi	X	X		X	X	X			X	X	X	
Google Docs	X			X	X	X		X	X	X	X	

ideas through a network where their (usually) anonymous contributions are immediately seen by everyone. Electronic brainstorming can also be done asynchronously over extended time, archiving information in its original form for later retrieval and further discussion. Both the anonymousness and the fact that learners have time to plan and rehearse their input before posting their ideas and feedback encourage candidness and limit the fear of evaluation.

(6) **Chatting** is the synchronous transmission of text-based messages between or among learners. The real-time interactive nature of chatting exercises learners' spontaneous written language production.

(7) **Voicethread** (www.voicethread.com) is a website (no software needed) where group exchanges can be gathered and shared in one place through collaborative multimedia slide presentations that contain still images, documents and/or videos. Learners can navigate slides and leave their comments through writing and/or speaking using a microphone, telephone, text, audio file or video webcam.

(8) **YouTube** (www.youtube.com) is a user-generated video-sharing website where individuals upload their own or view other people's videos as well as movie, TV and music clips. The wide array of easily accessed videos on almost any subject imaginable use authentic language in naturalistic venues that provide learners with excellent listening opportunities and cultural content to serve as topics for conversation and writing.

(9) **Twitter** (www.twitter.com) allows learners to hone the succinctness of their writing skills by texting 'tweets' of up to 140 characters through an online social networking service. Teachers will also find it ideal for collecting quick learner feedback filed into easily read lists by asking learners to 'hash tag' their texts.

(10) **Tumblr** (www.tumblr.com) provides learners with a space to post and peruse multimedia in the form of text, audio, still images, animation or video to a blog, called a 'tumblelog.' The versatile media options allow for the integration of the four skills and the availability of visualization alternatives provides scaffolding for language and multiple venues for feedback.

(11) **Skype** (www.skype.com) allows learners to synchronously communicate by voice, video and/or instant messaging, thus providing alternatives for the exercise of all four language skills. Other interesting features for language classroom use include the ability to group chat, store chat histories and edit previous messages.

(12) **Powerpoint or Prezi** both allow learners to make presentations that contain text, graphics, sound, movies, and/or other media but while Powerpoint is an at-cost software program constructed of individual pages or 'slides,' Prezi is a free web-based application tool that uses a single canvas. Presentations can be printed, shown live on a computer,

or navigated through by the user. For whole class viewing, the computer display can be projected using a data projector. The visualization provided and the potential integration of the four skills make these presentations an optimal language classroom resource.

(13) **Google Docs on Google Drive** allows for the creation of documents and presentations that can also be saved and sent via email. It is a collaborative tool that permits the editing of documents and presentations in real time which can be shared, opened, and edited by multiple users simultaneously. The features that make Google Docs interesting for our purposes is the ability for learners to synchronously collaborate on writing projects and upload photos for subsequent presentations that allow slide by slide exhibition.

The options listed (excluding mobile hand-held devices which are usually personally owned communication devices like cellular phones) are readily and publically available on the internet, but most demand that all users have an email account. Users can set up blogs, wikis, and discussion boards through a variety of free online providers while YouTube, Voicethread and Prezi are accessible directly through their own web addresses. Email accounts on servers like Yahoo!, Hotmail, and Gmail, among others, provide a synchronous chat function. To use Twitter, Tumblr, and Skype, all users need to set up a personal account at each web location.

Finally, we leave the technology modifications discussion with a few tips on combining specific technologies with techniques. The language learning diary figures prominently throughout our activities as a critical information source: as a de-briefing mechanism where learners use it as a space to reflect and provide feedback to teachers; as a storehouse of in-progress tasks (e.g. gathering naturalistic out-of-class data to be used for in-class interaction); and as a repository to house finished artifacts which teachers periodically collect and formatively assess. The language diary's importance demands extra deliberation concerning the form teachers want it to take. Although circumstances may limit some teachers' choices to paper and pencil versions, other teachers may have the infrastructure to contemplate learners' use of blogs, wikis and discussion boards. Teachers who want to transform the language diary from a reading and writing activity to a speaking and listening one may want to recommend the use of mobile hand-held devices to capture oral data which can be later re-played and used as the corpus for listening activities, and of course combinations of 'some' or 'all of the above' is another possible alternative.

Activities culminate in a de-briefing session which includes a specific prompt for reflection and discussion. This creates an ideal occasion for any of the following technology modifications: (a) Respond to a teacher-created thread on the class discussion board; (b) Create an entry in electronic language diaries (for written practice, use the word processing option; for oral practice, use the mobile, hand-held device option); (c) Post to learner's personal blog; (d) Tweet a response; or (e) Skype with peers. Beyond the motivation that this technology might arouse, it also solves the problems of unwieldy large groups and reticent learners, and depending on the technology chosen, it could focus on any of the four skills, be asynchronously collaborative, or synchronously interactive. Reiterating these technology modifications after each activity would have gotten redundant so we include them here as regular and reliable de-briefing techniques.

In conclusion, the kaleidoscope of individual differences among learners affect how well they respond to language learning, and while these differences are relatively stable features, they are also dynamic, interacting, and influenced by their learning contexts – where teachers play a pivotal role. Although a learner might, at times, experience considerable anxiety, defend long standing counter-productive beliefs about language learning, suffer from low motivation or perceive less-than-optimal aptitude, the teacher who stimulates that learner to greater self-awareness, provides a cooperative community-building environment, and focuses on success rather than failure, creates the positive-broadening emotions and attitudes that increase willingness to communicate in the TL and facilitate more effective learning. Furthermore, through strategy training and experimenting with style matching and stretching teachers provide balance, choice and individualization, and are rewarded in return with more self-regulated learners.

As you peruse this text and choose those activities you think your learners will benefit from, we trust that you have as much fun implementing these activities together with your students as we did in creating them!

1 Anxiety

From Premise...

Unchecked debilitating foreign language anxiety has destructive consequences on the language learners who suffer from it. Negative self-comparisons, excessive self-evaluations, worry over potential failures, concern over thoughts of others: these are some of the self-related thoughts that have anxious language learners focusing on their flaws rather than on their achievements, thus limiting the positive interaction and community-building that characterizes supportive language learning environments. In the following story, the 'cracked pot' is somewhat analogous to language anxious learners. He feels distress and shame over his flaws and even with evidence of the positive outcomes in the form of beautiful flowers, still needs to be encouraged.

A water bearer had two large pots, one hanging on each end of a pole he carried over his shoulders. The two pots were equal in size and splendor, except for the small crack along the side of one of the pots. At the end of the long walk from the stream to the master's house, the cracked pot always arrived only half full. For two years this went on daily, with the bearer delivering one-and-a-half pots full of water to his master's house. Of course, the perfect pot was proud of its accomplishments, knowing it had fulfilled its purpose each day. But the miserable cracked pot was ashamed of its imperfection, and that it was only able to do half the work of the perfect pot.

After two years of enduring this bitter shame, the pot spoke to the water bearer one day by the stream. 'I am ashamed of myself and I want to apologize to you.'

'Why?' asked the bearer. 'What are you ashamed of?'

'For these past two years I have only been able to deliver half my load because this crack in my side causes water to leak out all the way back to your master's house. Because of my flaws, you have to do all of this work, and you don't get full value from your efforts,' the pot said.

The water bearer felt sorry for the old cracked pot, and in his compassion, said, 'As we return to the master's house, I want you to notice the beautiful flowers along the path.'

Indeed, as they went up the hill, the old cracked pot took notice of the sun warming the beautiful wild flowers on the side of the path, and was cheered somewhat. But at the end of the trail, it still felt the familiar shame losing half its load, and so again, the pot apologized to the bearer for its failure.

The bearer said to the pot, 'Did you not notice that there were flowers only on your side of the path, and not on the other pot's side? That's because I have always known about your flaw, and I took advantage of it. I planted flower seeds on your side of the path, and every day while we've walked back from the stream, you've watered them. For two years I have been able to pick these beautiful flowers to decorate my master's table. Without you being just the way you are, he would not have this beauty to grace his house.'

To make an even stronger connection with how foreign language anxious students feel, take a moment to think about how you projected yourself in your TL as compared to your L1 as you first attempted to communicate. If you were like many other beginning TL speakers, while you probably considered yourself somewhat articulate in your first language – kind of funny ... sort of intelligent ... authentically you – you may have feared that others thought your jokes were not quite as funny, that they questioned your intelligence, and that the 'self' you communicated in your TL was somehow not the same person you were in your L1. It is this very awareness of the inability to authentically communicate who we are in our first languages when using our second languages that is the impetus for foreign language anxiety. These feelings can leave learners apprehensive about communicating, fearful of negative evaluation, and suffering from test anxiety (Horwitz et al., 1986). In the classroom context, anxious students have reported that the greatest source of their anxiety comes from speaking in front of peers (fearing being laughed at or ridiculed), making errors, and not communicating effectively (Price, 1991).

This self-realization might not be so bad if the manifestations of it were not so influential in the language learning classroom. There is nowhere for learners to hide when they freeze up during oral classroom activities, experience memory loss, or refuse to participate (Horwitz et al., 1986). Anxious students do not seem to handle language errors as effectively as more relaxed peers (Gregersen, 2003) partly because of the tendency to engage in negative self-talk and brood over poor performance. Doing so takes up space in working memory, which tends to reduce information-processing abilities (MacIntyre & Gardner, 1991c). Anxious learners exhibit avoidance behaviors by skipping class or putting off assignments. Some language learners tend toward perfectionism, adding unrealistically high personal performance standards to an already challenging learning process (Gregersen & Horwitz, 2002). Over time, the effects of language anxiety may culminate in lower proficiency and course grades, or in dropping out of language learning all together.

Although few specific classroom activities for reducing anxiety are outlined in the literature, researchers do give general guidelines for teachers to follow. Among these are the creation of student support systems and encouraging classroom environments that focus on sensitively correcting errors (Horwitz *et al.*, 1986); encouraging the overhaul of unrealistic expectations and counter-productive beliefs about language learning; incorporating more supportive, small group activities, and focusing on the meaning of the message rather than accuracy (Price, 1991). Language methodologists have also tried to remedy the maladies of debilitating anxiety by creating specific approaches that target negative affect. For example, the method, Desuggestopedia, attempts to 'de-suggest' the psychological barriers that are erected against the language learning process, and still another method, The Natural Approach, is designed to mimic as accurately as possible the way that children acquire their first language.

Throughout this chapter, we will examine what language classroom anxiety is, where it comes from, and by assessing its stigmatizing effects, draw some conclusions about the importance of this variable to language learning. After appraising how anxiety influences the four skills of reading, writing, speaking and listening, the chapter will conclude with what research suggests are general guidelines to consider for lessening anxiety's debilitating effects, followed by the introduction of specific activities teachers can implement in their classrooms.

Exploring Foreign Language Anxiety, Its Origins and Its Significance

What language anxiety is

Self-expression is intimately linked to self-concept. Language anxiety reflects the worry and negative emotional reaction aroused when learning and using a second language and is especially relevant in a classroom where self-expression takes place. Horwitz *et al.* (1986: 128) identify this phenomenon as 'a distinct complex of self-perceptions, beliefs, feeling and behaviors related to classroom language learning arising from the uniqueness of the language learning process.' To understand its origins, MacIntyre and Gardner (1991c: 297) propose that 'initially, anxiety is an undifferentiated, negative affective response to some experience in language class' and that 'with repeated occurrences, anxiety becomes reliably associated with the language class and differentiated from other contexts.' In other words, foreign language anxiety is situation-specific; learners may be anxiety-free in other environments, but upon entering the language classroom, they become anxiety-ridden.

Horwitz *et al.* (1986) discuss three interrelated concerns that work together in the specific milieu of the language classroom: communication apprehension, fear of negative evaluation, and test anxiety. The interacting parts consist of the realization that target language (TL) messages often are incomplete at best and incomprehensible at worst, leading to frustration and aborted communication. This tendency is exacerbated by the apprehension that nuanced self-expression in the TL is limited by impoverished vocabulary and inexperience with the nonlinguistic aspects of intercultural communication; self-expression is not as authentic as it would be in one's native language. This recognition of disparity is further intensified by frequent and often unreliable evaluations of learning, particularly the performance-based type of testing that occurs in the language classroom.

With this network of negative arousal jockeying for attention with plans to escape the misery, it is no wonder that language anxiety interferes with acquisition, retention and production of the TL. In its infancy, research into language anxiety centered mostly on speaking, as this was the skill that seemed to generate the most worry and concern for language learners. However, with further investigations and the realization that input and processing were also negatively impacted, researchers also began to look at anxieties in listening and reading as receptive skills providing input to the rest of the system, and writing skills that are linked to speaking as another avenue for language production.

At the input stage, anxiety arousal can produce shortfalls in attention and distraction as learners divide their energies between emotional drama and cognitive engagement, limiting the amount of linguistic information that is received and available to be processed. Thus, we encounter learners who hear or read new words but because of their inability to concentrate and encode, those words do not become part of their working vocabularies – the words seem to bounce off a wall of negative emotion and never enter the cognitive system. The effects of anxiety on processing the input are relative to the complexity of the task at hand – if the learners' abilities are commensurate with the task, little interference is likely to occur; but if the task is cognitively taxing, the combination of challenging task and high anxiety will result in difficulties during processing. In this case, learners may receive input in the form of a new word, but interference at processing does not allow them to mentally rehearse it or connect it to prior experience, again resulting in ineffective learning. Finally, interference occurring during the act of retrieving previously stored information typifies problems at the output stage (MacIntyre & Gardner, 1989). In these situations, learners may have processed the input and have it stored for future use, but because language anxiety is aroused, they sit with blank looks on their faces and mouths gaping, as they struggle to find that ever-elusive vocabulary item that they know they know.

Where language anxiety comes from

Sources of foreign language classroom anxiety abound. The causes of anxiety are at times closely associated with the learner and at others with the teacher; but the interaction between, and incompatibility of, learners' and teachers' styles may also be the trigger. Instructional practices, classroom procedures and language testing are also identified as anxiety generators (Young, 1991). Concerning those sources that reside in the learner, Bailey's (1983) study took aim at students' negative self-comparisons with other learners, the learners' perceptions concerning their relationship with their teachers, and their desire for teachers' approval. Beyond learners' competitive natures, which can prompt anxiety, MacIntyre and Gardner (1991b) noted that anxiety is often exacerbated by negative, self-degrading thoughts. They cited learners' own counter-productive reactions to a task as exhausting the cognitive energy necessary for the task itself, ultimately leading to an inability to process information. Excessive self-evaluation, worries over potential failure, and concern over what others think, divide their attention between the task and their own self-thoughts, thus sapping the learner of the cognition necessary for learning.

Young (1991) also cited learner beliefs and teacher beliefs as major contributors to foreign language anxiety, particularly when student beliefs collide with those of their teachers and with the reality of the nature of language learning. In terms of instructor beliefs, Young (1991: 428) contends, 'Instructors who believe their role is to correct students constantly when they make any error, who feel that they cannot have students working in pairs because the class may get out of control, who believe that the teacher should be doing most of the talking and teaching, and who think their role is more like a drill sergeant's than a facilitator's may be contributing to language learning anxiety.' (For a more extensive discussion on learner and teacher beliefs and how their mismatch creates negative effect, see Chapter 2.)

Error correction also can be a significant source of anxiety if it is not handled in ways that are welcomed by learners (Gregersen, 2003; Young, 1991). Students have reported that they feel teachers are on a mission to eradicate errors at all costs, and carry out the corrections with sarcasm or embarrassment. Gregersen (2003) contends that the relationship of errors and anxiety is cyclical: that as errors are made, learners become more anxious, and the more errors they make, the less they are willing to participate as they try to protect their social image. Without interaction in the language, anxious students support the cyclical impasse of negative emotion and decreased performance. Anxious learners tend to focus on the negative, believing their performance is riddled with more errors than they actually produce. MacIntyre *et al.* (1997) showed that non-anxious students overestimate their abilities and anxious students underestimate their abilities; in each case a cycle of self-fulfilling prophecy is triggered.

Finally, some types of activities and testing formats used in language learning classrooms provoke more anxiety than others. Activities and assessments that demand speaking in front of others have been reported by students as generating uneasiness. Oral class presentations, oral skits, oral quizzes and oral responses in class were the most anxiety-producing (Koch & Terrell, 1991). In the assessment arena, Young (1991) also counsels teachers that students are more comfortable when tests reliably measure classroom performance and target material covered in class with question formats and tasks that they have encountered before. Otherwise, frustration and anxiety are likely to ensue.

Significance of anxiety in language learning

Foreign language classroom anxiety results in a litany of specific manifestations that work together to debilitate learners' progress. MacIntyre and Gardner (1991c: 96) go so far as to say that in language learning, 'anxiety is one of the best predictors of success.' The multiplicity of anxiety manifestations cited in the literature, and their chicken-and-egg quality, makes the task of organizing them into a comprehensive and comprehensible framework daunting. However, four natural categories emerge: physical, emotional/affective, cognitive/linguistic and interactional/social. This typology helps us to think about how the symptoms of foreign language anxiety are expressed, but we must remember that the categories interact and work together dynamically. For example, an anxiety-provoking catalyst causes a physiological manifestation with increased heart rate and sweating palms, which in turn creates negative expectations that lead to worry and emotionality. This leads to cognitive interference from self-derogatory cognition, thus eliciting performance deficits. This whole cycle reinforces expectations of anxiety and failure (MacIntyre & Gardner, 1991c).

The physical realm
Anxious language learners report physical symptoms of increased heartbeat, tension, and trembling (Horwitz *et al.,* 1986). The question as to whether these physical sensations are the precursors to cognition or it is the other way around, is difficult to answer. According to MacIntyre and Gregersen (2012a), it might work either way, or both ways, but it is a quickly occurring process. Because it happens so quickly, it might not matter too much whether the 'jolt' comes from an external cue which causes the heart to race and unpleasant feelings and cognition to ensue, or if the thoughts of failure create an emotional response which then leads to physiological reactions, thus causing further unpleasant feelings and coping cognition. Either way, the key observation is that reaction quickly becomes coordinated between cognition,

emotion and physiology. A variety of automatic physical processes are triggered, some that increase arousal and other that reduce it, but cognition in the sense of thinking or problem solving is slower than physiology. For this reason, deliberate attempts to control run-away emotion are like trying to herd the cats back into the barn.

The unconscious physical reactions of students are also observed in their nonverbal behavior. With the purpose of giving teachers a starting point for identifying which students struggle with anxiety, Gregersen (2005) investigated the differences between how high anxious and low anxious learners communicate nonverbally. After decoding and interpreting learners' responses, she cataloged the following physical manifestations of anxiety: limited facial expression including brow behavior and smiling; less eye contact with the teacher; postures that were rigid and closed; and hand movements used more for self-touching and manipulating objects than in using gestures that enhanced meaning and turn-taking. With these observations, Gregersen (2005) was hopeful that teachers would take the first step of identifying who their anxious students are, so that with this information, remediating measures would be taken to help diminish anxiety's debilitating grip.

The emotional/affective realm

Anxious learners also have emotional or affective manifestations that hinder language progress. Among the counterproductive feelings anxious learners experience are: insecurity about speaking; fear of not understanding the teacher; panic at being unprepared; worry over the consequence of failure; embarrassment in volunteering responses; fear of teacher correction; confusion when studying for tests; incompetence in self-comparisons with other students; worry about being left behind as the class moves quickly; self-consciousness when speaking; feelings of being overwhelmed by grammatical rules and fear of being laughed at (Horwitz *et al.,* 1986). Other emotional manifestations include nervous laughter (Young, 1991), higher performance standards, procrastination, worry over the opinion of others, concern over errors, and negative reactions to imperfection (Gregersen & Horwitz, 2002). Finally, Phillips (1992: 22) discusses the 'influence of anxiety on the *attitudes* of students toward language learning and on their *intentions* to continue the study of a foreign language'. Anxious learners who are disturbed by evaluation are less likely to demonstrate positive attitudes toward language class and are less likely to continue language studies.

The linguistic/cognitive realm

In general, anxiety interferes with both TL proficiency and students' ability to produce the language (MacIntyre & Gardner, 1994). Horwitz (2001) documents the relationship between foreign language anxiety and achievement. From a top-down perspective, we understand that TL proficiency and classroom achievement are negatively influenced by language anxiety. From a bottom-up angle, there are linguistic and/or cognitive elements that are making that happen. Young (1991) reports a litany of symptoms: sound mis-representation, ineptitude in imitating sound patterns in the language, and forgetting learned linguistic information. Horwitz *et al.* (1986) cite an inability to distinguish sounds and structures as well as over-studying with no significant gains. They also cite unprepared, free speech as being problematic for anxious learners. Finally, anxiety-ridden students use less personal and interpretive speech, which impacts their ability to genuinely communicate (Steinberg & Horwitz, 1986).

The interactional/social realm

When anxious learners find themselves in physical, emotional and/or cognitive dilemmas, they invoke social image protection strategies that could take various forms. Being less apt to volunteer answers and participate in the classroom (Ely, 1986), anxious learners prefer to remain silent (Horwitz *et al.*, 1986). According to Schlenker and Leary (1982), anxious learners will proactively limit social exchanges. They will initiate and participate in fewer conversations, allow silence to hang heavily in conversation, and speak for shorter periods of time in front of an audience. To protect their images, anxious learners will rarely interrupt others but will give monosyllabic and frequent communicative feedback like head-nodding to keep their interlocutor talking. Shorter answers rather than longer, more detailed responses are to be expected. Anxious students avoid activities in class, act indifferently, go to class unprepared, sit at the back of the room to avoid interaction, or cut class altogether (Horwitz *et al.*, 1986).

Language anxiety across the skills

Research suggests that speaking may be the most often cited skill source for producing these debilitating feelings (Kim, 2009; Price, 1991), but recent investigations reveal the presence of language anxiety as learners listen, read, and write. Gregersen (2006) proposes that anxiety may be heightened when a foreign language learner is cognizant of a disparity in his or her abilities across the skills. That is to say, if a foreign language learner is mindful that he does not write as well as he speaks, and if writing is also perceived as important to him, his awareness of his deficiency will heighten his feelings of language anxiety in the writing domain.

Listening

Listening anxiety is particularly problematic as listening is a skill necessary for oral interaction. The speed and spontaneity of a native speaker talking in real time, with colloquial or incomplete expressions, often is cited as one of the catalysts for speaking anxiety; language learners must understand utterances in the moment. The comprehension of spontaneous speech is reduced when learners believe they must understand every word they hear (Scarcella

& Oxford, 1992). Listening to spoken words is a transitory event compared to reading the written word, so that any inattention to what is being said could result in an inability to capture the main ideas, or even to miss the message in its totality (Rivers, 1981). Elkhafaifi (2005) demonstrated that as anxiety increases, listening comprehension and course achievement decrease. This reinforces the MacIntyre and Gardner (1991a) findings concerning input interference and proficiency. Jones Vogely (1998) catalogued student reports of what they perceived as being the most influential sources of listening anxiety. In broad terms, language learners cited input and processing problems. Specifically, the input issues targeted the nature of speech, difficulty level, message ambiguity, absence of visual scaffolding, and low quantities of input repetition. Specific processing issues surfaced as a result of ineffective strategies, lack of processing time, and the impossibility of studying how to listen or check comprehension.

Reading

Even though reading allows foreign language learners to review and reread the passage, anxiety arousal still occurs during reading. The written word can be intricately complex and cognitively demanding, stretching and stressing attention, memory, perception and comprehension resources (Sellers, 2000). Furthermore, reading is a fundamental life skill and a critical means of foreign language input; reading causes its share of stress even in one's own first language. Saito *et al.* (1999) propose that unknown scripts or symbol systems that make rapid decoding difficult, combined with culturally unfamiliar content that is not conducive to schema activation, contribute to anxiety. Oh (1992) further noted that a lack of task familiarity, text difficulty, and/or learners' perceptions of task validity add fuel to the fire. Finally, highly anxious readers tend to experience 'more off-task, interfering thoughts than their less anxious counterparts' (Sellers, 2000: 512) thus limiting their recall of passage content.

Writing

Writing in another language, the final of the four skill areas, also presents obstacles to language learners. Like the other skill-related anxieties, foreign language writing anxiety can be differentiated from the other sources of anxiety. 'Although second language classroom anxiety and writing apprehension each claim to possess their own unique defining characteristics, they seem to share several assumptions, such as: negative affect toward certain aspects of communication, avoidance of certain kinds of social exchanges, and fear of being evaluated' (Cheng et al., 1999: 421). In a follow-up study, Cheng (2002) found that the self-perceptions held by learners concerning their second language writing competency were an accurate predictor of anxiety; learners who reported high self-perceptions of writing ability were less likely to feel writing anxiety.

Capitalizing on Anxiety: An Action Plan

There is not a single panacea that will rid the classroom of all negative affect. Given the nature of emotion, it would be foolish to try to eliminate negative emotion. There are, however, a series of measures that can be taken by any or all of the 'players' involved to make the experience less prone to disruption by negative emotion. The 'players' in the foreign language classroom are the teacher (who usually manages the instructional practices, classroom procedures and testing processes), the learner (who gruels over self-confidence and worries over potential failure), and the social milieu (created by the teacher and students interacting). Any of these constituents, individually or in combination, could be provocateurs or the remediators of language anxiety. Just as we may hold one or more of these 'players' responsible for the presence of anxiety, so too may we find in them the catalyst for solutions.

Player 1: Teacher

For teachers, researchers have suggested an assortment of guiding principles to help alleviate the challenges posed by foreign language anxiety that consider elements such as instructional practices, classroom procedures, and language testing. In discussing instructional practices, it is important for teachers to acknowledge the existence of anxiety (Horwitz, 1997a). Overt teaching of anxiety management strategies like relaxation techniques, positive self-talk and breathing exercises, as well as offering advice about language learning is recommended (Horwitz, 1997a; Kim, 2009). Systematic desensitization is one means by which teachers can help learners understand their personal anxiety-producing triggers, and through gradual exposure to the sources of anxiety through the imagination and anticipation, language learners can increase their comfort level in the real scenarios. Systematic Desensitization safely confronts the trigger(s) that provoke anxiety, giving learners a means to practice coping efforts. 'Desensitization for language learning anxiety may work for some learners because, put simply, a learner's language anxiety response to the imagined or anticipated situation closely resembles his/her anxiety response to the real situation' (MacIntyre & Gregersen, 2012a). Activities 1, 2 and 3 in the Activities section of this chapter provide step-by-step procedures.

Furthermore, while balancing the appropriate difficulty level of the language material presented, teachers need to promote student learning and performance that emphasize improvement over perfection (Ewald, 2007; Horwitz, 1997a) as in the wise proverb: the perfect is the enemy of the good. Teachers might give more opportunities for rehearsal and practice, personalize instruction, and use appealing, motivating materials. When the classroom is inserted in a culture where communicative activities are not the norm, teachers are advised to introduce them gradually so as to not wreak havoc on students' expectations (Kim, 2009).

Teachers might also consider scrutinizing their classroom procedures for anxiety triggers. One of the most commonly cited guiding principles in the language anxiety literature is to assess how error correction and feedback are handled. Through sensitivity, appropriate positive reinforcement, realistic expectations and promulgating the notion that errors are a natural and necessary part of the language learning process, learners are more likely to feel a greater sense of achievement. Judiciously rewarding learners for successful communication will reduce the fear that the teacher is perpetually focused on negatively evaluating performance (Ewald, 2007; Gregersen, 2003; Young, 1991). To turn the phrase, praise the good, don't wait for the perfect. Testing also needs to be carefully examined by teachers. Assessments that reflect instruction and that contain previously practiced item types will result in learners who are less stressed test-takers (Young, 1991). Researchers also suggest that teachers build classroom rapport by using humor and creating a welcoming, supportive environment (Ewald, 2007; Young, 1991) where the teacher is not perceived as the authority, but rather as a facilitator or coach. Gregersen (2005: 396) discusses the positive affective feelings generated by teacher immediacy which reflects nonverbal behaviors like leaning in toward another person, making eye contact, and having relaxed posture. She advocates paying attention to communicating approachability – 'not only does it behoove foreign language teachers to accurately *decode* students' nonverbal messages, but they should also effectively *encode* their affective messages as well.'

Player 2: Learners

The learner himself can help to effect positive change. While the teacher manages instruction, procedures and assessment, the individual learner is the master of his own mind. Learners who concentrate on their positive experiences benefit from increased achievement (Ewald, 2007).

MacIntyre and Gregersen (2012b: 113) discuss the applications of Fredrickson's (2001) 'Broaden and Build' theory to language learning. They note that '...positive affect functions differently from negative affect in human development. Positive emotion is qualitatively different from the more widely studied group of negative emotions, including anxiety. Whereas negative emotions tend to focus the individual on specific tasks, obstacles or threats (e.g. an anxiety reaction to being embarrassed), positive emotions work to broaden our thinking and build strengths for the future.' Positive emotion generates tendencies that facilitate language learning: joy urges play; interest urges exploration; contentment urges the savoring of positive events; pride urges the sharing of accomplishments; and love urges the creation of deep and meaningful relationships (see Fredrickson, 2001). According to MacIntyre and Gregersen (2012a: 193), positive and negative emotion are not opposite ends of the same spectrum; each has a different function. '...(P)ositive emotion tends to broaden a person's perspective, opening the individual to absorb the language. In contrast, negative emotion produces the opposite tendency, a narrowing of focus and a restriction of the range of potential language input.' Young (1991) suggests that the process begin with learners' acknowledgement of the existence of language anxiety followed by strategies such as positive self-talk, journal writing, and relaxation exercises. Activity 4 guides learners through an exploration of how positive emotions lead to action tendencies that differ from negative ones.

Player 3: The resultant 'being' of interaction

The third 'player' in our language classroom triad is the social milieu or the 'being' that is created as teacher and learners interact. The dynamics of any given group are as unique as any one human being, with the idiosyncrasies that emerge as two or more lives interconnect. The challenge then is to make this emergent creature an agent of positive change, generating positive emotion. How can teachers inspire the social milieu to stimulate affirming affect? 'There is one element on which Positive Psychologists agree: Building community, social networks and intimate relationships make people happy' (MacIntyre & Gregersen, 2012a). Lower anxiety is a potential by-product of human bonding and building relationships within the class. According to Young (1991: 428), the affective filter is low when a person feels 'club membership' and 'target language group identification.'

Friendly, caring environments that allow learners to verbalize their fears so as not to feel alone and where competitiveness, self-comparisons and a desire to out-do are eradicated gives learners an emotional space where they can foster community and grow as language learners. Pragmatically, how is this carried out? Many researchers advocate for the use of small groups where not only is the quantity and quality of interaction heightened (less teacher talk; more opportunities for individuals to speak), but learners can be more relaxed in an intimate group configuration and have their interaction tailored and learning personalized to their individual needs. Speaking in front of three rather than 30 people is much more affectively agreeable, and the negotiation of interaction more expeditious. Finally, the presence of role models within this social milieu is important to note.

Murphey (2001: 9) identified the benefits of observing a 'near peer' – a person who is near to us in the sense of being physically close but also close in characteristics such as age, ethnicity, gender, interests, and experiences. The benefits of near peers stem from learning that achievements are possible. 'Learners also find that they can be happy with small successes – they don't have to be frustrated believing that they have to be like native speakers. These learnings give them permission to try certain behaviors with hopeful expectations.' Further advice suggests that not only role models but also supportive conversational partners, students supporting

each other linguistically, socially and emotionally, may play a role in helping language learners avoid or overcome foreign language anxiety (Dewaele
et al., 2008). This support network can also be extended to the development
of literacy through the inclusion of dialogue journals, interactive writing
where learners exchange writing with the teacher or another learner.
Because it is a written exchange, it is less threatening and opens up new
channels of communication that provide a natural context for language and
literacy, while at the same time allowing learners to express themselves
and make sense of their own and others' experiences and feelings (Peyton,
2000). Social interaction and community-building play a critical role in
overcoming language anxiety. The remaining 11 activities will provide
opportunities for mutual encouragement, sharing emotional experiences
and strategies, increasing teamwork and cooperative effort, building rapport, eliminating competition, increasing realistic expectations and generating positive group dynamics.

To conclude the 'premise' part of this chapter, let's return to the story of
the 'Cracked Pot'. At some point, even before the pot communicated his
shame, the water bearer had already evaluated the situation and had the
foresight to plant some seeds that would ultimately capitalize on the cracked
pot's so-called 'defect.' What can we take from this parable to help deal with
foreign language anxiety? Teachers who have the foresight to create a supportive environment, highlight achievement rather than past failure, and
develop insight into the uniqueness of the individual learners in their care,
transform blemishes into blossoms.

... *To Practice*

Anxiety Activities

As teachers reflect upon issues of language anxiety through exploration of
the following activities, they must remain cognizant that anxiety can manifest in physical, emotional, linguistic or social behaviors. Teachers, individual
language learners and the class as a whole can pull together to create a network of support and collaboration.

The main affective aim throughout these activities is to create a classroom comfort zone where teachers, individual learners and the group as a
whole can capitalize on mutual encouragement and excel in language learning. Teachers will have the opportunity to review their instructional choices,
classroom procedures, and language testing practices; individuals will reflect
on their choices to focus on previous achievement and progress or past failure
and perfection; and the group will build community and social networks
that are fundamental to positive interaction.

**Anxiety-Reducing Activity 1: Systematic
De-sensitization: Constructing the hierarchy (adapted from
www.guidetopsychology.com)**

Fear is a habit; so is self-pity, defeat, anxiety, despair, hopelessness
and resignation. You can eliminate all of these negative habits with
two simple resolves: I can!! and I will!! – Unknown

Level: All

Procedure:

(1) Preface this activity by explaining that the next three activities,
grouped into consecutive steps, are part of a process called,
'Systematic Desensitization' (Wolpe, 1958), whereby learners will
construct a hierarchy chart, and participate in relaxation training
and desensitization sessions to reduce the intensity of negative-
narrowing emotional responses caused by situations that trigger FL
anxiety. The objective of this first activity is to have learners self-
reflect on their personal anxiety triggers, and create a hierarchy of
explicitly and vividly described triggers in order from least to most
anxiety provoking.

(2) Ask learners to each create an anxiety hierarchy where they list
10–15 scenarios associated with FL learning which cause them
varying levels of anxiety. To facilitate the prioritization process,
pass out index cards on which learners write one trigger per card
with a vivid, explicit and detailed description of the situation. For
example, if someone is fearful of being called upon in class by the
teacher without preparation, instruct him/her to write down the
specific situations in which this difficulty is experienced. Emphasize
that cards should have mild, moderate and severely anxiety-provoking situations.

(3) Next, instruct learners to rank order their items from the least
upsetting to the most upsetting by reflecting upon how badly it
would feel to be in that situation. Put the cards in that order and
number them.

(4) Finally, ask learners to finalize their hierarchies by prioritizing their
items beginning with those so mild that they would hardly evoke a
negative response and ending with the worst ones at the bottom. The
sequence of items should contain gradual bumps in severity from one
item to the next so that when they finish one item, the next one is
not too far away.

(5) De-brief this activity by allowing learners to share some of the triggers on their lists. Next, explain that as they work their way through
their hierarchies in the next two activities, they will begin with the
least anxiety provoking triggers and work progressively through the
hierarchy until they attain the last item – the trigger they define as
the most powerfully anxiety-provoking.

ASSESSMENT IDEAS:

Artifact: Hierarchy chart of anxiety triggers (on index cards)

Assessment questions: Did learners produce a personal hierarchy containing FL anxiety triggers that are both (1) vividly and explicitly
described in great detail; and (2) in order from least to most anxiety
producing?

Assessment ideas:

(1) Research suggests that the more vivid and detailed the descriptions
of the anxiety triggers are the better systematic de-sensitization
will work. To assess this, use peer assessment in the form of oral
interviews. In pairs, have learners go through each of the cards and
ask each other questions to stimulate the addition of at least six
more descriptors (adjectives or adverbs) to each card.
(2) To check whether each learner's hierarchy is an accurate and
fairly well-spaced progression of his/her anxiety, have learners do
the following self-assessment (adapted from www.guidetopsy-
chology.com):
     (a) Assign each trigger a number on a scale from 0 to 100 where
100 is the highest level of FL anxiety imaginable and 0 is complete relaxation. Write this number on the back of the corresponding index card.
     (b) Next, sort the cards into five piles, each representing a different
level of anxiety: Low (1–19); Medium/Low (20–39); Medium
(40–59); Medium/High (60–79); High (80–100). To meet the
requirement of a gradual anxiety progression, the goal is to
have roughly two cards in each pile (depending upon the
number of scenarios each individual created). If this is not
achieved on the first round of sorting, go back and re-evaluate
some items or create new ones.

Anxiety-Reducing Activity 2: Systematic De-sensitization: Relaxation Techniques (adapted from www.guidetopsychology.com)

There is no need to go to India or anywhere else to find peace. You will find that deep place of silence right in your room, your garden or even your bathtub. – Elisabeth Kubler-Ross

Level: All

Procedure:

(1) Preface this activity by explaining that the objective is to become acquainted with three relaxation techniques (autogenic relaxation, progressive muscle relaxation and visualization) and through experimentation, become aware of which techniques are personally more effective.

(2) Explain that the first technique is called 'autogenic' because it means that something comes from within the self, and in this technique, learners will use both visual imagery and body awareness to reduce stress.

(3) Ask learners to repeat words or suggestions in their minds to relax and reduce muscle tension. For example, ask them to imagine a peaceful setting and then focus on controlled, relaxed breathing, slowing their heart rates or feeling different physical sensations, such as relaxing each arm or leg one by one. Allow time for practice.

(4) The next technique is progressive muscle relaxation. Ask learners to focus on slowly tensing and then relaxing each muscle group. This helps them focus on the difference between muscle tension and relaxation and become more aware of physical sensations.

(5) Tell learners to begin by tensing and relaxing the muscles in their toes and to progressively work their way up to their necks and heads, or to work from their heads and necks down to their toes. Have learners tense their muscles for at least five seconds and then relax for 30 seconds and then repeat.

(6) Explain that the last technique will use visualization, forming mental images to take a visual journey to a peaceful, calming place or situation. As learners visualize, tell them to invoke as many senses as possible, including smell, sight, sound and touch.

(7) Guide visualization by having learners imagine relaxing at the ocean and thinking about the smell of the salt water, the sound of crashing waves and the warmth of the sun on their neck and shoulders. If students prefer, have them close their eyes and make themselves comfortable somewhere in the room.

(8) Ask learners to practice each of these and choose which one is the most successful. When learners are able to relax completely in three or four minutes by quickly running through one of the procedures, then they are ready to begin the desensitization sessions.

(9) De-brief this activity by asking learners to determine their success with each relaxation technique by assigning a 1 (effective), 2 (somewhat effective) or 3 (not effective) to each. Invite those learners who feel they have mastered one or more of the techniques to share any suggestions. Explain that well-managed anxiety allows learners to take advantage of positive-broadening emotions by forcing negative-narrowing emotion to recede into the background and that these relaxation techniques will benefit them physiologically (slower heart rate and breathing, lower blood pressure, increased blood flow to muscles, reduced muscle tension), cognitively (greater concentration), affectively (decrease frustration, increase confidence); and socially (slower conversation pace allows more time to process language).

MODIFICATIONS:

Emergent learners: Model the relaxation techniques alongside the learners and aid visualization by providing pictures that evoke tranquility.

Technology:

(1) Adding peaceful background music and video clips meant for relaxation during these techniques would be tremendously helpful.

(2) For teachers working at larger comprehensive institutions where physical education is also taught, find out if heart monitors are available. These instruments provide a more objective physiological measure of relaxation.

Anxiety-Reducing Activity 3: Desensitization Sessions
(adapted from www.guidetopsychology.com)

Somehow our devils are never quite what we expect when we meet them face to face. – Nelson DeMille

Level: All

Procedure:

(1) Preface this activity by explaining that desensitization occurs when learners, through repeated practice, can imagine their anxiety

triggers vividly and realistically in detail while feeling completely relaxed. When a learner can imagine a given item with no concern or worry, he/she can then move to the next item and repeat the process. Learners proceed from the least powerful to most powerful triggers.

(2)   Ask learners to get comfortable and induce relaxation using the most effective technique from Activity 2.

(3)   Invite learners to silently read an item from their hierarchies. The initial session targets the first item on the hierarchy while subsequent sessions will begin with the last anxiety trigger treated in the previous session.

(4)   Encourage learners to imagine themselves in their 'trigger' situation for a tolerable time (times will vary, but they should get progressively longer).

(5)   Tell learners to stop imagining their situation and determine their level of anxiety in that moment on a scale of 1–10, and then re-establish their relaxed state for about 30 seconds.

(6)   Have learners re-read their descriptions of the situations and once again imagine themselves in that scene for a tolerable time.

(7)   Tell learners to stop and determine their level of in-the-moment anxiety. If anxiety persists, have them return to Step 2; if their anxiety has dissipated, they may proceed to the next trigger. Repeat the steps.

(8)   De-brief this activity by getting learner feedback on the efficacy of this three-step desensitization process. Ask them to share their strategies for success and/or the obstacles that impeded them from reaching a relaxed state while imagining their anxiety triggers.

Anxiety-Reducing Activity 4: Making the most from urges (joy interest, contentment, pride, love)

The sharing of joy, whether physical, emotional, psychic, or intellectual, forms a bridge between the sharers which can be the basis for understanding much of what is not shared between them, and lessens the threat of their difference. – Audre Lorde

Level: All

Preparation:

On the floor, place five lines of masking tape, one for each of the five emotions of joy, interest, contentment, pride and love, with each end of the line representing the polar opposite of the feelings (e.g. 'complete absence of joy' on one end and 'overwhelmed with joy') on the other.

Procedure:

(1) Preface this activity by explaining that positive and negative emotions generate different kinds of urges or behaviors, and that through this activity, learners will be able to explore this idea.

(2) Write the following five words on the board: joy, interest, contentment, pride, love.

(3) Divide learners into five equal groups. Assign each group one of the five emotions. Ask learners to contemplate for a moment the intensity with which they feel that emotion on a 'normal' day. Remaining silent and communicating only nonverbally, tell learners in each group to line up on the tape in order, with those feeling the emotion most intensely on one end and those who experience it less on the other.

(4) Next, ask learners to turn to their neighbors and talk about what actions or urges the presence or absence of this emotion provokes in their lives. Ask them to try and understand their neighbor's feelings while they hone in on their own.

(5) In continuation, divide each group in half, with those feeling the emotion most intensely in one subgroup, and those who do not, in the other. Have each subgroup discuss their emotion among themselves and then create a role play that illustrates that emotion. The scenario is of their choice.

(6) Each subgroup then takes turns improvising their role play in front of the class. After each role play, discuss how that particular emotion can affect language learning and group dynamics. Most importantly, what urges spring from each emotion?

(7) Debrief this activity by explaining to learners that positive emotions lead to action tendencies that differ from negative emotions. Joy ignites the urge play, interest kindles the urge to explore, contentment awakens the urge to savor and integrate, and love inflames a continuing series of these human yearnings within protected intimate relationships (Fredrickson, 2001).

MODIFICATIONS:

Technology: Videotape the role plays and play them back for class discussion (Step 5).

Large groups: Form two groups for each emotion so group size remains manageable (Step 3).

Anxiety-Reducing Activity 5: Statues of Emotion: A Study of the Nonverbal

Nerves and butterflies are fine – they're a physical signal that you're mentally ready and eager. You have to get the butterflies to fly in formation, that's the trick – Steve Bull

Level: All

Procedure:

(1) Preface this activity by explaining to students that they will have the opportunity to be keen observers of their classmates, to look for physical manifestations of tension and to work together to make each other feel comfortable and relaxed.
(2) Direct learners to sit down. Ask them to feel the floor, the chair and the space around them, with eyes open or closed.
(3) Ask them to feel and then to replicate the emotion of anxiety, showing it in their faces and body language.
(4) Call out, 'Freeze!' directing everyone to freeze like a statue, holding their positions. Tell them, 'We are in the museum of anxiety.'
(5) Choose one individual to maintain his/her frozen pose and be the 'statue.' Ask the others to focus their attention on that person and describe different aspects of the statue, like the facial expression and posture.
(6) When the group has finished the discussion, repeat the exercise, but this time ask students to feel and replicate relaxation. Carry through the same process of freezing, electing one student to be the statue, and talking about what they see.
(7) Debrief this activity by letting learners know that when they feel anxious using their TL they are not alone and that pulling together as a team is necessary for optimal learning.

MODIFICATIONS:

Technology:
Rather than having learners visit a 'museum', invite them to a 'photo gallery' where photographs of their 'frozen' facial expressions and positions taken on hand-held mobile devices are posted on a group sharing website for comment (Steps 4, 5 and 6).

Large groups: Divide the whole group into smaller groups from the beginning of the activity and designate a statue in each small group.

Anxiety-Reducing Activity 6: Fear in a Hat

You can't wring your hands and roll up your sleeves at the same time. – Pat Schroeder

Level: All

Procedure:

(1) Preface this activity by explaining that language anxiety is common, and that acknowledging its existence is one of the first ways to alleviate its effects.
(2) Ask everyone to complete this sentence on a piece of paper: 'In this class, I am most concerned about....'
(3) Collect the papers, mix them up in a hat or box, and invite students to take a piece of paper and read about someone else's worry.
(4) Taking turns, individuals read aloud the fear of another group member and speculate and elaborate on what they perceive as the writer's intention. If the reader does not elaborate enough, ask one or more follow-up questions.
(5) When all of the anxieties have been read and elaborated on, discuss what the writers were feeling and what the readers noticed.
(6) De-brief this activity by reinforcing the idea that by sharing their concerns with others, individuals will realize that they are not the only ones who feel discomfort with certain elements of the language learning classroom.

MODIFICATIONS:

Technology:

(1) Use a Discussion Board prompt to complete the sentence (Step 2).
(2) Invite learners to comment on at least two other postings (Steps 3 and 4).
(3) Tell learners to discuss what they felt and noticed in their electronic journals (Step 5).

Large groups: Before beginning Step 4, place learners in smaller groups for reading aloud and providing elaboration.

Anxiety-Reducing Activity 7: Trigger and Strategy Mapping

Worrying is like a rocking chair, it gives you something to do, but it gets you nowhere. – Glenn Turner

Level: All

Procedure:

(1) Preface this activity by explaining that its purpose is to provide an opportunity for learners to share their anxiety triggers and strategies for overcoming their negative affect, and in doing so, to understand that they are not alone and to learn from one another.

(2) Place learners in groups with three to five students. Ask them to designate a 'recorder' and a 'reporter' in each group.

(3) Instruct the 'recorder' to take out two sheets of paper and draw a circle in the middle of each sheet with eight smaller circles around it. Then ask the recorder to draw a line between the center circle and each smaller circle. In the middle of the first sheet, have the 'recorder' write the phrase, 'anxiety triggers' and in the middle circle of the second sheet, to write the phrase, 'anxiety strategies.' Model this graphic organizer on the blackboard if necessary.

(4) Ask each group to fill in the eight bubbles on each paper. As the group brainstorms their ideas concerning what causes them to feel anxious in the language classroom, the 'recorder' is writing them down.

(5) Upon completion of the first bubble map, invite students to brainstorm strategies that they have used to relieve their anxiety. Again, the 'recorder' fills in the map.

(6) Encourage the small groups to talk about what they brainstormed together.

(7) Reconvene the whole group and have the designated 'reporter' read their bubble maps aloud to the whole class.

(8) De-brief this activity by asking learners if they encountered any similar answers among the groups and invite them to try out their classmates' strategies when they begin feeling uncomfortable in class.

Anxiety Reducing Activity 8: Sign Up Here, You're Not Alone!

The greatest mistake you can make in life is to be continually fearing you will make one. – Elbert Hubbard

Level: Intermediate/Advanced

In preparation:

(1) On six large pieces of newsprint or poster paper, write the following headings (Adapted from the Foreign Language Classroom Anxiety Scale – Horwitz *et al.*, 1986):
   (a) I worry about making mistakes in my (language being learned) class. Do you want to be corrected, and if so, what is the best way?
   (b) I get nervous when I don't understand every word the teacher says. What can the teacher do to help you understand more?
   (c) I don't understand why some people get so upset over (language being learned) class. What do you do so that you stay so calm?
   (d) I feel very self-conscious about speaking (language being learned) in front of other students. What instances make you more or less self-conscious?
   (e) I feel confident when I speak (language being learned). What instances make you more or less confident?
   (f) My (language being learned) class moves so quickly that I worry about being left behind. What does the teacher do that helps you stay ahead?
(2) Place the posters/newsprint around the room.

Procedure:

(1) Preface this activity by explaining its purpose is to share concerns and strategies about discomfort experienced in the language classroom and to give feedback to the teacher concerning ways in which learners' needs can be better met.
(2) Instruct learners to walk around the room and read the statements.
(3) Invite learners to sign their names on any of the sheets that represent something that is true for them and to add their comments to the accompanying questions.
(4) After everyone has had the opportunity to sign the sheets, ask one person who has signed the sheet to read the names of the people that have signed that sheet and read aloud any comments.
(5) De-brief this activity by discussing the different emotions that learners have expressed and the comments they gave as follow-up. What

are the biggest concerns? What are the strategies that the confident and less self-conscious learners use? What feedback have they given to the teacher to better meet their emotional learning needs?

MODIFICATION:

Technology:

(1) Create six wiki documents that gather and combine learners' input on each of the six items and accompanying questions (Steps 2 and 3).
(2) Print and distribute the six wiki documents for in-class discussion or open a separate Discussion Board for learners to give feedback (Step 5).

Anxiety-Reducing Activity 9: Proverbs to Pacify the Anxious

'I keep the telephone of my mind open to peace, harmony, health, love and abundance. Then, whenever doubt, anxiety or fear try to call me, they keep getting a busy signal—and soon they'll forget my number.' – Edith Armstrong

Level: Intermediate/Advanced

In preparation:

(1) On small slips of paper, write the following quotes/proverbs that focus on teambuilding and put them in a box. Make two or three slips for each quote, using the number of quotes necessary for the size of your class.
  (a) Teamwork: Simply stated, it is less me and more we. (author unknown)
  (b) A boat doesn't go forward if each one is rowing their own way. (Swahili proverb)
  (c) A single arrow is easily broken, but not ten in a bundle. (Japanese proverb)
  (d) It is amazing how much people get done if they do not worry about who gets the credit. (Swahili proverb)
  (e) You don't get harmony when everybody sings the same note. (Doug Floyd)
  (f) Overcoming barriers to performance is how groups become teams. (author unknown)
  (g) Light is the task where many share the toil. (Homer)

(h) In teamwork, silence isn't golden, it's deadly. (Mark Sanborn)
(i) Teamplayer: One who unites others toward a shared destiny through sharing information and ideas, empowering others and developing trust. (Dennis Kinlaw)
(j) There are few, if any, jobs in which ability alone is sufficient. Needed, also, are loyalty, sincerity, enthusiasm and team play. (William B. Given, Jr.)

Procedure:

(1) Preface this activity by explaining that it is a teambuilding activity where learners will have the opportunity to share their thoughts about insightful quotes on the subject.
(2) Ask learners to select one slip of paper from the box and read it silently to themselves.
(3) Explain that everyone in the room has someone with the same quote, and ask them to find that person.
(4) Allow learners to mingle and talk, sharing the quotes until they find their partners. Assure them that this is not a race.
(5) Once in pairs, have students discuss what the quote means.
(6) Reconvene the whole group and talk about the different quotes.
(7) Debrief this activity by asking the class to share what significance their quote has in their personal life and experience, particularly in language class.

MODIFICATION:

Large groups: In preparation, make three or four copies of each quote (depending on group size) and invite learners to work in groups of three or four (Steps 4 and 5).

Anxiety-Reducing Activity 10: Two Truths and a (Sort of) Lie

Rule number one is, don't sweat the small stuff. Rule number two is, it's all small stuff. –Robert Eliot

Level: All

Procedure:

(1) Preface this activity by explaining that besides being a team-building activity, this exercise is meant to focus their attention on favorable classroom experiences as this will in turn promote higher affect.

(2) Invite learners to write down two favorable language classroom experiences they have had and one that they have not had yet, but wish they would.

(3) Ask learners to get together with a partner and take turns sharing their two truths and the 'sort of' lie, asking the listener to guess which is which.

(4) Reconvene the whole group and have each interviewer report on the three experiences shared by the interviewee and see if the whole group can guess which favorable experiences actually happened and which was a projection.

(5) Debrief this activity by explaining that by projecting a hoped-for experience, learners can anticipate future positive action. For teachers, this provides a glimpse of students' future hopes.

MODIFICATION:

Large groups: Reconvene to smaller groups of four or five for reporting/ sharing (Step 4).

Anxiety-Reducing Activity 11: Building Teams, Constructing Sentences

Many great ideas have been lost because the people who had them could not stand being laughed at. – Author Unknown

Level: Intermediate/Advanced

In preparation:

(1) If there is no blackboard in the classroom, hang two pieces of newsprint on which students may write.

Procedure:

(1) Preface this activity by explaining that its purpose is to highlight the importance of individuals cooperating in a group task by collaborating on teams in a race to be the first to complete a group sentence.

(2) Divide the students into teams of equal numbers – roughly five to eight members each. (The number of learners in each group will dictate the length of the sentence they must form.) If one group has one more than the other, one person may participate twice.

(3) Invite the teams to line up ten feet from their blackboard or news-print and give the first person in the line a piece of chalk or marker.
(4) Explain the following rules:
   (a) Each team player takes turns adding one word to the sentence.
   (b) The player goes to the board, writes one word, runs back, gives the next player the chalk or marker, and then goes to the end of the line.
   (c) Team members cannot discuss the sentence or plan it as they await their turns.
   (d) The sentence must contain the same number of words as there are members on the team, and players may not add a word between words that are already written.
(5) De-brief this activity by explaining that a strong sense of community fosters the team spirit and positive energy that characterize supportive language classrooms. Make the analogy of collaborate sentence-building to cooperative language learning.

Anxiety-Reducing Activity 12: Have You Ever … Yikes! Yahoo!

Comedy is defiance. It's a snort of contempt in the face of fear and anxiety. And it's laughter that allows hope to creep back on the inhale. – Will Durst

Level: All

In preparation:

(1) Create two lists of items that are tailored to your particular learners that begin with the phrase, 'Have you ever…?' Items should be carefully constructed so as to not provoke embarrassment, ridicule, or unpleasant reactions.
(2) One list should contain incidents that would encourage learners to commiserate with each other over 'unsuccessful' communication attempts they have encountered in their past language learning experiences, like 'Have you ever frozen up in a public speech?' or 'Have you ever sat at the back of the classroom to avoid being called on by the teacher?'
(3) The other list should contain celebratory events that will allow learners to share in each other's successes, like 'Have you ever used (language being learned) to buy something?' or 'Have you ever answered

the phone and found a (language being learned)-speaker and actually knew what they wanted?'

(4) Place chairs in a big circle.

Procedure:

(1) Preface this activity by explaining that it is going to be an active, fun way to explore and celebrate the rich diversity of experiences that learners have brought to the classroom.
(2) Ask participants to take a seat somewhere in the circle. Explain that you will call out different experiences one by one that may or may not apply to them as individuals; if the item applies, run into the middle, jump in the air, and do a high five with anyone else who runs in. Continue until you have exhausted your two lists.
(3) De-brief this activity by explaining that verbalizing one's fears and past experiences as well as sharing successes may increase classroom rapport and group identification, which in turn creates a comfort zone in the language classroom.

MODIFICATION:

Emergent learners: Explain the formulaic expression, 'have you ever. . .?' and make sure that the phrases provided to complete the statement are within the proficiency constraints of the participants.

Anxiety-Reducing Activity 13: Headlining Memorable Language Learning Moments

Memory is a child walking along a seashore. You never can tell what small pebble it will pick up and store away among its treasured things. – Pierce Harris

Level: Intermediate/Advanced

Procedure:

(1) Preface this activity by explaining that its purpose is to create strong support networks among learners in order to alleviate negative affect or a high affective filter.
(2) Ask students to write down two memories from their language learning experience: one that brings them joy; another that evokes uneasiness.

(3) Invite students to create a title for each memory as if what they wrote is a newspaper story and they are creating a pithy headline that captures its essence.

(4) Have students form small groups of five or six to talk about their memories and combine them into a single document using scissors and glue.

(5) As they work in their groups, have them answer the following questions:

(a) Do the memories reveal important themes in one's past as well as present language learning experience?

(b) Is the memory accurate? Are the details meaningful? Are these memories accurate depictions of reality, or have they been subjectively 'created'?

(c) How does sharing uncomfortable memories with others make group members feel? Is there a greater sense of solidarity and less of feeling alone?

(d) How does sharing successful memories allow others to share in achievement?

(6) De-brief this activity by asking learners whether working in small groups and sharing their experiences helped minimize the competitiveness, self-comparisons, and desire to out-do one another that sometimes characterizes the classroom environment.

Modification:

Technology: Use a free newspaper-making website like www.wordpress. org to create a single electronic document of all learners' memories/stories (Step 4).

Anxiety-Reducing Activity 14: Group-Tell-A-Story

That the birds of worry and care fly over your head, this you cannot change, but that they build nests in your hair, this you can prevent. – Chinese proverb

Level: Intermediate/Advanced

In preparation:

(1) Arrange chairs in circles with four to six seats.

Procedure:

(1) Preface this activity by reinforcing the notion that realistic expectations are necessary for maintaining a positive attitude toward language learning and that the following tasks will give them an opportunity to explore them.

(2) Put students in groups of four to six. Give each group one sheet of paper and dictate the following ambiguous situation for a recorder to write down: 'Once upon a time, there was a language learner who had completely unrealistic expectations about his language class.'

(3) In groups, invite each learner to add another sentence to the story and pass it around the circle, each student adding a new sentence and passing it on so that there are different stories circulating in each group.

(4) Invite one reporter from each small group to read their story aloud to the whole group.

(5) Repeat this exercise, but with a different lead sentence: 'Once upon a time, there were two language learners: one who was constantly focusing on his mistakes and the other who was able to celebrate small victories.'

(6) Again, invite a reporter to share their small group's story.

(7) De-brief this activity by explaining that by changing negative self-related cognition to a focus on positive achievement, learners will not only increase their progress, but will also be more content in class. This may also be an occasion for a discussion on the nature of language learning.

Anxiety-Reducing Activity 15: Taking the Group's Pulse

'No one is moved to act, or resolves to speak a single word, who does not hope by means of this action or word to release anxiety from his spirit.' – Ali ibn-Hazm

Level: All

Procedure:

(1) Preface this activity by explaining that its purpose is to take the group's 'pulse' and to draw attention to how group dynamics are influenced by emotion.

(2) Ask each learner to write one word on a piece of paper to describe how he/she is feeling at that moment.

(3) Divide the class into small groups based upon their expressed emotion (i.e. stressed/worried; happy/content; angry/annoyed, etc.)

(4) Invite each group to discuss their mood state among themselves and then produce a role play that illustrates that mood. Their choice of scenarios is limitless.

(5) Improvisation is critical, so give enough time to create the parameters of the scenario, but not enough to seek perfection through practice and rehearsal.

(6) After each role play, ask the whole group to discuss how the defined mood of that group influenced the group dynamics, examining things like communication patterns, body language, and group cohesion.

(7) Invite the audience to congratulate the actors where they saw them successfully communicate. Reiterate that improvisation is process and not perfection.

(8) De-brief this activity by highlighting that foreign language anxiety is often reduced when learners are rewarded for successful communication and that learning and improvement are much more important to healthy emotional pulses in the classroom than perfection is.

MODIFICATION:

Technology:

(1) Videotape the performances (Step 4).
(2) Play them back for audience feedback (Steps 6 and 7).

2 Beliefs

From Premise...

Beliefs are shaped by perceptions and often assimilated by choice. The synergy among beliefs, perceptions and choice is poignantly illustrated in the story of the wealthy father who took his son on a trip to the country so that the son could see how the poor lived.

After spending a day and a night at the farm of a very poor family, the father asked his son on the way home, 'How was the trip?'

'Very good, Dad!' he exclaimed.
'Did you see how poor people can be?' the father inquired.
'Oh, yes, Dad!'
'So what did you learn?'

Without a blink, the son answered, 'I saw that we have a dog at home and they have four. We have a pool that reaches to the middle of the garden; they have a creek that has no end. We have imported lamps in the house; they have the stars. Our patio reaches to the front yard and is enclosed by a gate; they have the whole horizon.'

Those insights left the father speechless. Then the son added, 'Thanks, Dad, for showing me how poor we are!'

This story demonstrates how fundamental the element of choice is when viewing beliefs through a teaching lens. Belief systems define perceptions, which in turn determine the manner of response. With this sequence in mind, individuals can choose to evaluate their beliefs and then choose to change them. Although many of life's events are out of one's control, individuals always have within their power the decision about how to respond to them. Although some long-held, dogmatic beliefs may be resistant to change and more stubbornly embraced than others, if teachers perceive them as un-malleable or impossible to change and do not take steps to propose counter-arguments, learners remain oblivious to new and progressive ideas that could propel their proficiency further. Teachers, too, have choices.

Insert yourself into this scenario: You are a relatively new ESL teacher and you just got a dream job teaching in another country that you have always wanted to experience. You spend months agonizing over your syllabus, meticulously creating materials and grueling over lesson plans. You arrive in your newly adopted culture, begin implementing all your plans and materials and the day arrives for you to give your first important formal, summative assessment. Much to your chagrin, the majority of your students fail.

At this point, you have a choice: how will you respond? You may or may not have had control over all the variables that comprised the failure equation, but now you can certainly take control of how you respond to them. That part of your life and your teaching will always be within your power. You shape your own reality through your beliefs. Everything begins with a choice.

Exploring Beliefs, Their Origins and Their Significance

What beliefs are and where they come from

Whether called 'mini-theories,' 'insights,' 'assumptions,' or 'filters of reality' (Arnold, 1999; Hosenfeld, 1978; Omaggio, 1978; Riley, 1980), language learners and teachers enter classrooms with a wide array of beliefs. These pre-conceived ideas may revolve around the nature of language learning and how difficult it will be, whether innate ability predisposes success; the strategies that work effectively; and expectations and motivations, among others. These beliefs may be unconsciously gleaned from observation and imitation or consciously acquired through listening to others' advice on how learning best transpires (Wenden, 1999). Past experience, particularly that obtained in other language learning environments combined with culture and personality work together to create self-constructed, and very individual, concepts of learning (Ellis, 2008).

Teachers be heartened! Whereas beliefs may be firmly held products of long-term development, many experts support the notion that they may be malleable as learners partake in new situational experiences, reflect on their learning process, adjust attributions for their successes and failures, revise earlier assumptions or develop new ones and receive instruction congruent with effective beliefs (Ellis, 2008; Mori, 1999; Wenden, 1999). Because of their basic and pervasive power to influence the language learning process, a chapter elucidating language learners' beliefs and exploring activities to transform them into facilitative agents of progress rather than counterproductive impediments has a place in our current agenda to create an emotional/psychological comfort zone for learners.

All beliefs are not created equal: some facilitate learning and others have the opposite effect. But how do we differentiate and recognize positive and negative beliefs?

Significance of beliefs in language learning

According to Horwitz (1988), exposure to widespread and occasionally conflicting notions about language learning accompany our students to class and influence behavior. These beliefs range from helpful to damaging, with a wide berth for neutral beliefs that apply well at times and not-so-well on other occasions. Whether other people agree or not, learners act upon their beliefs as if they were true (Stevick, 1980). For example, some learners might believe that language learning is strictly a matter of translating from their first language or that it is mostly a matter of memorizing vocabulary. Such beliefs are neither overwhelmingly helpful nor damaging, but they exert their influence on the student's approach to the language. For this reason, beliefs have an influential role in learning outcomes, experience and achievement (Sukui & Gaies, 1999), and the development of insight into the self and the learning process (Oxford, 1990a). With this in mind, let's take a look at the detrimental influence of counterproductive beliefs and the positive implications of those that are helpful.

The negative consequences of counter-productive beliefs are manifested in students who may assign excessive significance to aspects of learning that are beyond their locus to control. Some beliefs can prevent embracing a responsible, proactive position to learning and limit the independence of the learner. An individual who believes that aptitude is necessary for language learning and that she does not have it will approach learning differently than an individual who perceives him/herself as having a gift for language who will differ again from the learner who sees aptitude as multidimensional and a matter of finding personal strengths as a learner. Harmful beliefs may lead to a strict reliance on less effective strategies, resulting in a negative attitude towards learning and autonomy (Victori & Lockhart, 1995). Other debilitating consequences of counterproductive beliefs include classroom anxiety (Horwitz et al., 1986) (see our chapter on Anxiety) and poor cognitive performance (Reid & Hresko, 1982), as beliefs connect into the larger emotion and motivation systems.

On the other hand, positive, helpful beliefs have the opposite effect on classroom performance. Mori (1999) powerfully argues for the encouraging effects of learner beliefs when suggesting that positive beliefs could compensate for one's limited ability as demonstrated in those students who believe that intelligence can be increased and who ultimately outperform those who are initially equal or even superior in ability but believe in a predisposition toward aptitude. Effective learners develop insightful beliefs about language learning processes and their own skills in choosing and implementing operational strategies that may compensate for possible weaknesses (Anstey, 1988). This, in turn, has a facilitating effect on students' learning, as they perceive themselves as initiators of their own learning and become more self-reliant and seekers of their own potential. These students tend to be more proactive, allowing them to take charge of their learning whatever the situation may be (Victori & Lockhart, 1995).

Language learners' beliefs can be assessed on a variety of continuums. Using the idea of a continuum to conceptualize beliefs allows us to think of each belief as falling somewhere between two extremes gradually moving from one end to the other. First, beliefs can be resistant to change on one end and easily malleable on the other. Those resistant to change have most likely been developed over a longer period of time than those that can be readily changed. Another continuum is that which assesses the 'erroneousness' of the belief, extending from that supposition which completely contradicts current empirical SLA research to that which is aligned with current thoughts and trends. Although SLA research literature applies the word 'erroneous' to certain beliefs, we will use the term 'ill-advised' from now on. Research trends come and go with time and further investigations and their results should 'advise' – not dictate – our response. We also believe that 'erroneous' is far too categorical a term to label personally held visions. A third continuum, the counterproductive/productive dichotomy, suggests that there are beliefs that propel students to greater language learning proficiency and those that impede it. Conceptualizing these continuums enables teachers to measure progress toward ultimate attainment of positive, productive beliefs when taking those counter-productive beliefs and transforming them into facilitating action cues.

Capitalizing on Beliefs: An Action Plan

The action plan in continuation is composed of five steps, all working together to reach the common goal of making language learning beliefs facilitative rather than debilitating. The five phases include: (1) Identify your teacher beliefs; (2) Make student beliefs known to the teacher; (3) Increase student awareness of their beliefs and evaluate them for effectiveness; (4) Address the mismatch between teacher and student beliefs; and (5) Confront ill-advised beliefs. These five steps are followed by a series of language learning belief categories that serve as a guiding framework for this chapter's activities and provide opportunities for teachers to work through the five-step action plan.

Identify your teacher beliefs

It seems obvious that just as learners' beliefs will influence their behavior, so too do teacher beliefs impact the way they teach. As beliefs shape the way teachers behave, we need to be aware that real and effective change in teachers' practices can only occur through a change in their beliefs (Kennedy, 1996). To modify these beliefs, Breen (1991) suggests that teachers evaluate their beliefs considering actual classroom events and that through promoting teacher reflectiveness, teachers will connect classroom action and personally held language learning beliefs. Consciously accessing this self-knowledge or taking a personal belief inventory of the language learning ideas held most fervently, allows teachers to make more informed decisions concerning their instructional choices and methods (Horwitz, 1985).

Make learner beliefs known to the teacher

Wenden (1986) suggests that effective language learning necessitates that teachers ascertain what students believe about their learning by using instructional strategies that encourage students to scrutinize these beliefs and their potential influence on how learning is approached. The information gleaned through teachers' investigations into their learners' beliefs should act as a determining factor in the appropriate support for the individual learners (Cotterall, 1995). On the other hand, instruction cannot be tailored to each belief of each student, thus putting the teacher in the position of dealing with groups of students. The investigation of beliefs which inform different behaviors in the language classroom will therefore be useful in building teacher awareness of different learner types that need accommodation (Horwitz, 1999). At the same time, teachers need to be evaluating the data and distinguishing the functional from the dysfunctional beliefs, and planning accordingly (Benson & Lor, 1999).

Students form correct and incorrect assumptions about a wide range of factors that will affect their learning. They have beliefs about cognitive variables, such as intelligence, innate ability, age and motivation; and how they impact language learning. They have beliefs about their strengths and weaknesses and their self-concept as learners. They also have some knowledge about the task of language learning, its difficulty and their role in the whole process. Learners also develop some ideas about using certain strategies and about their potential effectiveness. Effective teachers often consider making decisions based upon this knowledge, which students themselves bring to the task of language learning, and help learners modify it if it is potentially impeding their learning and potential for autonomy (Victori & Lockhart, 1995).

Furthermore, beliefs, in part, determine students' receptivity to various instructional practices as well as their selection of language learning strategies. As learner beliefs are often founded on limited knowledge and experience and often vary among student groups, Horwitz (1997b) suggests that teachers determine their own students' beliefs in order to more effectively explain the purpose of classroom activities. When the purpose is explained, couched in the knowledge of what learners believe, receptivity may increase.

Increase student awareness of their beliefs and evaluate them for effectiveness

When students examine their own beliefs and evaluate their effectiveness when placed alongside new incoming information about how languages are learned and within the context of their personal increasing proficiency, they may be able to modify ill-advised or counterproductive beliefs. This evaluation of beliefs is particularly crucial for rectifying those situations where learners may be misplacing blame for failure. False attribution may preclude proactive measures on the real cause of ineffective learning (Peacock, 2001a). For example, the learner who believes that innate aptitude plays a large role in language learning and who also believes that he is not innately gifted may give up on learning because it is beyond his abilities.

Address the mismatch between teacher and student beliefs

Kern (1995) found that a mismatch between teacher and learner beliefs might create tension in the classroom. In his study, he found that, although teachers and learners had relatively few conflicts in their beliefs, those that were found presumably were attributable to the teachers' greater experience as both language learners and teachers. For example, although both learners and teachers optimistically agreed that almost everyone can learn a second language, teachers were apt to be more realistic with the amount of time that it takes to become proficient. Teachers who have made their beliefs explicit are equipped to deal with the belief conflicts with their students more overtly.

It is only through conscious awareness of personal beliefs that teachers can compare their notions about language learning with those of their students. Although many teachers may believe that language learning is most effective through communicative, meaning-based activities, their students may believe that learning is fostered through form-focused grammar tasks. This mismatch could cause disjointed attitudes between teacher and students and needs to be overtly addressed.

Confront specific ill-advised beliefs

Concurrent with the need for teachers and students to reflect on their beliefs and address the mismatches between them, teachers and students also need to confront ill-advised beliefs. According to Horwitz (1988), this may be most effectively done by providing new information through habitual discussions about the nature of language learning. Armed with the information of what students believe, teachers can work to 'counteract or reinforce (beliefs) as appropriate' (p. 292). Additionally, through examples and instructional practices, teachers can also expose students to the holistic nature of language learning. Concurring with the need for students to rectify their ill-advised assumptions about language learning through a more informed understanding of the nature of language acquisition, Dörnyei (2001) expands this by also suggesting that students need to have reasonable criteria for progress as well. His argument advocates for students to be made aware of the variety of ways that mastery of a second language can be achieved and that learners need to define their own way, using their own strategies and discovering for themselves the techniques which best suit their learning.

When discussing the nature of language learning, knowledge falls into three categories: knowledge about the person, the task and strategies. Person knowledge includes learner beliefs about the cognitive and affective factors that mediate learning; task knowledge taps into views of how language works and what tasks are involved; and strategic knowledge encompasses beliefs about strategies and an understanding of general principles determining strategy choices (Flavell, 1979).

Ill-advised beliefs need to be modified through learner self-examination and reflection in order to purge preconceived notions and prejudices which might interfere with language learning (Horwitz, 1988). If this does not occur, learners' misconceptions and excessive attribution of importance to factors external to their own action will blind them to their personal responsibility in the learning process, which in turn will make it less likely that they will adopt a responsible and active attitude in their approaches to learning. Learner autonomy could be weakened or even lost (Victori & Lockhart, 1995). Although self-examination and reflection will illuminate some counterproductive beliefs that are specific to certain individuals, research into second language acquisition also has highlighted some beliefs that may cause problems for a majority of learners.

Language learning beliefs categories

Research on language learning beliefs presents a plethora of typologies that lists and/or classifies the beliefs reported by learners or observed by investigators. A perusal of the lists generated by Horwitz (1988) and Cotterall (1995) provides an indication of the breadth of possibilities of learners' belief systems as a starting point for capitalizing on learners' beliefs, including those specific learner beliefs that need modification to increase a learner's potential for success. These will be further addressed with specific tasks in the Activities section of this chapter. In the first five belief sets addressed in continuation, Horwitz (1988: 285) seeks to 'describe specific beliefs and to discuss the potential impact of these beliefs on learner expectations and strategies,' using the instrument she created, the Beliefs About Language Learning Inventory (BALLI). The beliefs exposed in the remaining six sets are the result of Cotterall's (1995: 195) sampling of learners in her quest to 'gauge their readiness for the changes in behavior and beliefs which autonomy implies.'

Difficulty of language learning

'Difficulty of language learning' is the title given to Horwitz's (1988) first set of beliefs and includes items such as 'Some languages are easier to learn than others,' and 'It is easier to speak than understand a foreign language.' She also includes an item that examines participants' beliefs concerning how long it takes to become fluent in their target language (TL). In this group of beliefs, counter-productivity could be found on either end of the scale. If the task of language learning is perceived as relatively easy and quickly achieved, learners might become frustrated when their progress is slow. On the contrary, if learners believe it will take an enormous amount of effort, they could become discouraged and apply themselves minimally to the task. The same problem of extreme positions on the scale is found with beliefs about the time investment necessary to become fluent. Experienced teachers understand that learners who believe fluency will be attained quickly, in a matter of semester hours in the classroom, are underestimating the necessary timeframe. On the other hand, learners who are more pessimistic may be unduly so, making them give up before they even begin. Activities 2 and 3 in the 'Practice' section of this chapter address learners' beliefs about issues of time and effort in language learning difficulty.

Foreign language aptitude

In her second category, 'Foreign language aptitude,' Horwitz (1988: 287) includes items such as 'It is easier for children than adults to learn a foreign language', and 'Some people are born with a special ability which helps them learn a foreign language.' Counterproductive beliefs that may need modification in this group are held by those learners who believe that some people are incapable or less capable of learning a second language. This promotes negative expectations for those who put themselves in the low ability group and encourages self-doubt and low expectations. Furthermore, an adult who believes that the window of opportunity for language learning slams shut upon entrance into adulthood will have lower aspirations of success than one who has a firm grasp of the SLA research that suggests that adults indeed learn faster than children (Lightbown & Spada, 2006). Activity 4 targets beliefs about aptitude.

Nature of language learning

Horwitz's (1988: 288) third grouping is 'The nature of language learning' and includes items such as 'Learning a foreign language is mostly a matter of learning a lot of new vocabulary' and 'Learning a foreign language is mostly a matter of translating from my first language.' Specific ill-advised beliefs in this subset are those that consider memorization, grammar and translation as the only means to achieving language learning proficiency. These notions lead learners to invest time and energy in tasks and activities that SLA research suggests are not the most effective means of garnering second language proficiency. Memorizing vocabulary lists, doing fill-in-the-blank grammar worksheets and translating from L1 into TL alone do not necessarily result in speaking fluency or enhanced listening comprehension. Learners can process their beliefs concerning the nature of language learning in Activities 5 and 6.

Strategies

'Learning and communication strategies' is Horwitz's (1988: 290) fourth set and includes items such as 'It is important to repeat and practice a lot,' 'It is important to speak a foreign language with an excellent accent' and 'You shouldn't say anything in the foreign language until you can say it correctly.' Problematic beliefs in this category are once again located on the extreme ends of the scale. Students with an over-concern for correctness might be reticent to participate in communicative activities where the objective is to concentrate on meaning as much as on form. On the other extreme, learners who single-mindedly embrace communicative practices may cringe when teachers make corrections that interrupt their fluent utterances. Furthermore, if a learner perceives that language attempts should only be made when accuracy is assured, the necessary risks that SLA research suggests are necessary for improvement will not be taken. Activities 7 and 8 juxtapose learners' beliefs about the importance of communication and fluency as it relates to form and accuracy.

Motivations and expectations

Horwitz's (1988: 290) final group, 'Motivations and expectations' contains items such as, 'If I learn to speak this language very well, it will help me get a good job,' and 'I would like to learn this language so that I can get to know its speakers better.' In this set, teachers may want to focus on learners who report beliefs that language learning has little or no integrative or instrumental value. In these cases, one concern is that when language study becomes more arduous both in time and effort than originally estimated, some learners might renounce language study. Activity 9 will allow learners to work through their motivations and expectations.

Teachers' roles

Cotterall's (1995) research specifically targets learners' beliefs about their readiness for autonomy. Her first factor, 'Role of the teacher' includes items such as 'The teacher should always explain why we are doing an activity in class' and 'I like the teacher to tell me what to do.' Learners who perceive the teacher's role as dominant and authoritative do not fit the profile of autonomous learners. These counterproductive role beliefs include: The teacher must offer help, tell learners what their difficulties are, specify the amount of time learners need to spend on an activity and explain its purpose, and tell learners what to do. We temper this idea with the cautionary note that not all learners are equally autonomous and teachers must be more directive in some cases. Learners will explore their beliefs about the role of teachers in Activity 10.

Role of feedback

A natural segue from the 'Role of the teacher' is the 'Role of feedback' and follows with statements such as 'I find it helpful for the teacher to give me regular tests' and 'I need the teacher to tell me how I am progressing.' Cotterall (1995) proposes that some learners find the notion of feedback hard to separate from the role of the teacher. Whereas autonomous learners believe in the necessity of self-monitoring progress and the self-evaluation of effort, dependent learners believe the teacher is responsible for giving regular tests and informing about progress. Autonomous individuals understand the importance of seeing progress and using feedback from a variety of sources, including both self- and teacher-assessment processes. The role of feedback in learners' beliefs systems is processed in Activity 11.

Learner independence

Cotterall's (1995) third factor, 'Learner independence' is characterized by beliefs such as 'I like trying new things out by myself' and 'Learning a language is very different from learning other subjects.' Students without a clear idea of what they need English for, those who are unwilling to try out new things and those who do not have strategies for language learning that are different from other subjects likely do not operate independently in their quest for increased language skills. In tandem, Activities 12 and 13 provide opportunities to raise awareness of learners' beliefs about their own independence and to work at increasing it.

Role of previous general learning experiences

The fourth factor contained two beliefs and sought to differentiate between knowing how to 'study languages well' and 'study other subjects well.' Cotterall (1995: 200) relates this to 'an individual's assessment of his/her ability in relation to study in general' and proposes that learners' perceptions of their previous language learning experience influence their confidence, and as this is a key component in autonomous learning, she suggests that teachers 'need to explore with learners their "myths" about themselves and to promote reflection on the language learning process.'

Role of previous language learning experiences

Cotterall's (1995) fifth factor, 'Experience of Language Learning' contains two beliefs: 'I have been successful in language learning in the past' and 'I have my own ways of testing how much I have learned.' Learners who respond favorably to these beliefs can distinguish between being able to use their language and formally studying it. Effective learners integrate the positive input from past experience into self-affirming auto-evaluation. Cotterall (citing Flavell, 1979) directly relates beliefs about metacognition to a learner's approach to language learning. Person knowledge (which embraces cognitive and affective variables), task knowledge (how the language functions and the duties necessary to carry out the language learning mission) and strategic knowledge (the deliberate intentional acts invoked to achieve a purpose) are all used by autonomous learners to further their language learning aims. The main objective in Activities 14 and 15 is to process learners' beliefs about their previous general and language learning experiences in order to increase their confidence and self-efficacy.

Learner approaches to studying

Finally, 'I study my target language the same way I study other subjects' and 'Talking to the teacher about my progress is embarrassing for me' compose Cotterall's (1995) final factor of 'Approach to studying.' This belief addresses learner confidence and language learning experience. Learners who believe they are powerless to impact their learning outcomes are less likely to be autonomous. Activity 16 provides an opportunity for language learners to set goals and reflect upon their willingness to take measured risks.

The 'premise' part of this chapter provided information concerning the nature of language learning beliefs, where they come from and their significance, and also highlighted the specific helpful and harmful beliefs that we will target in the upcoming activities section. With these investigations, we can go beyond the anecdotal to corroborate which ill-advised beliefs learners maintain that contradict current SLA research concerning effective language learning practices and the nature of language learning, and work toward encouraging learners to make alternative choices. To conclude this part of this chapter, we would like to leave you with a story from Buddhist philosophy that poignantly illustrates the dangers of clinging to destructive 'truths'.

This is the story of a widower who dearly loved his five-year-old son. While the father was away on business, thugs burned his entire village and stole his son. Upon the father's return, he saw the charred ruins and panicked. Sobbing uncontrollably, he took the burnt corpse of a child he thought to be his son, cremated him in a ceremony, collected the ashes and put them in a beautiful urn that he kept with him constantly. Afterwards, his real son escaped from the thieves and found his way home, arriving at his father's new cottage late at night. He knocked on the door. Still in tremendous grief, the father asked, 'Who is it?' The son exhausted yet elated answered, 'It is me, Papa! Open the door!' In his agitated state of mind and convinced his son was dead, the father thought that some young village boys were taunting him and he shouted, 'Go away!' and he continued to cry inconsolably. After some time, the child left, and they were never to see each other again.

Although beliefs about language learning will not result in such dire consequences as related in this story, the moral of it is nonetheless evident: Sometime, somewhere, you believe something to be the truth. If you cling to it so much, even when the truth comes in person and knocks on your door, you will not open it.

... To Practice

Beliefs Activities

As language learners work through the following activities, keep in mind these multi-faceted, simultaneously targeted goals: to clarify your teacher beliefs, to increase understanding of learners' beliefs; to enhance learners' self-awareness and self-evaluation of their beliefs; to address any mismatches between what you and your students believe; and to confront specific ill-advised beliefs. Although the activities may differ conceptually, the affective aim is similar: to process language learning beliefs and modify them when necessary in interaction with others. As teachers listen and interact, they too achieve greater understanding of their learners' beliefs.

Beliefs Activity 1: De-bunking Language Learning Myths through Affinity Mapping

Man is made by his belief. As he believes, so he is. – Johann Wolfgang von Goethe

Levels: All

Procedure:

(1) Preface this activity by explaining that according to the Merriam Webster dictionary, a 'myth' is 'a popular belief or tradition that has grown up around something or someone ... an unfounded or false notion.' For example, it's an enduring *myth* that money brings happiness. To check for understanding, ask learners for examples of commonly held myths in their cultures.

(2) Write this open-ended question on the board: 'What language learner myths do you hold? Model one from the 'premise' part of this chapter. Distribute several post-it notes to each student and ask learners to answer it with one idea per post-it note.

(3) Through communicating non-verbally, ask learners to organize all of their ideas by what they perceive as 'natural' categories.

(4) Converse about the sorting exercise and come up with a name for each category.

(5) To debrief this activity, review and discuss the group categories. Discuss what implications there are if or when these beliefs are held as the truth.

MODIFICATIONS:

Emergent learners: Provide vocabulary for both potential myths and possible category titles from which they can choose.

Large groups: Place students in groups of five for the activity (Steps 3 and 4). De-brief in the same groups (Step 5).

Technology: To prime students' learning and to increase understanding of 'myths,' find a video on YouTube of a particular myth or type 'common cultural myths' in the search engine and surf until a suitable one for your group is found.

Beliefs Activity 2: Difficulty of Language Learning Fishbowl (Effort needed)

If I have the belief that I can do it, I shall surely acquire the capacity to do it even if I may not have it at the beginning. – Mahatma Gandhi

Level: Intermediate/Advanced

In preparation:

(1) Arrange four to five chairs in an inner circle with the remaining chairs arranged in a concentric circle outside.

Procedure:

(1) Preface this activity by explaining that the objective is for learners to explore their beliefs about the difficulty of language learning, particularly as concerns the amount of effort needed, so that those with extreme viewpoints might align their ideas to a more moderate position.

(2) Ask for three or four volunteers (one less than the number of inner circle chairs) to take a seat in the inner circle to discuss some of their beliefs about language learning.

(3) Direct the rest of the students to take seats in the outer circle. Clarify that any member of the audience can, at any time, occupy the empty chair and join the discussion, but that when this happens, a member of the inner circle must take a seat in the outer circle to free up a chair.

(4) Explain that the purpose of the discussion is not to come to a consensus but rather to allow those who so desire to give their opinion, whether that be their own belief or one that they think others might have.

(5) Introduce the following belief and allow the participants to start discussing the topic: 'Some languages are easier to learn than others.' The discussion continues with participants entering and leaving the inner circle while the entire audience listens in on the discussion.

(6) When all volunteers have had the chance to speak concerning that particular belief, introduce the following: 'The language I am trying to learn is: (a) very difficult; (b) difficult; (c) of medium difficulty; (d) easy; (e) very easy.' Allow the same conversational process to run its course.

(7) If time permits, introduce the following prompt: 'Rank the following foreign language skills in terms of difficulty: reading, writing, speaking and listening.' Let the students discuss.

(8) De-brief this activity by reminding learners that beliefs found on both ends of the 'difficulty' continuum could be hazardous; that if one perceives language learning as 'too easy,' learners might become frustrated if their progress slows, whereas on the other hand if learning is perceived as 'too difficult', learners may become discouraged and apply themselves minimally.

MODIFICATION:

Emergent learners: Although emergent learners may not have the linguistic ability necessary to discuss at length their rationale for their beliefs, they should – with enough scaffolding – be able to answer the questions with a show of hands thus providing the teacher with information about their beliefs.

Technology: Consider using Voicethread for this activity to move learners from writing to speaking. Create a different thread with each question and ask learners to post their own ideas and to comment on those posted by others by using webcams, computer microphones or telephones.

Beliefs Activity 3: Stand Where You Stand: Difficulty of Language Learning (Time investment)

If you believe in what you are doing, then let nothing hold you up in your work. Much of the best work of the world has been done against seeming impossibilities. The thing is to get the work done. – Dale Carnegie

Level: Intermediate/Advanced

In preparation:

(1) Place a line of masking tape on the floor from one wall of your classroom to the other.

Procedure:

(1) Preface this activity by explaining that the purpose is to explore learners' beliefs about the time investment necessary to learn a language, and to raise awareness about the hazards of maintaining extreme positions.
(2) Ask learners to respond to the following statement by choosing a number that best supports what they believe: 'If someone spent one hour a day learning a language, how long would it take him/her to become fluent? (1) less than a year; (2) 1–2 years; (3) 3–5 years; (4) 5–10 years; (5) You can't learn a language in one hour a day.'
(3) Explain to learners that each end of the tape represents the polar positions on the scale. Invite them to line up with notebook and pencil in hand on the tape in the order of the strength of their response, discussing their belief with the person on their right and then on their left and why they hold that belief.
(4) Tell each learner to list the reasons in writing of the person to their immediate right and left. This encourages each individual to reflect upon at least one reason for their belief and not opine, 'Just because.'
(5) When students are finished, ask for volunteers to summarize their interviews.
(6) De-brief the session by explaining that beliefs found on both ends of the 'time commitment' continuum are risky: Underestimating the time necessary may lead to frustration when fluency is not immediately attained while overestimating the time may result in undue pessimism.

MODIFICATIONS:

Emergent learners: Emergent group members should be able to form the timeline which would provide important 'learner beliefs' information to the teacher, but they may have difficulty in articulating complex reasons for it and in summarizing peer interviews.

Technology: To provide writing practice and time to plan and rehearse, the summary of the interviews from Step 5 may be posted to an online discussion board.

Beliefs Activity 4: Debate on Foreign Language Aptitude

What we can or cannot do, what we consider possible or impossible, is rarely a function of our true capability. It is more likely a function of our beliefs about who we are. – Anthony Robbins

Level: Intermediate/Advanced

Procedure:

(1)   Preface this activity by explaining that learners will explore their beliefs about aptitude and age and how they influence language learning. Explain that this is especially problematic for those individuals who believe themselves to be members of one of those unfortunate groups who would likely generate negative expectations.

(2)   Divide the students into two groups. In the first group, present the belief: 'It is easier for children than adults to learn a foreign language.' By a show of hands, invite learners either to work in a group that is preparing arguments to support that belief or to work in a group that is organizing arguments to oppose it. In the second group, state the belief, 'Some people are born with a special ability which helps them learn a foreign language.' Follow the same volunteering process as the other belief.

(3)   Inform all those who had volunteered to work on the team to draft arguments to support the belief that they will now oppose it, and all those who had volunteered to work in the group to oppose the belief will now argue in support of it.

(4)   Give learners in all four groups several minutes to create a list of arguments. Each group elects one person to represent their assigned position.

(5) Invite the two opposing sides of the 'special ability' belief to present. Then invite the opposing sides of the 'children learn more easily' debate to present.
(6) After the initial presentations, tell groups to reconvene to create rebuttal arguments and choose one person to represent them. Instruct each side to give their arguments.
(7) De-brief this activity by presenting second language acquisition research on the idea that although children may learn better in the long run, adults tend to learn faster (Lightbown & Spada (2006): How Languages Are Learned). Also present research on aptitude that is available in Chapter 3 in this volume. Confronting these 'myths' with kernels of SLA 'truths' may help to modify learner beliefs in the direction of more positive expectations of success.

MODIFICATION:

Technology: Voicethread has a feature for class debates. Learners can post information for the first four steps (i.e. mostly information gathering) in either written or oral form, but stipulate that learners must post using oral technology (webcams, computer microphones, and telephones) to actually present their arguments (Steps 5 and 6). De-brief learners through a teacher blog posting.

Beliefs Activity 5: Gallery Walk to Clarify the Nature and Difficulty of Language Learning

When you believe 'I can do it', the 'how to do it' develops. – David Schwartz

Level: Intermediate/Advanced

In preparation:

(1) Place posters with the following 'loaded' beliefs around the room:
    (a) Learning (language being learned) is a long and difficult process.
    (b) Learning (language being learned) can be accomplished quickly and easily.
    (c) (Language being learned) is learned best by studying grammar and vocabulary.

(d) (Language being learned) is learned best by speaking and inter-
     acting in the language.

(e) Anyone can learn (language being learned).

(f) Only children and people with special abilities can learn (lan-
     guage being learned).

(2) Feel free to modify these statements according to those beliefs that
     you consider your students need most to clarify and evaluate.

Procedure:

(1) Preface this activity by highlighting the idea that the beliefs learners
     maintain about language learning influence their behavior, and
     while some beliefs are helpful, others may be counterproductive.
     The purpose of this activity is to clarify some of these beliefs and
     heighten learners' self-awareness.

(2) Randomly assign learners to a poster.

(3) Give each group a different colored marker.

(4) Ask the small group in front of the poster to discuss the belief and
     write down their remarks.

(5) Invite each group to shift to the next poster and repeat the exercise.

(6) When all of the groups have visited all of the posters, ask them to
     return to their original poster and discuss and analyze the responses
     of the other groups.

(7) Debrief by asking learners if they had changed their opinions and
     what the implications of holding one belief over another would have
     as they continue their language learning journey.

MODIFICATIONS:

Large classes: Invite learners to reflect on the de-briefing question in their
language learning diaries and collect them sporadically for teacher reflection and to inform future instructional decisions.

Technology: Place the six 'loaded' learner belief statements on the class
Discussion Board as teacher threads and tell learners to post responses
to three of them and to respond to two of their peers' comments.

Beliefs Activity 6: Rotating Stations on the Nature of Language Learning

In the province of the mind, what one believes to be true either is true or becomes true. – John Lilly

Level: Intermediate/Advanced

In preparation:

(1) Preface this activity by explaining that it is meant to clarify learners' beliefs about the importance of culture, context, vocabulary, grammar and translation in language learning so that ultimately they are able to put each into perspective in relation to the others.
(2) Create six 'stations' around your classroom each containing a large piece of poster paper/newsprint/blackboard with one of the following six titles:
   (a) Is culture important? Why or why not? If so, how?
   (b) Is learning (language being learned) in (country where language is spoken) better than in another setting? What can I do to enhance my learning here?
   (c) Is vocabulary important? Why or why not? If so, how?
   (d) Is grammar important? Why or why not? If so, how?
   (e) Is translating from my first language a good thing? Why or why not? If so, how?
   (f) Is learning (language being learned) the same as other school subjects? Why or why not? If so, how?

Procedure:

(1) Divide learners into six small groups and place each group at one of the stations. Give them five minutes to discuss each belief and to record their ideas on the poster/newsprint/blackboard with a marker.
(2) Invite learners to move to new a station. Tell them to continue their discussion considering the ideas they find from the previous group. Repeat this process until all six groups have commented on all six beliefs.
(3) Reconvene the whole group and read the students' responses from the posters. Discuss.
(4) De-brief this activity by explaining that whereas grammar, vocabulary and translation all have a role in language learning, it is best to balance these with other communicative activities. Discuss the role of culture in language learning and talk about

ways that learning in a second language context may be different from that of a foreign language context.

MODIFICATIONS:

Technology: Consider using wikis to answer the above six questions by creating documents that are collaborative, owned by all, and revisable. Format six wikis with a title corresponding to each of the questions above. Follow the low tech steps, but rather than shifting groups physically around the room, begin by assigning one question to each group to begin the wiki. When every group has written down their ideas, exchange the wiki and have the next group revise and add. Continue exchanging the wikis until all the groups have had a chance to collaborate on all the documents.

Beliefs Activity 7: Human Graph on Form/Accuracy vs. Meaning/Fluency

Whatever you believe with feeling becomes your reality.– Brian Tracy

Level: Intermediate/Advanced

In preparation:

(1) Put up four signs on four opposing walls with the opposing walls representing different viewpoints.
   (a) On one wall, post the following statement: 'I agree that learning a foreign language is mostly a matter of learning a lot of grammar rules.'
   (b) On the opposite wall, post the following statement: 'I agree that if I heard someone speaking the language I am trying to learn, I would go up to them so that I could practice speaking the language.'
   (c) On the other set of opposing walls, place these statements: 'If you are allowed to make mistakes in the beginning, it will be hard to get rid of them later on,' and 'It's ok to guess if you don't know a word in the foreign language.'

Procedure:

(1) Preface this activity by explaining that your objective is to provide an opportunity for learners to explore their beliefs about the

importance of fluency versus accuracy in language learning with the purpose of transforming extremes into more balanced perspectives.

(2) Invite students to position themselves in the room according to their position on those axes. For example, students might arrange themselves on an axis reflecting agreement that language learning is a lot of grammar, and a second that mistakes should not be allowed.

(3) Once learners are in the four main areas defined by their responses on the 'graph', tell them to clarify their position about the nature of language learning and their communication strategies relative to the people around them.

(4) Ask a representative from each quadrant to make another group of four. Each learner receives two minutes to summarize the general idea of their initial quadrant.

(5) De-brief the session with a discussion on the importance of a balance between accuracy and fluency. Explain that this is achieved by implementing strategies that allow for both grammar and communicative pursuits. Also explain the hazards of taking an extreme position on 'correctness': that an over-active monitor may impede fluency, whereas an under-active one may lead to incomprehensibility.

MODIFICATIONS:

Technology: As a follow-up to the classroom activity, create a hash tag and have learners 'Tweet' one important epiphany that they experienced through participating in this task.

Beliefs Activity 8: Role Play on the Importance of Meaning and Communication

I know that you believe you understand what you think I said, but I'm not sure you realize that what you heard is not what I meant.
– Robert McCloskey

Level: Intermediate/Advanced

In preparation:

(1) (Adapted Story, original found on 'Aspiring to Greatness' website) Make one copy per group of the following adapted story from www.aspiringtogreatness.com:

One day I was lying on the bed, reading, when my mother came into the room. She held out a vase – a rather ugly vase.

She asked, 'Would you like to have this vase?'

I replied quickly, 'No, I don't want it.'

As she turned to walk away, my inner voice implored, 'Wait a minute, don't let her walk away. Find out more.' So I asked, 'Where did you get it?'

She said, 'Oh, I got it when I filled an order.'

Filled an order? I thought – no communication here. So I asked, 'What do you mean, filled an order?'

'Well,' she said, 'when I was a little girl, the Smith Company mailed catalogs to people. I would take the catalog around the neighborhood, and I'd get people to order from it. When I filled an order and sent it in, they gave me a prize. One time, I got a porch swing for my family.'

Now you have to understand that my mother is 81 years old. She is one of six children in a family that her father deserted when she was quite young. Money was real hard to come by. My grandmother managed to keep the family together through the years, although I don't know how. For my mother to win a luxury like a porch swing was a significant accomplishment. Although she no longer had the swing, she had the vase – a vase full of meaning – which she offered to me. Instantly I said, 'Mom, I want the vase.' Now it sits in a prominent place in my living room. It symbolizes a precious meaning which my mother and I share: Unless you and I are sensitive to the other person and hear meaning, we may well have a communication problem.'

Procedure:

(1) Preface this activity by drawing learners' attention to the idea that language learning is much more than grammar, vocabulary and translation; that learning a language is about seeking meaning.

(2) Place students in groups of five and distribute a copy of the story to each group.

(3) Assign the following roles, one to each member:
   (a) Starter: Begins the discussion by reading the story.
   (b) Wrapper: Summarizes the discussion at the end.
   (c) Optimist/Pessimist: Present good/bad side.
   (d) Investigative Reporter: Poses questions and searches for details about the story.

(4) Ask the 'Starter' to read the story aloud. If there are language difficulties with vocabulary or meaning, have learners discuss them in the group. Circulate to clarify any precise language questions students could not decipher for themselves.
(5) Ask the 'Investigative Reporter' to compose a list of questions to ask his/her group members about the story that will help illuminate some of the finer important details and discuss the story.
(6) Ask the 'Pessimist' to present those issues the story raised that could be seen as opportunities for improvement. When he/she is done, ask the 'Optimist' to point out the positive events in the story.
(7) At the end of the discussion, ask the 'Wrapper' to summarize the group's discussion and highlight important points.
(8) De-brief learners by asking them to share their thoughts about the activity. Explain that language learning differs in very human ways from the study of other academic subjects. Impress upon them the need to seek sensitivity and enter their interlocutor's frame of reference; to search for the reasons why their interlocutor receives and responds to messages as he or she does; to look for genuine interaction.

MODIFICATIONS:

For emergent learners: Teachers may need to scaffold with more pre-reading strategies through activating existing schema about family communication patterns, providing vocabulary assistance and simplifying some of the more complex syntax.

Large groups: The de-briefing may not allow everyone to share so as a follow-up activity, invite learners to journal about experiences when they were involved in a 'miscommunication' and how it was resolved (or not!).

Technology: Projecting the story on to a screen through a data projector saves a few trees. Learners might also enjoy creating their own inspirational stories using animation features from their computer desktop applications (e.g. Microsoft Office).

Beliefs Activity 9: Generating Beliefs Statements on Motivations and Expectations

They can conquer who believe they can. – Virgil

Level: All

Procedure:

(1) Preface this activity by explaining that learners' motivation and persistence will increase with heightened awareness of the value inherent in being able to use another language.
(2) Divide the class into groups of four students. Come up with six endings to the open-ended statement: 'With (language being studied), I can....' Provide the example, 'travel to (country where language is spoken).'
(3) Reconvene the whole group to share responses. Compose a learner-generated list on the board.
(4) De-brief this activity discussing all of the instrumental and integrative reasons for learning another language. When learners see the value in language learning they are more likely to continue even when the time and effort necessary turns out to be more than originally anticipated.

MODIFICATIONS:

Technology: Brainstorm electronically so learners can post anonymously. Invite them to read the list and post a reflection to the class electronic Discussion Board under a teacher created thread (*With this language I can...*). Prioritize five top favorite ideas. Provide rationale (Steps 2 and 3).

Beliefs Activity 10: Think/Pair/Share Teacher's Role

It's lack of faith that makes people afraid of meeting challenges, and I believe in myself. –Muhammad Ali

Level: All

Procedure:

(1) Preface this activity by explaining that learner autonomy is critical in approaching language learning tasks and that through the next steps learners will explore their beliefs about the role of the teacher.

(2) Pose the question: What is the role of my language teacher?
(3) Ask learners to brainstorm independently in writing for 4–5 minutes.
(4) In partners, discuss responses for 3–4 minutes.
(5) Reconvene the group. Invite volunteers to share their ideas. List them on the board.
(6) Ask learners to partner again with the same person and respond to the prompt, 'What could I do for myself that I had previously expected the teacher to do? Allow 3–4 minutes for conversation.
(7) De-brief this activity by inviting students to share any insights they gleaned during their exploration of their perceptions of the teacher's role. Were they able to recognize that beliefs that put the teacher in a dominating role could, in some cases, be counterproductive to independent learning?

MODIFICATIONS:

Technology: Electronically brainstorm the two prompts. This converts the activity from a predominantly listening/speaking to a reading/writing focus. Learners read the brainstormed lists and answer the de-briefing questions on the Discussion Board using a teacher created thread (*My role/Teacher's role*).

Beliefs Activity 11: Nominal Group Technique to Clarify the Role of Feedback and Self-Monitoring/Evaluating

Others believing in you is nice but worthless if not matched by your own thought.– Scott Moore

Level: All

Procedure:

(1) Preface this activity by telling learners that its objective is to enhance their beliefs about the importance of learner autonomy and to discover new learner-driven ways to monitor and evaluate their progress.
(2) Pass out an index card to each learner and ask the question, 'How can I self-monitor or self-evaluate my learning more effectively?'
(3) Allow learners enough time to write their answers.
(4) Ask learners to turn their cards over and answer this second question: 'What other sources (besides the teacher) could I look to in order to receive feedback on my language progress?'

(5) Collect the cards and re-distribute them.
(6) Invite students to take turns reading and defending the answer/opinion on their card as if it were their own.
(7) List the responses on the board. With input from learners, cluster and tally them.
(8) De-brief this activity by reiterating the importance of exploring other sources beyond the teacher in their individual process of self-monitoring and self-evaluation. Stress that autonomous language learners are continually monitoring their learning and assessing their efforts.

MODIFICATIONS:

Emergent learners: After re-distributing the cards, give learners time to write down some ideas and share them with a partner rather than have them speak spontaneously in front of the whole group.

Large groups: Carry out this entire activity in groups of five or six so that everyone has an opportunity to read and defend what is written on the card. Have small groups list, cluster and tally their responses to hand in for teacher review.

Technology: Show a video from YouTube that uses the TL a bit beyond learners' current proficiency as a stimulus for reflection. With specific language and situations in mind, learners are better equipped to formulate strategies.

Beliefs Activity 12: Minute Paper on Learner Independence

If people believe in themselves, it is amazing what they can accomplish. – Sam Walton

Level: All

(1) Preface this activity by explaining that research suggests that learners are more autonomous when they have clear beliefs of what they can use their new language for and that those who are willing to take risks with the new language will usually fare better.
(2) Pass out a blank index card to each student. In one minute, learners write a thoughtful but brief response to the following prompt: What do you believe you can use (language being learned) for? Collect the anonymous responses.

(3) Read each of them out loud.
(4) Pass out another blank index card to each student. In one minute, learners write a response to a new prompt: 'What new things are you willing to try as we continue learning (language being studied) together?
(5) Read these new cards out loud.
(6) De-brief this activity by asking students to comment on any risk-taking strategies they developed. Discuss the implications of success and failure with the new strategies.

MODIFICATIONS:

Large groups: Put learners into groups of five or six and have them read back the 'minute papers' and de-brief.

Technology: Search YouTube for a video that uses language that is a bit beyond learners' current proficiency of someone using the TL in the culture where the TL is spoken. After reading the first question, but before handing out the first index card, show the video as a means of stimulating more precise learner feedback to the two questions posed.

Beliefs Activity 13: Stand and Declare Your Learner Independence

Believe it can be done. When you believe something can be done, really believe, your mind will find the ways to do it. Believing a solution paves the way to solution. – Dr David Schwartz

Level: Intermediate/Advanced

Procedure:

(1) Preface this activity by explaining that learners will reflect upon their previous experience with language learning and attempt to transform their positive beliefs into effective strategies for autonomous learning.
(2) Write the following statements on the board. Tell learners to use a scale from one to five to represent the strength of their agreement or disagreement (1 = strongly agree; 2 = agree; 3 = neither agree nor disagree; 4 = disagree; 5 = strongly disagree):
    (a) Learning a language is very different from learning other subjects.
    (b) I know how to study languages well.

(c) I have been successful in language learning in the past.

(d) I have my own ways of testing how much I have learned.

(3) Recite the first and second beliefs, 'Learning a language is very different from learning other subjects' and 'I know how to study languages well.' Tell learners who responded that they 'agreed' or 'strongly agreed' to either question to form a group at the front of the room. Ask members of the group to answer the following questions:

(a) What are your most effective strategies for studying/learning language?

(b) How do you study language differently than other subjects?

(c) How did you come to use the strategies that you do?

(4) Tell that group to sit down and then recite the other two beliefs: 'I have been successful at language learning in the past' and 'I have my own ways of testing how much I have learned.' Again, tell learners who responded that they 'agreed' or 'strongly agreed' to form a group at the front, but this time, ask these questions:

(a) To what do you most attribute your success?

(b) What have you tried that was *un*successful?

(c) Tell us your most successful self-assessment strategies.

(5) De-brief this activity by explaining that not all strategies are effective for all learners, but listening to others about their successful learning experiences is a good way to begin looking at one's own.

MODIFICATIONS:

Technology: Consider making an online survey for this activity by accessing one of the many quick and easy survey creation websites. With the results, teachers can either continue with the in-class activity above or have the 'agreed' and 'strongly agreed' respondents create threads and write their responses on the class Discussion Board to which the respondents who answered they 'disagreed' or 'strongly disagreed' must respond with their reflections about the feasibility of the proposed ideas.

Beliefs Activity 14: Guided Imagery and Dialogue Journaling for Learner Confidence

You must start with desire, keeping in mind that with the magic of believing you can obtain what you picture in your mind's eye. – Claude M. Bristol

Level: Intermediate/Advanced

Procedure:

(1) Preface this exercise in guided imagery by informing learners that it is meant to help them get in touch with their expectations, assumptions and fears about language learning. Explain that research demonstrates that language learners who believe that they have the ability to impact their own learning outcomes are more autonomous. Through this exercise, learners imagine what success looks like.

(2) Invite learners to get comfortable, close their eyes if they wish, and listen to the following narration:

This is Good!

Author: Unknown

(Downloaded from: http://www.inspirationalstories.com/11/1120.html)

> *The story is told of an African king and his close friend with whom he had grown up. The friend had a habit of looking at every situation that ever occurred in his life (positive or negative) and remarking, 'This is good!'*

> *One day the king and his friend went on a hunting expedition. The friend's job was to load and prepare the guns for the king. The friend had apparently done something wrong in preparing one of the guns, for after taking the gun from his friend, the king fired it and his thumb blew off.*

> *Upon examining the situation the friend remarked as usual, 'This is good!'*

> *To which the king replied, 'No, this is NOT good!' and proceeded to send his friend to jail.*

> *About a year later, the king was hunting in a dangerous and secluded area. Cannibals captured him and took him to their village. They tied his hands, stacked some wood, set up a stake and bound him to the stake. As they came near to set fire to the wood, they noticed that the king was missing a thumb. Being superstitious, they never ate anyone that was less than whole. So they untied the king, and sent him on his way.*

As he returned home, he was reminded of the event that had taken his thumb and felt remorse for his treatment of his friend.

He went immediately to the jail to speak with his friend. 'You were right,' he said, 'it was good that my thumb was blown off.'

And he proceeded to tell the friend all that had just happened. 'And so I am very sorry for sending you to jail for so long. It was bad for me to do this.'

'No,' his friend replied, 'This is good!'

'What do you mean, 'This is good'? How could it be good that I sent my friend to jail for a year?'

'If I had NOT been in jail, I would have been with you.'

(3) Ask learners to respond to this reading in the form of a dialogue entry in their language learning diaries, making as many personal connections between the story and their own language learning journey.
(4) Tell learners to exchange their entries with a partner and write comments alongside their partner's thoughts. Return the journal to the original writer and read what the partner shared.
(5) De-brief this activity by talking about individual responsibility, learner autonomy and the role of teacher as facilitator rather than dominating force.

MODIFICATIONS:

Emergent learners: Find a different inspirational story with more basic vocabulary and simpler syntax or invent another. After scaffolding the selected or invented story with a vocabulary preview and activating learners' schema about its themes, present the story and continue with the dialogue journals.

Large groups: De-briefing in the whole group format might get unwieldy considering the number and variety of learner responses. To facilitate learners' processing, stop at several intervals during the de-briefing and ask for a volunteer to summarize or paraphrase what has just been said.

Technology: Accompany the guided imagery with music appropriate to the story's theme.

Beliefs Activity 15: Self-efficacy and Attribution Wagon Wheel

Sometimes I've believed as many as six impossible things before breakfast. – Alice, from Lewis Carroll's, *Alice in Wonderland*

Level: All

In preparation:

(1) Place chairs in multiple concentric pairs of circles, each containing an inner and outer circle with four chairs each. The inner circle chairs face outward, whereas the outer circle chairs face inward, creating pairs of chairs.

Procedure:

(1) Preface this activity by explaining that learners who maintain positive beliefs about their personal ability to make a difference in their own learning will be more effective goal-setters, so the purpose of this task is to draw their attention to successful experiences.
(2) As students file in, ask them to take a chair in any of the concentric circles. When everyone is seated, with each pair facing each other, tell them that they will have five minutes to discuss the following question with their partner: 'Can I influence my own language learning outcomes? What would this look like in action?' Invite them to brainstorm and come to a common understanding of the topic.
(3) At the end of the allotted time, learners on the outside circle rotate one seat to the right. Pose the next question for the newly formed pair: 'Using your previous successful and unsuccessful experience, brainstorm a list of methods for self-assessing your language learning.'
(4) Do this two more times with the following two prompts so that each of the four people in the inner circle have had an opportunity to interact with every member of the outer circle: 'Tell your partner about one instance when you have used (language being learned) successfully and how that made you feel,' and 'Share with your partner a specific instance when you have set a specific language goal, created steps to meet it and the result.'
(5) Debrief this activity by reminding students of the importance of maintaining positive beliefs concerning self-efficacy and attribution. Learners with strong self-efficacy beliefs tend to exert greater efforts to meet challenges, whereas those with considerable doubt decrease their efforts or give up.

MODIFICATIONS:

Emergent learners: Provide simplified prompts and scaffolding while circulating among the dyads.

Technology: Use Skype. If teachers want learners to practice spontaneous oral language, follow the format above, using the videoconferencing function. If teachers want learners to practice writing, use the chat function. To facilitate the exchange of partners, have the four pair combinations prepared in advance with one partner on 'List A' and the other on 'List B,' so that when the teacher calls 'time' for a partner exchange, the partner from 'List A' calls the individual from 'List B' with no confusion over who makes and receives the call.

Beliefs Activity 16: Pyramids to Setting Goals and Taking Risks

To accomplish great things, we must not only act, but also dream; not only plan, but also believe. – Anatole France

Level: Intermediate/Advanced

Procedure:

(1) Preface this activity by explaining that when learners are willing to take risks with the language, they will see positive outcomes in their language learning, and that risk-taking is also a positive element in setting language learning goals; to reach high, but not unrealistically so. These two elements, risk-taking and goal setting, are worth their 'thought time' to evaluate and ultimately incorporate into their belief systems.
(2) Write the following two questions on the board: (a) How can I take more risks in learning language?; and (b) What are some reasonable goals I can set right now?
(3) Pair learners and ask them to respond to the questions in a brainstorming session.
(4) Ask two groups of two to join each other and combine their suggestions and limit their proposal to their top five for each question. Allow them to prioritize their lists for themselves.
(5) Continue combining learners until the entire class has reconvened and developed their top five ideas for the two prompts.
(6) De-brief the class by inviting students to continually be setting realistic goals and overtly thinking about how they can take calculated risks.

3 Cognitive Abilities: Aptitude, Working Memory and Multiple Intelligences

From Premise . . .

'You care for nothing but shooting, dogs and rat catching,' said one father to his son.

In his autobiography, the son later wrote, 'I was considered by my father, a very ordinary boy, rather below the common standard in intellect.'

'Mentally slow, unsociable and adrift forever in his foolish dreams,' was how one teacher referred to her student. The pupil was later expelled and refused admittance to a polytechnic school and had his PhD dissertation dismissed as irrelevant and fanciful.

'I have an idiot for a son,' said another father whose opinion was corroborated by the boy's uncle who said he was, 'uneducable.' Described as the worst pupil in the elementary school, this young man was also later denied admittance to art college.

Was Charles Darwin, the father of the theory of evolution, really 'below the common standard in intellect?' Was Albert Einstein, the famous physicist, truly 'mentally slow?' Was Rodin, the sculptor of The Thinker, an 'idiot' and 'uneducable?' One can only imagine the disservice to humanity that would have resulted if individuals who later went on in life to do great things had listened to the voices around them. These true-to-life scenarios are evidence of the enigmatic nature of human aptitude, intelligence and ability, and underscore the prudence that must be exercised as we move from premise to practice in conceptualizing, assessing and applying teaching practices to capitalize on them.

When individuals say they have a 'knack' or a 'flair' for something, they seem to be connoting that their prowess is a predisposition that comes 'naturally' to them. Is this a genetic endowment? If so, can this natural 'trait-like' predilection also be nurtured? Does it exist with language ability? Some students may boast to having a talent for learning language in instructional settings, whereas others brag about 'picking up' the language while immersed in a second language environment. Do both of these scenarios fall under the rubrics of 'aptitude' and/or 'intelligence?' A number of individuals may score highly on traditional intelligence tests. Will they be more likely to earn high marks on language aptitude tests as well? Is assessing an individual on only mathematical and verbal intelligence a fair and accurate measure of learning ability? Or are there other just as important intelligence types? Experienced language teachers intuit that language learning is extremely complex and happens in stages. Is aptitude a single, unitary concept or is it composed of a number of cognitive factors making up a composite measure, which might include the variable of a 'working memory' (WM)? If it is multi-variant, do different components of aptitude relate to specific stages in the acquisition process?

Throughout this chapter, we will attempt to answer these questions by examining the research on language learning aptitude, WM and multiple intelligences (MIs), first by investigating their inter-relationship as cognitive ability variables and then by breaking them into their separate domains where we will define them, explain their importance and provide guidelines for effective pedagogy. The Activities section will transform the aptitude, WM and MIs research premises into classroom practice through the provision of research-based activities.

Exploring Cognitive Abilities, Their Origins and Their Significance

None of the concepts of *ability, aptitude* or *intelligence* have a universally accepted theory or definition, but they are, for the common layperson, interchangeable and capture the stages involved in processing information and obtaining new knowledge. When a person is thought to have 'language aptitude' most people would equate that with 'language learning ability.' Intelligence, on the other hand, has a broader meaning. When not accompanied by an adjective such as 'verbal,' *intelligence* implies a generic kind of aptitude that is not limited to a precise performance domain but is transferable to a variety of acts.

Strictly speaking, the term *language aptitude* needs pluralization as it is made up of a variety of cognitive features forming a composite measure that has traditionally referenced an individual's general capacity to learn a foreign language. One of the component parts of aptitude is WM. Wen and Skehan (2011: 35) make a convincing case for modifying existing aptitude constructs to include three important '(pre)conditions': (1) WM capacity varies among individual TL learners in measurable ways; (2) WM is a persistent and pervasive presence in numerous phases of SLA and cognitive processes; and (3) WM components correlate highly with features of TL performance and development. Likewise, intelligence shares language aptitude's composite make-up and involves a range of cognitive factors that overlap between them as we will see later in the chapter when we explore MIs. The multi-componential nature of mental abilities implies that variation will exist within the individual considering particular skills; that is to say, just because an individual may demonstrate strong verbal abilities does not mean he will excel in reasoning (Dornyei, 2005).

Exploring Aptitude

What language aptitude is

Early studies of language aptitude characterized it as a stable cognitive feature – an important distinction, for if language aptitude were malleable or easily influenced by other environmental factors like training or previous language learning familiarity, Carroll (1973) suggested that aptitude would simply be a pseudonym for relevant experience. Whether it is fixed at birth or shaped by early experience, Carroll remained neutral, suggesting that genetic determination or early experience both produce the results of having it constrained by roughly the age of four. Furthermore, when aptitude was measured via Carroll and Sapon's (1959) widely used and still influential Modern Language Aptitude Test (MLAT), it did not predict whether an individual can learn a foreign language or not; it predicted the rate at which a person could learn (Skehan, 2002). From the beginning, aptitude was conceived as a multi-variant construct, consisting of four components: phonetic decoding ability (codification, assimilation and recalling phonetic material), rote memory (ability to recall foreign language information), and two features embodying the grammatical skill – grammatical sensitivity (capacity to identify grammatical functions of words and/or phrases in sentence structures) and inductive language learning ability (the ability to figure out the rules that constrain language use in specific linguistic contexts) (Carroll, 1981).

The significance of language aptitude

Simply stated, the importance of language aptitude lies in its strong predictive accuracy of academic success in a wide variety of contexts (Dornyei, 2005; Dornyei & Skehan, 2003; Ranta, 2008). It has significant influence in the realm of TL learning and is ranked among the litany of individual differences that consistently impact language achievement. In fact, Ehrman and Oxford (1995) discovered that aptitude was the ID variable most powerfully correlated with TL proficiency. With this empirical support and the impressive correlations that aptitude has consistently demonstrated with faster and better language learning, why have language practitioners in recent years been somewhat reticent in picking up the aptitude gauntlet? A walk down memory lane might provide some answers.

When John Carroll (1962, 1973) pioneered his early studies in language aptitude, the Audio-lingual method with its roots in Behaviorist Psychology was the current rage. Instructed learning environments with tightly teacher-controlled 'repeat-after-me' and slot-substitution drills were in vogue. With almost exclusive attention on form to the near exclusion of meaning, teachers had little access to language materials that recognized the uniqueness of the individual learner and assumed their uniformity. Amid this clamoring for structured input and practice-oriented activities, Carroll conceptualized his theories on language aptitude. However, during the 1970s and early 1980s, the methodological pendulum swung the opposite direction, and most ideas associated with Audio-lingualism became somewhat taboo. Instructed learning fell out of favor; naturalistic techniques gained popularity. With this paradigm shift came an awareness of the learner as an individual – not only as a being that cognitively processes language information, but as a person who feels and emotes as he is engaged in learning. Learner-centeredness became front-page news and aptitude – interpreted as a determination of a learner's fixed endowment of immutable language learning capacity – was perceived as being counterproductive to encouraging individual effort and stimulating motivation to those handicapped with low aptitude. Thus, aptitudes' waning importance in teaching circles may be attributed to three factors: (1) out-dated methodologies; (2) greater awareness of the learner as an individual, including the affective domain; and (3) the perception of aptitude as anti-egalitarian (Skehan, 2002).

Fast-forward to another decade. TL aptitude research is experiencing a revival, much of which is accelerated by scholars who are exploring ways of connecting language to advancements in SLA investigations (Dornyei, 2005). According to Robinson (2007: 258), the reasons are two-fold: (1) theories of learning have become much more contextualized and 'mapped onto cognitive processes and (2) aptitude is now perceived as dynamic and a 'potentially trainable concept' where the abilities that contribute to aptitude are influenced by the interaction between context and processing demands. With these advancements, an appropriate working definition for *language aptitude* for this chapter comes from Ranta (2008: 144): 'A learner's aptitude reflects strengths and weaknesses in a range of cognitive abilities that underlie the language development process and which interact with other factors such as motivation and opportunity.'

However a perusal of the pedagogical literature reveals that language practitioners have not yet incorporated the potentially revolutionary information that is now available. Leaving aptitude (and intelligence) to be framed as extraneous to language classroom practices and to allow it to languish in its misinterpretation as irrelevant, out-of-touch and undemocratic does not do justice to contemporary accounts of how aptitude can be reframed in situational contexts, connecting cognitive abilities to specific acquisitional processes. In the following section of this chapter, we will reveal some of the rich connections that have been made and attempt to formulate innovative pedagogical guidelines to align recent research advancements with classroom practices.

Recent findings on aptitude

Robinson: The compositional nature of aptitude and its dependence upon task and context

Robinson's (2001, 2002, 2005, 2007) work on aptitude involves the study of cognitive abilities combined with other ID factors in a range of trait complexes, and how these complexes interact with instructional and situational variables to support learning in various learning situations or conditions. By placing components of aptitude into a hierarchy of complexes (i.e. optimal blend of ID variables particularly conducive to resourceful learning), Robinson takes a more differentiated view of aptitude that guarantees an improved paradigm for examining how aptitude impacts the efficacy of specific instructional activities (Ranta, 2008) and has more predictive power than traits viewed separately (Dornyei, 2005). His paradigm combines the situational dependence of learning abilities and their combined influence thus allowing aptitude to be framed as a dynamic construct that takes into account the synergy of learner variable combinations and the cognitive load of specific TL learning tasks and teaching practices.

Robinson (2002: 114) suggests:

> ...cognitive abilities or 'aptitude complexes' are differentially related to language learning under different psycholinguistic processing conditions. Such conditions can be described at the situational level of classroom instructional treatments; at the more constrained situational level of the specific pedagogic tasks that learners perform in classrooms; and at the cognitive level of implicit, explicit, and incidental learning processes. Matching learner's strengths in particular aptitude complexes to options in the delivery of learning conditions and instructional techniques at each of these levels, then, is therefore an important element in the delivery of optimally effective classroom exposure and practice for second language (L2) learners.

For example, rather than addressing aptitude holistically, Robinson recommends that we look at elements of aptitude such as 'aptitude for focus on form via recasts' consisting of the capacity to 'notice the gap' and 'memory for contingent speech' which is made up of a learner's individual utterances together with their partner's recasts. The ability to notice the gap is made up of the combination of perceptual speed and pattern recognition, whereas memory for contingent speech is made up of WM capability and the rate of WM (Ranta, 2008). In investigating the association between language aptitudes and learning methods/situations, Robinson proposes that language aptitude can only be viewed within the context of the teaching method being used, and that aptitude is neither fixed nor immutable. He defines three interacting entities: (1) conditions to exposure (implicit, incidental and explicit); (2) a variety of cognitive resources (e.g. pattern recognition and/or processing speed); and (3) higher-order abilities (e.g. noticing the gap and/or metalinguistic rule rehearsal). These second-order skills can then be combined into aptitude complexes that exercise an optimal impact on learning in particular circumstances (Dornyei, 2005).

Skehan: Components of aptitude are linked to specific SLA phases

Like Robinson, Skehan (2002) perceives aptitude as multi-faceted, but rather than linking it with tasks and situational contexts, Skehan contextualizes it in the stages of the SLA process. Although the linking of specific SLA stages to their corresponding aptitudinal constructs is still a work in progress, the ideas provide interesting advances in our understanding of language learning not only in formal classroom contexts, but in incidental learning as well. Skehan (2002) proposes that the stages of SLA can be defined in four macro-components: noticing, patterning, controlling and lexicalizing. Noticing is the realization that some element of language form is worthy of attention. If aptitudinal individual differences are found at this stage, we must assume that some individuals can more effectively notice form in this way than others. Being able to process sound is not enough – WM and attentional management are necessary to work with the particular form sometime in the future. Patterning permits the learner to analyse, process, make generalizations and then extend the noticed input. This aptitude component includes the ability to modify initial perceptions and to uptake feedback. Control incorporates the internalization of rule-based generalizations – proceduralizing the noticed and patterned input. Finally, lexicalizing is establishing 'a repertoire of linguistic expressions, which can be accessed very quickly and without need for extensive internal computation' (Skehan, 2002: 92). Hence, phonemic coding ability is pivotal in the initial phases of acquisition where noticing occurs; grammatical sensitivity is most pertinent at subsequent stages when patterning emerges; and memory becomes primary in the final lexicalizing stage where learners reach fluency.

Capitalizing on Aptitude: An Action Plan

The pedagogical significance of linking aptitude to stages in SLA processes is partially found in the notion that aptitude is relevant not only for traditional, form-focused teaching contexts where grammar is overtly addressed, but also in settings where learning is implicit. Because naturalistic language learning contexts do not supply learners with selected and sequenced language input as an instructed setting does, learners must extract structural information from their target language (TL) interactions on their own, thus making individual differences in aptitude even more consequential. This does, however, presuppose that learners are focused as much on form as they are on meaning during their TL interactions (Dornyei & Skehan, 2003).

Individualize instruction through task-based learning in groups

Cook (2001) provides practical advice for operationalizing the classroom relevance of aptitude by suggesting that teachers provide instruction adjusted to the individual aptitude profile of each learner which can be done through task-based learning and the use of group work structures. When individualizing instruction, teachers must decide whether they want to work with either a matching or compensatory principle: Should one teach to the strengths of each learner so as to provide potentially greater opportunities for success (matching principle)? Or should one teach to learners' weaknesses so as to stretch their limitations (compensatory principle)? Skehan (2002), for example, has weighed in on this dilemma suggesting that it is preferable to stretch learners' limitations rather than teach to their strengths because the components of aptitude are linked to particular stages in the learning process.

Teach explicitly

Ranta (2008) also enters the matching vs. compensating argument when she outlines how to help learners with limited analytic dexterity figure out the rules and justifies the importance of this skill by claiming that good language learners are able to manage an array of analytic and de-contextualized tasks even though the task did not specifically encourage the development of that expertise. 'The aim of remediation for less analytic learners is to help them to extract information about linguistic structure from the communicative input and thus "see the trees in the forest"' (Ranta, 2008: 148). One way to do this is to first explicitly teach a 'rule of thumb' for the given form followed by some type of consciousness-raising task. In doing this, teachers provide information about how grammar works that is accessible to all learners. Ranta (2008) also provides insight into how learners with weak phonological skills can improve their ability to encode sounds and words in their TL. She cites the importance of auditory abilities as a precursor to language learning success by implicating its role in segmenting speech into words, syllables, phonemes and in connecting these segments with graphemic counterparts. This must be done in real time because of its relevance in subsequent stages of processing and its crucial role in the earliest stages of vocabulary acquisition (Skehan, 1998). For learners who are limited in these phonological skills and the encoding of sounds, Ranta (2008: 149) proposes 'a multisensory structured learning approach where learners see, hear and write the language simultaneously' and focuses on the overt instruction of spelling-sound correspondence, morphology and syntax.

> Lessons are sequenced from simple to more complex and include continual review of previously learned letters and sounds. The most important feature of this approach is that new material is always presented such that students use their visual, auditory and tactile-kinesthetic skills. This means they pronounce the sounds and write at the same time. (Ranta, 2008: 150)

Activities 1 through 4 in the upcoming Activities section are grounded in Skehan's four macro skills. Activity 5 provides a template for matching and compensating for learners' aptitudinal strengths and weaknesses.

Exploring Working Memory (WM)

What WM is

Progress in cognitive psychology, particularly in the realm of WM, has also contributed to a framework that allows more specific predictions and greater accuracy in the testing of memory aspects that may contribute to language learning success. As far back as Carroll's early studies in language aptitude, memory had been defined as one of its primary component parts, and was the principle focus of a portion of the MLAT where associative short-term memory tasks and linguistic analytic skills were tested (Hummel, 2002). WM corresponds to those processes implicated in the synchronized storage and processing of input in real time (Baddeley & Hitch, 1974), and comprises four subsystems – two short-term storage domains made up of the phonological loop and the visuo-spatial sketchpad, a central executive directing the course of information between these domains and additional cognitive processes, and the episodic buffer where different types of information are momentarily stored and integrated. The three short-term storage domains act as information repositories managed by the central executive, and momentarily maintain a restricted quantity of information that is accessible for only a few seconds before it disappears. Storage is limited both by the quantity of information that can be preserved and the length of time that the information is accessible (Baddeley, 2000). Verbal input is processed in the phonological loop thus making it the element that holds the most promise for researchers and practitioners interested in language learning and processing (Juffs & Harrington, 2011).

The significance of WM

Juffs and Harrington (2011) review a variety of studies investigating the role of WM in TL learning, including its impact on sentence processing, phonological memory, vocabulary learning, spoken output, extensive TL reading and writing, general proficiency and studying abroad. Concurring with Skehan, one of the major themes that emanates from the WM data is that its influence changes over the course of development – in other words, WM may play a different role in early vocabulary acquisition than it does in later grammar use.

Addressing the much discussed theme in aptitude research concerning the role of attention, Juffs and Harrington (2011) suggest that WM research may be a means through which a deeper understanding of the role of attention in SLA may be achieved. Their cumulative findings suggest that WM is not a unitary construct and that its role varies depending on the age of the TL learners, the task and the linguistic domain:

> The dual functions of WM (storage and processing) vary in importance according to the L2 domain, and it is clear that the various WM subsystems may change in their importance over time and domain. How these subsystems interact, and the role they play in constraining L2 performance, remains unanswered. It is important to emphasize that the effect of WM as a constraint on L2 performance will differ by L2 domain, and evidence for its presence or absence in an area (e.g. sentence processing) may tell us little of the role it plays in other, arguably more important, domains (discourse comprehension). (p. 159)

Furthermore, the significant role that WM plays in SLA begs the question as to whether WM is a trait – with fixed individual characteristics – or a dynamic processing state whose capacity and efficacy is influenced by features such as domain knowledge and learner goals. Juffs and Harrington (2011) take the middle ground when they suggest that individual differences in WM capacity are generally stable yet can also change as a result of experience – its dynamic nature being reflected in the learner's organization of knowledge and experience. Engle (2007) likens it to the combination of trait and state elements in anxiety where there is a stable pattern of behavior across tasks, but that the behavior can be influenced at any time by the conditions of a particular task.

Capitalizing on WM: An Action Plan

Systematically avoid WM failure through specific steps

Educational researchers in WM propose a variety of classroom and teacher interventions to support learners with poor WM. Put simply, they suggest that WM failures need to be avoided to prevent learning from being delayed or impaired. The first step is to identify WM overload through warning signs that include inadequate recall, inability to heed instructions, place-keeping problems and leaving tasks incomplete. Because an excessive cognitive load is caused by long and complex sentences, unfamiliar and meaningless subject matter and challenging cognitive processing tasks, teachers may want to consider limiting the quantity of material to be remembered, increasing the meaningfulness and familiarity of the material, simplifying mental processing and reorganizing complex tasks. This can be done through increasing the meaningfulness and familiarity of the material through *schema* activation, the *repetition* of important information by the teacher and/or peers, encouraging the use of memory aids through *visualization*, realia or other learning aids (e.g. wall charts, posters, spelling aids, dictionaries, memory cards, audio recorders and computer software), and by helping learners to develop their own *strategies* that support memory, including asking for help, rehearsing, note-taking, invoking the long-term memory and implementing organizational strategies (Gathercole & Alloway, 2008).

Refrain from confusing 'speedy' with 'high aptitude' and 'slow' with 'low aptitude'

Teachers may be tempted to equate high aptitude and speediness with the categorical thinking that an individual who processes faster is a better language learner, thus implying that a lower aptitude/slower processing learner is less capable. This thinking could potentially create a vicious cycle wherein the high aptitude learner gets better instruction, more practice, patience, and the benefit of the doubt while we wait for the low aptitude person to drop the course and confirm expectations. Considering WM ideas, aptitude is more about tasks and abilities falling in line to generate speed, and less about possibilities. Most learners develop an adequate vocabulary and communicate well enough to function day-to-day. Some got there easily, others with difficulty, but equating high initial speed of learning with the projected long-term outcome for an individual could prove detrimental.

Incorporate multi-modal support

Some of the pedagogical implications arising from WM research target attentional resources and how they can be manipulated in the best interests of language learners. Because language learners low in WM may be at a disadvantage in communicative classrooms where the primary emphasis is on listening, Hummel and French (2010) suggest the incorporation of visualization wherever possible. Supplementary multi-modal support with greater visual scaffolding might be found in multi-media tools or even the learner's own writing. Additionally, computer-assisted language learning techniques like online synchronous chat reduces a learner's cognitive burden and increases planning time for low WM learners. When language is automatized, less WM processing is required, so fluency based exercises and activities aimed at automatizing word recognition and retrieval are helpful. They also advocate for limited amounts of reading aloud to promote some rehearsal and to encourage the phonological loop feature of WM. Sunderman and Kroll (2009) link WM to attentional capacity and therefore recommend measures that suppress competing pressure from the L1 and assisting learners to focus on TL forms.

In sum, the WM is a temporary input storage and processing system that is extremely limited by both time and space constraints. The key to minimizing WM failure for optimal learning is to manage and reduce the processing and storage demands placed upon it – to essentially de-clutter it – in order to prevent WM overload and free up attentional resources. Activities 6 through 13 in the upcoming Activities section provide a template for teachers to implement as they attempt to maximize the storage and processing capacity of language learners' WM as they focus on form.

Exploring Multiple Intelligences (MIs)

What MIs are

The perception of language aptitude as monolithic, fixed and anti-egalitarian caused it to fall from grace with the advent of communicative teaching methods and a greater understanding of the affective needs of the language learner. It has been replaced by a contextualized notion of aptitude that is situation- and task-dependent, is linked to SLA processes and embodies functions of the WM. A similar transformation has occurred with the related notion of intelligence. Once perceived as having two or three main strands (logical/mathematical, linguistic and spatial) and tested via traditional IQ tests, the definition of intelligence has been expanded, mainly through the extensive work of Howard Gardner (1983), who challenges the traditionally singular view and proposes that intelligence falls into seven different areas:

(1) Linguistic intelligence is the ability to use words effectively in speaking and writing, demonstrating sensitivity to sounds, meanings and functions of language.
(2) Logical-mathematical intelligence is the ability to use numbers effectively, reason well and see logical and numerical patterns.
(3) Spatial intelligence is the ability to create mental models of the visual-spatial world with sensitivity to colors, shapes and sizes and the relationships between them.

(4) Bodily kinesthetic intelligence is the ability to use one's body for self-expression and problem-solving.
(5) Musical intelligence is the ability to recognize, alter, and distinguish musical forms through sensitivity to rhythm, pitch and melody.
(6) Interpersonal intelligence is the ability to understand the feelings, motivations and moods of others, and to respond to them appropriately.
(7) Intrapersonal intelligence is the ability to understand oneself, knowing self-strengths, weaknesses and emotional states, and to exert self-discipline.

Gardner (1991: 12) presents his theory in his own words:

> I have posited that all human beings are capable of at least seven different ways of knowing the world – ways that I have elsewhere labeled the seven human intelligences. According to this analysis, we are all able to know the world through language, logical-mathematical analysis, spatial representation, musical thinking, the use of the body to solve problems or to make things, an understanding of another individual, and an understanding of ourselves. Where individuals differ is in the strength of these intelligences – the so-called profile of human intelligences – and in the ways in which such intelligences are invoked and combined to carry out different tasks, solve diverse problems and progress in various domains.

The significance of MIs

Gardner (1993) suggests that each intelligence has a natural process of development called a 'developmental trajectory' which is initiated at different times and moves through stages from a universally experienced 'raw patterning ability' to a 'symbol system' and finally to a 'notional system' with developmental peaks occurring at diverse times in an individual's lifetime. Although everyone has the potential to develop each intelligence to a higher level of functioning through exposure and training, an adequate competency level is developed by most people for each intelligence. Although Gardner (1983) identifies and scrutinizes the seven intelligences independently, he does this only to distinguish the central features of each intelligence. He proposes that only in very extraordinary instances does one intelligence exist by itself and that the intelligences interact in complex ways, thus making it imperative that individuals are perceived as a 'collection of aptitudes' rather than being identified by the conventional single IQ measure. Revealing a 'pluralistic panorama of learners' individual differences', the various individual intelligences are personal tools that each person possesses to process new information and to store it in easily retrievable ways when needed for use. Considered of neutral value, no intelligence is judged as superior to the others (Arnold & Fonseca, 2004: 120). In sum, each of these frames is autonomous, changeable and trainable and they interact to facilitate the solution of daily problems (Armstrong, 1999).

Capitalizing on MIs: An Action Plan

Nurture all MIs through balanced instruction and task variation

As every learner has the capacity to exhibit all of these intelligences (albeit some more highly developed than others in certain individuals), the challenge in language classrooms is for teachers to foster learning environments that nurture the advancement of all seven intelligences. Balanced instructional presentations and the selection of tasks and activities that encourage the composite of all MIs benefits everyone and exposes learners to the most advantageous means through which underutilized intelligences can be stretched (Haley, 2004). Gardner (1991: 13) suggests: 'Genuine understanding is most likely to emerge and be apparent to others if people possess a number of ways of representing knowledge of a concept or skill and can move readily back and forth among these forms.' To allow for this, Christison (1996) gives language teachers advice on examining their best instructional practices and strategies in light of learner differences. First, activities that are frequently used must be examined and categorized in order to track what intelligences are being addressed. She recommends four actions to work with intelligences: (1) awaken the intelligence; (2) amplify the intelligence; (3) teach for/with the intelligence; and (4) transfer the intelligence. A second way to teach from a MI perspective is to deliberately plan lessons so that the different intelligences are represented.

Modify what is already being done

Presenting occasions for individuals to learn in their most receptive ways capitalizes on their potential for achievement in the classroom and in real life (Armstrong, 1994). Incorporating MIs into the learning environment does not necessitate a major reconstruction in methodology or curricula in that supplementing and revising existing activities with creative and innovative ideas will usually suffice (Campbell, 1997). For example, focusing on interdisciplinary units, providing activities that center on a theme, utilizing cooperative learning and supplying a selection of tasks and activities all provide the structure where MIs can be well represented within the context of instruction. In offering a choice of tasks, teachers are not necessarily targeting specific intelligences but rather they are providing learners with the opportunity of capturing and processing information in their preferred way, as well as promoting the development of their other intelligences (Arnold &

Fonseca, 2004). To conclude, to attempt to address all of the individual MIs of every learner in every language class would be enough to send even the most sane teacher over the edge; rather it is a matter of offering a balanced approach where different 'windows on the same concept' are incorporated (Gardner, 1993). Activities 15 through 17 guide teachers through a series of thematically organized, interdisciplinary tasks using cooperative learning and offering a choice of tasks while simultaneously awakening, amplifying, teaching for and with learners' intelligences, and finally transferring the learning and making it relevant for learners.

To conclude the premise part of this chapter, it is important to review previous misnomers in order to learn from them. In the past, learners endowed with language aptitude were perceived like comic strip heroes with cosmic linguistic powers: invincible in their phonetic decoding, unassailable in their memory capacity, and indestructible in their automatization of language forms. Those unlucky many that tested low on the language aptitude scale were relegated to the cartoon role of the damsel in distress with no hope of ever being rescued: irretrievably lost amid the complexity of sentence patterns, dismal memory functions and miserable retrieval processes. Because aptitude had historically been erroneously classified as an immutable predisposition immune to teacher intervention, it had been an undesirable topic for language teachers: why would a sensitive, responsive language teacher even want to know aptitude scores if it only led to the unequal treatment of learners and language-lethal self-fulfilling prophecy?

The conversation has changed. Aptitude, although still a bit more inflexible than other ID variables, is no longer perceived as immune to teacher intervention. Our contemporary understanding of aptitude considers it a complex and changing variable, so although a learner may demonstrate a strong complex of aptitudes and abilities at one stage of the learning process under specific learning conditions and/or tasks, another phase in the acquisitional process, a change in the learning environment, or the manipulation of a task may induce a variation in an individual's aptitude. Thus aptitude is, as a stand-alone construct, a dynamic variable. Furthermore, advancements in cognitive psychology have highlighted the important role of the WM as a component of language learning aptitude, and with these modifications have come a wide array of pedagogical implications to nurture and expand WM capacity.

Likewise, research on intelligence has also taken a pedagogically favorable turn. Instead of the focused attention on verbal and mathematical intelligence that dominated IQ testing in the past, new developments in intelligence research focuses on a variety of intelligences working together to create a complex of skills. No longer are only the virtues extolled of those endowed with the ability to solve advanced trigonometry problems and exhibit verbal dexterity. The educational community now understands that humans possess a number of distinct intelligences that manifest themselves in different skills and abilities, all of which are necessary for human advancement and world peace.

However, the cognitive abilities of aptitude (including WM) and intelligence are inserted into an even larger 'psycho-emo-cogni' system as one of a myriad of individual differences which together create a *symbiotic, synergetic* relationship whose *dynamism* plays out in every language learner. Entities are said to be symbiotic when there is a close, prolonged association between two or more agents, but whose relationship does not necessarily benefit each one (http://wordnetweb.princeton.edu). Thus we can say that aptitude, a cognitive variable, is in a symbiotic relationship with other psychological ID variables because it has been associated closely and 'prolongedly' (a strategically chosen word allowing the authors to escape an unequivocal position on the nature vs. nurture and immutable vs. malleable debates among ID researchers) with factors like anxiety, motivation and other variables covered in this book to create the Composite Language Learner. However the association of any of these ever-changing variables (e.g. high FL anxiety and low motivation), when coupled with aptitude does not necessarily create the beneficial psycho-affective environment where cognitive abilities could flourish.

Furthermore, the relationship between cognitive abilities and other ID variables is *synergetic* because *synergy*, like symbiosis, also denotes the interaction or cooperation of two agents, but unlike symbiotic relationships, *synergetic* ones produce a combined effect greater than the sum of their separate effects. These two ideas – synergy and symbiosis – are often mistaken for each other or even misused but are concepts that teachers can look for in their learners. That is to say, teachers need to understand that the effect of cognitive abilities as an isolated feature of the language learner is much more powerful in combination with other psychological variables like motivation and anxiety – either to negatively narrow or to positively broaden.

An important morale-boosting caveat for language teachers as they consider the symbiotic, synergetic and dynamic relationship of the more stable (but not inflexible) cognitive abilities such as aptitude, WM and intelligence with other more readily modified affective and psychological ID variables is that, although research suggests that aptitude explains a relatively large portion of variability among learners, other IDs such as motivation, which are more susceptible to teacher intervention, may ultimately result in being much more robust explanatory variables in TL learning (Juffs & Harrington, 2011). In other words, a highly motivated, self-confident learner who may have a dispositional tendency toward low cognitive abilities still has a fighting chance to acquire high proficiency in a TL.

Teachers committed to the principle of learner-centeredness should therefore address not only the real-life goals and learning preferences of students but also their cognitive processing needs. It is admittedly a daunting
prospect. Nevertheless, accommodating the aptitude profiles of their
learners is one way that teachers can provide instruction that will help
their students become the best language learners they can be. (Ranta,
2008: 151–152)

Throughout this chapter, we have maintained that cognitive abilities
play an active role in language learning, and although they may be somewhat
stable features (perhaps in specific domains), we believe that cognitive
abilities and attentional variables can be changed or manipulated through
instruction and experience thus making it possible to transform the recent
research developments on aptitude, WM and intelligence into classroom
practice.

...To Practice

Cognitive Abilities Activities

The first four activities are packaged together to energize Skehan's
four macro-components of aptitude: noticing, patterning, controlling
and lexicalizing. As teachers plug their chosen TL forms into the activity
template, they inherently modify the difficulty of the activities to meet
the proficiency needs of their specific learners. Feel free to replace the
examples we have provided in the instructions with models that are
commiserate with the proficiency of your learners and the language forms
you target. If learners provide positive feedback during the de-briefing
procedures, consider using these aptitude-heightening activities again –
alone or in combination – and substituting different language forms. It is
important to remember that aptitude is composite and in flux, so while a
learner may demonstrate a strong complex of aptitudes at one stage of the
learning process under a specific learning condition and/or task, another
phase in the acquisitional process and a change in the learning environment may dynamically influence how aptitude manifests. Activity 5 is an
example of how to match and compensate learners' self-reported aptitudinal profiles.

The main tenets undergirding the WM activities (6 through 13) combine
the features of repetition and rehearsal of input, visualization, increasing the
meaningfulness of the material by building new schema and activating the
old, and providing opportunities for learners to experiment with a variety of
WM enhancing strategies, while benefiting from form-focused instruction.

Two sets of four activity sequences guide learners through an innovative template that we are calling 'SRVS Working Memory Enhancement.' We include instructional interventions firmly grounded in WM research and propose a four-phased design where learners: (1) 'Schemactivate;' (2) Rehearse/Repeat; (3) Visualize; and (4) Strategize. Like other activities targeting cognitive abilities presented in this chapter, the difficulty of the task and the requisite proficiency level of the learner depend on the linguistic structures that the teacher wishes to target.

Activities 15 through 17 target Multiple Intelligences and together provide a template for meeting the intelligence needs of many different learners in the same classroom. Although the hotly debated question in language aptitude research concerning whether teachers should match or compensate for learners' strengths and weaknesses in the creation of classroom tasks is also applicable to MIs, MI experts answer it by suggesting that teachers should account for all learners' predispositions by integrating balanced instructional presentations and selection of tasks and activities that encourage the composite of all intelligences (Arnold & Fonseca, 2004). Readers will notice that the series is based upon an interdisciplinary theme that integrates cooperative learning and a choice of tasks. Thus, rather than creating learning opportunities that either match or compensate learners strengths or weaknesses, teachers who are MI savvy will incorporate multiple ways for learners to capture and process information. Activities 15 through 17 are adaptations of Christison's (1996) series of steps that include awakening, amplifying, teaching for, and transferring MIs.

Cognitive Abilities Activity 1: Noticing Forms in Natural Input through Language Learning Diaries

Genius is nothing but a great aptitude for patience. – George-Louis De Buffon

Level: All

Procedure:

(1) Preface this activity by explaining that its purpose is to prompt the 'noticing' of specific features of the TL to increase learners' awareness of language forms in a range of contexts to help consolidate new knowledge and that 'noticing' is particularly important when interacting in naturalistic settings.

(2)   Choose a language form being covered in class ('much' vs. 'many' for example). Ask learners to listen for it in their daily, out-of-class interactions for the next two weeks. Tell learners to make entries in their 'language diaries,' recording noticed language elements and giving a short description of the context in which it was used. Insist that language patterns and collocations are also recorded (an important caveat for Activity 4). By recording the language information, they become explicitly aware of the form used in context.

(3)   After two weeks, with a variety of 'noticed' examples with their patterns and collocations, ask learners to:

(a)   Form pairs and exchange diaries.

(b)   Compare what partners noticed and recorded with teacher-provided expert models of the same form (also refer back to class notes).

(c)   Look for any correspondences and mismatches found between partner's 'data' and the corresponding TL norms. For example, extending the 'much vs. many' example from above, learners may have heard and recorded: 'I have *many* girlfriends,' or 'How *much* time do you have.' In comparing it to the expert model, the partner realizes that this is correct (a correspondence). However, the learner may have heard and recorded, 'I have *many* time,' so when the partner compares it to the correct form, he or she realizes that it does not conform to the model (a mismatch).

(d)   Make a written list of the mismatches – without correcting them – and pass the diary and list back to the original writer who will then correct the mismatches.

(4)   De-brief this activity by explaining that by 'noticing' the mismatches in both data sets – their own and those of their partner's, learners begin to 'notice the gap' – i.e. pay attention to correct and incorrect language forms, which is the starting point for modifying their interlanguage and increasing TL accuracy.

MODIFICATIONS:

Technology:

(1)   'Noticed' language forms can be entered electronically in written form via word processing or posting them to learners' personal blogs (Step 2).

(2)   To use this as a listening/speaking activity, audio record 'noticed' language forms on a mobile, hand-held device (Step 2).

Cognitive Abilities Activity 2: Patterning Language through the Circulating Papers Technique

From a sequence of these individual patterns, whole buildings with the character of nature will form themselves within your thoughts, as easily as sentences. – Christopher Alexander

Level: All

Procedure:

(1) Preface this activity by explaining that its purpose is to give learners experience in modifying their initial perceptions of how a new language form functions, uptaking feedback from interlocutors when appropriate, and making a habit of generalizing and looking for language patterns to increase their aptitude.

(2) Tell learners to use the 'noticed' form-focused naturalistic data from the previous activity and select three correct examples of the chosen language form and write them on a piece of paper, leaving space to number from one to five between them (for example, Student A used the following examples from his learning diary: 'I have many girlfriends.' 'How much time do you have?' and 'I have many friends' and leaves space for five sentences beneath each phrase).

(3) In small circles of five, ask learners to pass their three examples to the person on their right and spend three minutes reading, analyzing, processing, making generalizations and extending the noticed input from the examples by making one more original sentence for each in the space provided. (Using the above example, Student B reads, 'I have many girlfriends' and then generalizes from that and writes, 'I have many cats' and then proceeds to the second and third examples.)

(4) Instruct learners to pass the papers again to the right and use the second space provided under each example to repeat the procedure. Exchange papers a total of five times until the original writer has his or her paper again.

(5) De-brief this activity by asking learners to silently read through the peer feedback and discuss the examples with group members.

MODIFICATIONS:

Technology:

(1) If an oral format was used to record learners' noticed input, have group members exchange their mobile hand-held devices and rather than read the TL forms from a written diary, they listen, write down what they hear and follow the same procedures as above (Steps 1–3).

(2) If teachers want to maintain the listening/speaking format rather than transforming it into a reading/writing exercise, ask one group member at a time to play back the language forms recorded on the hand-held device and have other group members say aloud their patterned sentences (Steps 1–3).

(3) Have learners exchange written electronic diaries as attachments to emails (for word processed entries) or access partners' blogs and post to create the new sentences (Steps 2 and 3).

Cognitive Abilities Activity 3: Controlling Language Input through 4/3/2 Talks

(This activity is adapted from Nation's (1989) 4/3/2 procedure and is meant to help learners proceduralize language – Skehan's third aptitudinal macro-component.)

> Language should be an ever developing procedure and not an isolated occurrence.– Robert Smithson

Level: All

Procedure:

(1) Preface this activity by explaining to learners that its purpose is to enhance their aptitude by internalizing the form-focused rule that had been targeted in their data collection from Activity 1 and later patterned in Activity 2.

(2) Tell learners to each prepare a four minute talk using the same language form from the previous two activities (including unused material from Activity 1), so that through repetition, they gain greater control over the language form and learn to proceduralize it.

(3) Pair learners. Tell partners to take turns delivering the four minute talks, but in THREE minutes.

(4) Ask learners to switch partners. This time, tell pairs to take turns delivering their four minute talks, but this time in TWO minutes.

(5) Tell learners to use the following rubric for a short peer assessment:
   (a) 3 = Uses the TL form in a variety of ways. Demonstrates the fluency that comes through having internalized the TL form. Uses complex sentences. Speaks with little hesitation.

(b) 2 = Uses the TL form but with little variation. Demonstrates some fluency, but has not completely internalized the TL form. Uses simple sentences. Speaks with some hesitation
(c) 1 = Does not use variation with the TL form. Demonstrates limited fluency and internalization of TL form. Uses simple sentences with many errors. Speaks with a lot of hesitation.

(6) Invite learners to exchange and discuss peer feedback giving justification for the score earned.
(7) De-brief this activity by asking learners whether the number of their hesitations decreased with the re-telling of each story and whether their sentences became more complex (as Nation (1989) discovered). Discuss not only how their iterations changed with time constraints and multiple opportunities but how this also influenced the control they gained over the language form being targeted.

MODIFICATIONS:

Technology:

(1) For teachers whose learners have access to hand-held video recording devices such as cellular phones or ipads, ask learners to videotape each other's two talks (Steps 3 and 4).
(2) Using the same rubric as outlined in Step 5, tell learners to self-assess their own performance, hence increasing responsibility for their own learning.
(3) To de-brief (Step 7) for videotaped performances, tell learners to upload video files to Voicethread and have viewers post comments on at least two of their classmates' set of talks.

Cognitive Abilities Activity 4: Lexicalizing: Building Your Repertoire of Linguistic Expressions (Adapted from the Lexical Approach [Lewis, 1993]).

'For imagination sets the goal picture which our automatic mechanism works on. We act, or fail to act, not because of will, as is so commonly believed, but because of imagination. – Maxwell Maltz

Level: All

Procedure:

(1) Preface this activity by explaining that its purpose is to increase aptitude by concentrating on word chunks or word combinations to access language more quickly and with less concentration.

(2) Ask learners to review the language patterns and collocations recorded in their diaries in Activity 1, notice any lexical chunks, and highlight or circle them. Tell them to list all chunks or patterns on a separate piece of paper. Ask them to choose five and then take out five small sheets of paper, and head each paper with one set of word chunks. (Highlighting, and then listing, and then heading each paper with the same word pattern serves as repeated exposure to the lexicalized unit.)

(3) In dyads (who share the same L1, if possible), tell learners to exchange the five papers each headed by a different lexicalized phrase and:
   (a) guess the meaning from context,
   (b) categorize the word chunks,
   (c) use summary words to characterize its meaning, and
   (d) juxtapose the learner's native language translation of the TL chunk and compare.

(4) Ask learners to return the papers to their original owner, review their partners' work and exchange feedback.

(5) De-brief this activity by soliciting students' input on how using language patterns, collocations and word chunks positively increases their fluency and what plans and/or strategies they might consider to increase their aptitude by making these units more 'noticed,' 'patterned', 'controlled' and 'lexicalized' (Skehan, 2002).

MODIFICATIONS:

Technology:

(1) Options for learners who electronically recorded their TL forms (Steps 2–4):
   (a) listen to their own recording, write the list of their chunks, pass it to their partner and continue the activity; or
   (b) do this as a listening and speaking activity with one partner listening to the others' recording and responding to the four prompts orally.

(2) Create wikis headed by the patterns/collocations/word chunks that learners exchange and answer prompts. This technology is ideal for allowing the exchange of work among more collaborators.

Cognitive Abilities Activity 5: Matching and Compensating Aptitudinal Strengths through ZPD Peer Teaching

Do not train a child to learn by force or harshness; but direct them to it by what amuses their minds, so that you may be better able to discover with accuracy the peculiar bent of the genius of each.' – Plato

Level: All

Procedure:

(1) Preface this activity by explaining that the tasks will accommodate learners' individual aptitudinal profiles by matching some tasks to their strengths and compensating for limitations in others. Learners explore what Vygotsky (1962) calls the 'Zone of Proximal Development (ZPD)' where each have a chance to be the more 'expert' peer who moves the others from their current level of understanding or knowledge closer to their aptitudinal potential.

(2) Place learners in two groups according to their responses to the following statements:
   (a) I am better at identifying sounds and words when I hear my TL than I am at figuring out the rules (the 'expert analyzers').
   (b) I am better at figuring out the rules of my TL than I am at identifying distinct sounds (the 'expert sound coders').
   If groups are numerically unbalanced, ask volunteers who perceive their aptitude in both statements to be relatively equal to change to the lower populated group. If that does not create balance, use teacher intuition and knowledge of individual learners to move students from one group to the other.

(3) Partner two learners who raised their hand to letter *a* with two learners who indicated letter *b*. Partner and pair until all learners are placed and each group of four contains two 'expert analyzers' and two 'expert sound coders.'

(4) Tell groups to agree on a naturalistic out-of-class task (at least five minutes long) through which they can gather TL input. (Choice is a valuable element of all aptitude-heightening activities.)

(5) Ask each group member to write down as much language as possible (i.e. a 'text') to be used later in an in-class activity. Possible options:
   (a) listen to a TL song;
   (b) watch a five minute segment of a TL television show, news broadcast, or YouTube;

(c)   engage a speaker in a five-minute TL conversation; or

(d)   suggest another naturalistic data-gathering task.

(6)   In class, explain that the pair of 'expert sound decoders' and the pair of 'expert analyzers' have different teaching tasks using the 'text' from the out-of-class activity.

(7)   Tell the 'expert sound coders' to plan a multisensory mini-lesson that engages the other pair in simultaneously seeing, hearing, and writing extracts from the chosen 'text,' and then create **three** exercises to use the new vocabulary. (For example, the 'experts' choose three particularly challenging sounds or vocabulary items that were used in the 'text' and create three flash cards with corresponding images, so that as the 'experts' hold up the card, the 'pupils' say the word out loud, see the image and the written form, and write the word themselves. The emphasis should be on the direct and explicit teaching of spelling-sound relationships. An exercise for using the new vocabulary is, for example, to use the word in a new sentence– but with the caveat that the 'experts' make their tutorial *multisensory*.)

(8)   Tell the 'expert analyzers' to extract at least **three** language rules from the text and plan a short tutorial for the other pair, including a consciousness-raising exercise for each rule. (For example, for one of the rules, the 'experts' demonstrate how the adjectives 'many' and 'much' are used in the text, follow it with an explicit explanation of the rule, and conclude with three fill-in-the-blank exercises.)

(9)   Instruct the 'expert sound coders' to present their tutorial on sounds/spelling/vocabulary development and follow it with practice opportunities.

(10)   Next, instruct the 'expert analyzers' to illustrate their expertise on language forms and provide practice exercises.

(11)   Once both the 'coders' and the 'analyzers' complete this phase of the activity, explain that this exercise was meant to MATCH their self-reported aptitude to the class activity, but that now you want them to COMPENSATE – that is, to stretch their limitations. Tell them to switch roles: the 'expert sound coders' are now the 'expert analyzers' and vice versa.

(12)   Repeat the entire activity. Using the same source of authentic language found in the written 'texts,' tell each pair to create another mini-lesson, but this time the pair who previously taught sounds, spelling and vocabulary now analyzes and teaches a grammatical form found in the text but different from the one previously taught. The pair who had originally presented grammatical forms now

teaches different elements of sound, spelling and/or vocabulary. Re-emphasize that the 'sounds/vocabulary' lesson uses multisensory tasks and the 'grammar' lesson targets attention to form and structural analysis of the language. Remind learners to create another short assessment tool. Tell pairs to prepare and take turns teaching, participating in and assessing the peer-directed lessons.

(13)   De-brief this activity by asking learners to compare their experiences of learning language when their aptitudinal strengths were matched as opposed to when they were compensated. Solicit feedback on their response to peer instruction, the group work model used, and task-based learning – all pedagogical implications suggested in the research on aptitude (Ranta, 2008).

MODIFICATIONS:

Emergent learners:

(1)   Provide options (Step 4) with simplified language to create their 'text' like an exchange between TL learners in the TL.
(2)   If learners provide positive feedback, use it multiple times to:
   (a)   target specific problematic sound/spelling/vocabulary TL features for learners with less aptitude for phonetic de-coding and auditory segmentation; and
   (b)   focus on difficult TL constructions for those with less aptitude for pattern analysis and grammatical sensitivity.

Technology: Tell 'experts' to use computer assisted technology (i.e. flash cards that have moving images and sound or rule explanation through a Powerpoint or Prezi presentation) to prepare, present and assess their peers through the form analysis and sound decoding exercises.

Cognitive Abilities Activity 6: S for Schemactivation in SRVS: Working Memory Enhancement for Action Verb Tenses

It's a poor sort of memory that only works backwards. – Lewis Carroll

Level: All

Procedure:

(1)   Preface this activity by explaining that WM failures often manifest in ways that many learners have probably experienced. Ask learners

if they have ever put their keys somewhere and later could not remember where, or if they have ever spent time looking for their lost car in a parking lot because they could not remember where they had parked it. Share experiences. Explain that memory lapses may be attributable to an overload in their WM – the place limited in time and space where information comes in for processing and temporary storage – and that theirs may have been overloaded so that attention had not been paid to their actions.

(2) Explain that one memory strategy experts recommend is to verbalize everything – that is, talking to oneself – as the action is being done. So, for example, as you are putting your keys on the counter, you say aloud (or subvocally), 'I am putting my keys on the counter,' or as you are parking your car, you say aloud, 'I am parking my car next to the oak tree in the third row from the sidewalk.'

(3) Ask volunteers to verbalize what they are doing right now. Answers may include present continuous structures like, 'I am sitting in language class' or 'I am answering the teacher's question' or 'I am twiddling my pencil.'

(4) Then ask, 'What did you do an hour ago?' Allow learners to respond. To finish the schema activation, ask 'What will you do in an hour?' (Teachers may prefer to target past and future continuous tenses by asking 'What were you doing an hour ago?' and 'What will you be doing in an hour?'). If learners prefer explicit form-focused instruction, review how the tenses work or provide model answers to questions.

(5) De-brief this activity by explaining that it was meant to 'activate learners' schemas' or in other words, to tap into previous background knowledge or experience to prime learning for new but related information. Ask individuals to share other related effective memory strategies.

MODIFICATIONS:

Large groups:

(1) Divide students into groups of five or six. All learners will then have the opportunity to take turns using the past, present and future tenses. If overt grammar instruction is necessary, bring them back into whole group format.

(2) Maintain small groups to discuss de-briefing prompt. For teacher feedback purposes, ask a group reporter to take notes.

Technology: To de-brief, learners post effective memory strategies to the classroom discussion board to make the information accessible to the class.

Cognitive Abilities Activity 7: R for Repeat/Rehearse in SRVS: Working Memory Enhancement for Action Verb Tenses

Twice and thrice over, as they say, good is it to repeat and review what is good. – Plato

Level: All

Procedure:

(1) Preface this activity by explaining to learners that they will repeat and rehearse the language forms from the last activity's schema activation. They will answer similar questions for the next week, but with a few modifications.

(2) Instruct learners to pause in whatever they are doing three times a day for the next week. This task will be more effective if they remember to pause at different times of the day during different activities. During their pause, learners sub-vocally verbalize answers to the following three questions: *What am I doing? What did I do an hour ago?* and *What will I do in the next hour?*

(3) Tell learners they must remember their utterances long enough to record them in their language diaries at first opportunity so they may refer to them later for another class activity. (WM is also enhanced through the strategy of writing things down.)

(4) De-brief this activity by asking whether sub-vocally repeating or rehearsing helped learners remember what they were doing in the moment. How many had difficulty remembering their answers until they could write them down? Did writing things down help them remember better?

MODIFICATIONS:

Technology: Use hand-held devices to record oral data in the form of an electronic language diary (Step 2).

Cognitive Abilities Activity 8: V for Visualize in SRVS: Working Memory Enhancement for Action Verb Tenses (Note: Pair this activity with 9)

> To accomplish great things we must first dream, then visualize, then plan... believe... act! – Alfred A. Montapert

Level: All

Procedure:

(1) Preface this activity by informing learners that visualization is another way to stimulate memory thus improving the ability to learn new language forms.

(2) Tell learners they will be using the week-long recording of their present, past and future on-the-spot activities to participate in 'visual storytelling.' Pair learners and ask them to consult their diaries and share experiences from the previous week.

(3) Ask pairs to combine their data by forming three lists of all the utterances by categorizing entries into 'Present,' 'Past,' and 'Future' columns. Using this corpus, invent a completely original story with new protagonists, settings, conflicts, etc. accompanied by pictures, whether hand-drawn, from magazines and newspapers, or actual photos.

(4) Ask each pair to take turns telling their stories through visuals. Tell the audience to use the pictures the storyteller provides to stimulate their visual representations of the words as they are spoken.

(5) De-brief this activity by asking learners whether they achieved the same level of visualization when listening as when they created their own stories. Solicit input on how different learners use visualization as a catalyst to remember things.

MODIFICATIONS:

Large classes:

(1) Where the number of dyads precludes the delivery of effective presentations to the whole group, combine three of the dyads to present their visual stories in front of each other.

Technology:

(1) To share experiences from the previous week, invite learners to synchronously 'chat.'

(2) Rather than using the 'ancient art' of storytelling with low tech visuals, have learners explore digital storytelling by interweaving

digitalized still and moving images and sound into their narratives. In digital storytelling, learners use digital tools to tell their stories (sometimes even interactively) in compelling and emotionally engaging formats, usually in under eight minutes through web-based stories, interactive stories, hypertexts and narrative computer games. If learners have access to media production techniques, hardware and software, including technology such as digital cameras, digital voice recorders, iMovie, Movie Maker and Final Cut Express (just to mention a few), audiences for their productions need not be limited to classmates. New technologies allow the sharing of insightful and creative ideas through the internet, YouTube, compact discs, podcasts, and other electronic distribution systems.

Cognitive Abilities Activity 9: S for Strategize in SRVS: Working Memory Enhancement for Action Verb Tenses

When you're prepared, you're more confident. When you have a strategy, you're more comfortable. – Fred Couples

Level: All

Procedure:

(1) Preface this activity by informing learners that invoking specific strategies, like note-taking, also improves WM.
(2) While listening to peers' stories, tell learners to take notes – a strategy known to enhance WM because it frees up attentional resources.
(3) Join three of the pairs to make groups of six. Tell groups to combine the three stories and create the front page of a newspaper – with headlines and pictures using paper, pens, and scissors. As asking questions is another strategy that WM researchers suggest to avoid WM failures, tell learners to ask questions to the pair of original storytellers as they work.

MODIFICATIONS:

Large groups: Maintain the same groups from the previous activity.

Technology:

(1) Take audio notes via hand-held devices or written notes electronically via word processing (Step 2).

(2) Make electronic newspapers (Step 3). Many free student newspaper templates are available online, allow for easy importation of both text and visuals, and come with easy-to-follow instructions. For example, surf and explore the following: http://jc-schools.net/tutorials/classnews.html and https://docs.google.com/previewtemplate?id=1e8Layh1rHXU2qw WFSh9SlS-bTZAxeH-VlOw4BOn-tcU&mode=public).

Cognitive Abilities Activity 10: S is for Schemactivation in SRVS: Working Memory Enhancement for Formulaic Expressions

To know that we know what we know, and that we do not know what we do not know, that is true knowledge.' – Henry David Thoreau

Level: All

Preparation:

(1) Post five large pieces of newsprint or poster paper around the room (large black or whiteboards also work) with one of the following 'language functions' as a heading on each: *greetings, introductions, apologies, asking and receiving directions* and *expressing gratitude.*

Procedure:

(1) Preface this activity with an experiment:
    (a) Say the following 13 words slowly: 'Hello, how are you? Fine thanks. And you? I am well, thank you.' Have learners immediately repeat them back in a choral response.
    (b) Do the same 'repeat after me' exercise at the same rate but with the following 13 words: *pink, jumped, always, her, the, shirt, quickly, big, run, winter, he, dog, there.*
    (c) Ask which series was easier to repeat. Most will agree that the first string of 13 words was easier. This is because learners' WMs were able to 'chunk' the language into three formulaic utterances – essentially automatizing their language to decrease the informational overload on the WM.
(2) Draw attention to the five newsprint sheets hanging around the room. Clarify each heading with a model phrase (for example, to model *greetings* refer to the opening exercise: 'How are you?'; to model *introductions* offer: 'I would like you to meet so and so.').

(3) To activate background knowledge concerning formulaic expres-
    sions, divide learners evenly into five groups. Assign each group to one
    newsprint sheet. Have them brainstorm for two minutes as many
    formulaic expressions as possible that correspond to the function and
    write them down. While writing, tell learners to say the phrase aloud
    to stimulate the multi-sensory structured learning that is cultivated
    through simultaneously pronouncing and writing language.
(4) Call time. Tell each group to move to the next piece of newsprint
    and repeat the exercise. Do this five times so all groups respond to
    all the language functions. (Keep these lists posted for Activity 11.)
(5) De-brief this activity by surveying the comfort level of learners in
    using formulaic expressions. Ask whether this activity produced
    unfamiliar formulaic expressions. Which are the most and least
    commonly used when learners interact outside of class?

MODIFICATIONS:

Technology:

(1) To increase learners' visualization of the language functions (Step 2),
    search YouTube for short clips of interlocutors authentically using
    them in natural settings. Enter information like 'greeting examples'
    in the search engine, and a myriad of examples pop up – even some
    specifically devoted to ESL learners!
(2) Rather than walk around the room responding on newsprint sheets,
    rotate the lists of formulaic expressions via wikis.

Cognitive Abilities Activity 11: R is for Repeat/Rehearse in SRVS: Working Memory Enhancement for Formulaic Expressions

We are what we repeatedly do. Excellence, therefore, is not an act but
a habit. – Aristotle

Level: All

Preparation:

(1) Write the following adverbs on small slips of paper and put
    them in a hat (or bag): *happily, sadly, hurriedly, slowly, peacefully,
    angrily, fearfully, excitedly, joyfully, nervously, sincerely, dishonestly,
    timidly, forcefully.*

(2) Keep the five lists of formulaic expressions from the last activity visible to the whole class.

Procedure:

(1) Preface this activity by explaining that language functions must be accompanied by the correct nonverbal cue. For example, an apology delivered with 'joyful' intonation and a comical facial expression would not be accepted by the receiver. Tell learners they will practice matching verbal messages with nonverbal cues while rehearsing and repeating the formulaic expressions from the previous activity and pay attention to those combinations of intonation and formulaic expressions that do not seem to match.
(2) Ask a volunteer to draw an adverb from the hat and read the initial formulaic expression from the first list aloud to the class using the voice inflection and nonverbal cue intrinsic in the adverb. (Remember that reading aloud promotes rehearsal and encourages an efficient phonological loop!) Set adverb aside until the whole list from the first newsprint is read. Start again with all the adverb words returned to the hat for the next list.
(3) Repeat this process until all the formulaic expressions from all five newsprint sheets have been 'interpreted.'
(4) De-brief this activity by asking learners to single out which formulaic expressions did not match their delivery. Discuss how interlocutors might respond upon hearing the incongruence between what speakers say and how they say it. Did repeating and rehearsing enhance WM for retaining and later retrieving formulaic expressions?

MODIFICATIONS:

Technology: To make this activity more game-like, there are a variety of free educational sites that randomize names and information. For example, in the following site: (http://classtools.net/education-games-php/fruit_machine/), plug the adverbs into the space provided rather than throwing them into a hat. Assign one of the formulaic expressions from the brainstormed list to the learner who is 'up', and hit 'enter.' The adverb that comes up will dictate the learner's intonation of the expression. With the 'typewriter' feature from the website, the adverb randomly appears by individual out-of-order letters, thus inciting a bit of fun anticipation.

Cognitive Abilities Activity 12: V is for Visualization in SRVS: Working Memory Enhancement for Formulaic Expressions

Visualize this thing that you want, see it, feel it, believe in it. Make your mental blue print, and begin to build. – Robert Collier

Level: All

Procedure:

(1) Preface this activity by explaining that formulaic expressions from the previous lesson will be learned by participating in two ways:
  (a) As audience members, learners visualize and hear the phrases as they are acted out.
  (b) As performers, learners use multi-modalities (through body movement, seeing, hearing, writing, and reading).
(2) Tell learners to re-form the five groups from the previous activity. Assign one sheet of newsprint to each group. Ask them to create a role play, using the formulaic expressions found on their list and writing it out in its entirety. Because increased planning reduces the cognitive burden on the WM, give adequate time to plan, write and practice.
(3) Have each group take turns presenting its role play.
(4) De-brief this activity by soliciting feedback on whether role play is an effective way to visualize language forms. What did learners do to remember their lines for their presentations?

MODIFICATIONS:

Technology: Ask learners to consider how these language functions change when blogging, chatting and emailing. Instead of asking learners to role play, ask groups to collaborate on writing a blog, chat, or email exchange using the various functions of greeting, making introductions, apologizing, asking and receiving directions and expressing gratitude (Steps 2 and 3). De-brief with a whole group discussion on how language functions change with technology and what the differences imply.

Cognitive Abilities Activity 13: S is for Strategize in SRVS: Working Memory Enhancement for Formulaic Expressions

Repetition of the same thought or physical action develops into a habit, which, repeated frequently enough, becomes an automatic reflex. – Norman Vincent Peale

Level: All

Procedure:

(1) Preface this activity by explaining that in order to fully automatize the formulaic expressions explored in class, learners will use an individual organizational strategy suggested by WM experts.
(2) Ask learners to copy all five lists of formulaic expressions into their language diaries.
(3) Assign one list for review every homework session. As learners master an expression, instruct them to put a check mark by it, but to still briefly review expressions from previous study sessions before attacking the new list for the day.
(4) De-brief this activity by asking learners whether they use lists as mnemonic devices and whether they feel a sense of satisfaction as items are crossed off. For learners who do not habitually use lists, challenge them to use this strategy in the future to enhance their WM.

MODIFICATION:

Technology:

(1) Tell learners to record (either as voice or text) their lists into an electronic portable device so reviewing can be conveniently done anywhere and at any time when learners encounter a five minute pause from other activities.
(2) Often learners have the best intentions to meet their daily study obligations, but sometimes they just seem to forget or get sidetracked with other activities. To meet their daily review responsibilities, tell learners to set an alarm on their cell phones for five opportune times during the next five days. When the device sounds, learners are reminded to review their lists.

Cognitive Abilities Activity 14: Awakening Multiple Intelligences: Know Thy Intelligence Self

The awakening of potentialities of human beings is the most impor-tant thing in life – unknown

Level: All

Procedure:

(1) Preface this activity by introducing 'nonverbal communication' as the interdisciplinary theme for the next series of lessons. Tell learn-ers that this means all that we communicate without words (Knapp & Hall, 2010). Besides 'awakening' their specific intelligences, tell learners that the objective is also to raise awareness of the impor-tance of nonverbal communication in second/foreign language acquisition – that too often so much attention is paid to the verbal modality to the exclusion of important nonverbal functions in the communication process.

(2) Ask learners to close their eyes and imagine a time in the last few days when they relied on nonverbal communication to achieve understanding with a friend or family member. Invite them to reflect upon the critical role of nonverbal cues when considering an exchange between TL speakers and their potential language diffi-culties. Tell learners what Singelis (1994: 275) said: 'The fact that at least one communicator is working in a second language means the verbal content may not be as clear as it would be in an intracultural interaction. Consequently, the reliance on nonverbal communica-tion may be even greater than normal.'

(3) Tell learners to brainstorm a list on the board of how humans com-municate without words. Compare their list with the following codes and add any absent ones: vocalics (intonation), gesture, facial expression (eye behavior), posture, proxemics (use of space), chrone-mics (use of time) and touch.

(4) List the following five MIs on the board: mathematical, spatial, linguistic, physical, and musical. Using the descriptions of the MIs found in the 'Premise' part of the chapter, describe each of them. Tell learners that interpersonal and intrapersonal intelligences will be targeted later in the series of activities.

(5) Tell each learner to select the MI with which he or she feels most comfortable. Have learners form groups accordingly. Equalize as much as possible the number of students per group by asking learners in an over-represented group if they have another choice

commiserate with their preferences (the importance of same-size groups will be seen in Activity 15 where learners participate in a Jigsaw task). Match the following (mostly) nonverbal codes to each group:

(a) Mathematical: Chonemics (use of time to communicate).
(b) Spatial: Proxemics (use of space to communicate) and touch.
(c) Physical: body language, gesture, posture and facial expression.
(d) Musical: Vocalics (intonation– how we use our voices to communicate without words).
(e) Linguistic: Word choices (how specific word choices modify messages' meanings).

(6) Next, write the following prompts on the board:
(a) communicate that you are enjoying someone's company,
(b) communicate that you are unhappy with something someone has said,
(c) communicate that you are angry with someone.

(7) Clarify that although the verbal channel is optimal for imparting ideas, the nonverbal mode is considered more effective for conveying feelings and emotions (Kang, 2000). Explain that the group task is to decide how the prompts on the board are best communicated through their chosen code and then model it. The following instructions take into account how differences among the codes dictate changes in the groups' responses to the prompts:

(a) The first two groups silently act out the prompt. For example the 'spatial intelligence' group silently role plays proxemics by giving a hug; whereas the 'physical intelligence group' might gesture excitedly.

(b) The 'musical intelligence' group has two options: Use the same series of sounds but change the vocal cues to correspond to the cue, so for example they utter: 'eeeeeeaaaaa!' as an expletive of joy (situation a), unhappiness (situation b), or anger (situation c); or the can repeat the 'I am...' portion and fill in the blank with 'enjoying your company,' 'unhappy', or 'angry' using the appropriate intonation.

(c) The mathematical group has a more complicated job owing to the nature of how time communicates. They have two options: either silently role play a more elaborate scenario adding more nonverbal codes from the other groups to model how time is a powerful nonverbal communicator; or they opt to verbally describe a scenario or create a story from the teacher-provided prompt.

(d) The linguistic group uses the verbal channel to talk about how different words can be used to evoke the same or different emotions for each prompt. Ask this group to focus on the subtleties and connotational differences among different word choices to express the same emotion. Use at least three 'synonyms' to say the same thing, but be able to explain their differences (e.g. furious/annoyed/upset).

(7) Ask each group to model the three prompts using their nonverbal (or verbal, when applicable) code.

(8) De-brief this exercise by asking learners whether the MI they chose was 'awakened' by the code they role played. What were some of the criteria used by the groups to decide how to express each prompt? Do different cultures express these emotions differently? If so, how?

MODIFICATIONS:

Emergent learners: Although the actions that learners must DO in this activity are easily performed by learners of all proficiency levels, emergent learners may need teachers to scaffold the explanations and descriptions through more visuals, body language, the provision of definitions, and possibly L1 translation.

Technology: Some learners feel more comfortable in front of a camera than a live audience as cameras allow groups to stop, start and rewind and to perform without a large group watching. If technology is available, give learners a choice as to whether their code is presented 'live' or 'recorded.'

Cognitive Abilities Activity 15: Amplifying Multiple Intelligences: Task Collaboration of the Like-Minded

It is not the IQ but the I Will that is most important in education. – unknown

Level: Intermediate/Advanced

Procedure:

(1) Preface this activity by highlighting learners' answers from the de-briefing of the previous activity. Explain that powerful cultural influences affect the way individuals nonverbally express themselves. Called 'display rules,' these are culturally specific restrictions

understood by most in-group members concerning how much emotion individuals may overtly express (Knapp & Hall, 2010). For example, a male in one culture may openly cry in public, but that same man in another culture exhibiting the same behavior would be entering into culturally taboo territory.

(2) Ask groups to amplify their assigned MI (spatial, physical, musical, mathematic, or linguistic) by investigating its corresponding code (proxemics, gesture/body language/facial expression, intonation, chronemics and word choice – necessarily verbal) and comparing and contrasting the display rules of two different cultures.

(3) If the class is composed of learners from the same culture, use their home culture as the point of comparison/contrast. However if the class is multicultural, opt for the culture with the largest number of students originating from it so as to secure as many cultural informants as possible. Choose the second culture from among those cultures that predominantly speak the TL. For example, if you are teaching French in Spain to Spanish speakers, your home culture is Spain, and your comparison/contrasting culture will be chosen from among countries that speak French, like Quebec, Cameroon or France. To bring relevance to this activity, agree upon two cultures: one that corresponds to the TL and the one which provides a first culture to the greatest number of learners.

(4) Using cultural informants, library resources, the internet, movies and television, previous knowledge, teacher-provided material, observing people or any other information source, tell each intelligence group to research how their nonverbal code is exhibited in both cultures. For example, for a group of Japanese students learning Chinese who self-reported 'mathematical intelligence,' they will research and compare how people in Japan perceive or use time compared to how Chinese people use time. Tell group members to take copious notes on a Venn diagram (showing points of similarity and differences) to use in the next activity or to collect for possible formative assessment.

(5) De-brief this activity by asking learners to share their speculations on how these cultural differences in specific nonverbal display rules influence cross-cultural misunderstanding.

MODIFICATIONS:

Emergent learners: Provide scaffolding to emergent learners to understand instructions and explanations, particularly visualization. Allow simpler notes in the Venn diagram.

Large classes: If the class has more than 25 (i.e. more than five people per group in the previous activity), make as many groups of five as possible dispersing any remaining individuals throughout the class.

Technology: Investigation of nonverbal behavior is extraordinarily enhanced with access to electronic media and websites like YouTube where learners see interlocutors using nonverbal behavior in authentic interactions. If learners have access to electronic media and/or the internet, invite them to peruse YouTube and other visual media sources. Tell groups to save the entirety of their research findings as a separate video or audio file for future use and teacher formative assessment.

Cognitive Abilities Activity 16: Teach for/with the Multiple Intelligences: Task Collaboration of the Unlike-Minded

Language grows out of life, out of its needs and experiences... Language and knowledge are indissolubly connected; they are inter-dependent. Good work in language presupposes and depends on a real knowledge of things. – Anne Sullivan

Level: Intermediate/Advanced

Procedure:

(1) Preface this activity by asking whether learners have ever had any cross-cultural communication misunderstandings owing to the inability to send and/or receive nonverbal messages. Ask learners to share their experiences.
(2) Create five new groups by placing a representative from each intelligence group into the new one, i.e. each new group will be composed of one person from each of the original mathematical, spatial, linguistic, musical and physical groups who has become an expert on one specific nonverbal code from the two cultures under investigation.
(3) Tell groups to consult the Venn Diagrams or the electronic files from the previous activity and draw upon everyone's newly developed specialized nonverbal expertise to creatively present a project that demonstrates how the two cultures interact and communicate cross-culturally using the five different codes, highlighting both similarities and differences. Student choice concerning the form it takes is paramount. Suggest: (a) live performance options like role play, newscasts, or visual story-telling; or (b) written but visual

options like a travel guide, a series of 'Dear Abby' letters with pictures (i.e. members of the newspaper audience write in asking for advice, and Abby wisely responds), or some posters using the universally recognized red circle (with or without the line through it to indicate 'Not Permitted' or 'Permitted'). Allow learners a wide berth in their creativity and plenty of time to prepare and rehearse.

(4) Before preparation begins, write the following questions on the board. Peers will provide anonymous written post-performance feedback considering the following pre-established criteria/questions:
   (a) Was the performance original?
   (b) Were all five nonverbal codes included? Which was the most attention-grabbing?
   (c) Were both similarities and differences between the cultures highlighted? Which were the most surprising?
   (d) How well had the group rehearsed in preparation for their presentation, both in terms of language use and delivery of content?

(5) After sufficient preparation and rehearsal time, number the groups in the order of their performance and tell audience members to take out the corresponding number of papers – one for each group. (Unless teachers choose otherwise, the performing group does not critique itself.) In response to each group, ask every peer reviewer to provide at least one positive comment for every constructive criticism offered. Remind reviewers that the questions from Step 4 should guide their feedback.

(6) Invite groups to present their live performances and/or written projects. After each group presents, ask audience members to write feedback. Collect the feedback, organize it by groups, and return it to the corresponding performers. Allow time for groups to absorb and discuss their classmates' feedback.

(7) Solicit responses about the difficulty of having expertise in one area of intercultural nonverbal behavior but being required to arrive at a consensus with four other 'experts' to create and present projects. How did it feel giving and receiving both negative and positive peer assessments? Explain that these abilities to work together in groups and to participate in peer feedback sessions are part of the sixth intelligence, called *interpersonal intelligence* – defined as the ability to understand the feelings, motivation, and moods of others, and to respond to them appropriately.

(8) De-brief this activity by asking language learners to tap into their intrapersonal intelligence by responding to the following prompt in their language learning diaries: What did I learn about

my interpersonal intelligence, the intelligences of my group members, and the strengths and weaknesses of my other intelligences through this project experience?

Modifications:

Emergent learners:

(1) Provide a modified list of performance options that learners are capable of executing.
(2) Simplify the peer feedback prompts, possibly with the provision of an easily read rubric necessitating only numerical responses.

Technology: With the availability of electronic and digital technology, learners' performance options are greatly enhanced. Rather than a live role play or hand-written projects, learners could record their own personally enacted videos, create a collage of public access videos from the internet, or design Powerpoint or Prezi presentations, among limitless others.

Cognitive Abilities Activity 17: Transfer Multiple Intelligences: A Teacher's Wish List

In seeking knowledge, the first step is silence, the second is listening, the third is remembering, the fourth is practicing, and the fifth – teaching others. – Solomon Ibn Gabirol

Level: Intermediate/Advanced

Procedure:

(1) Preface this activity by outlining its goal: To make the recent activities involving MI relevant to learners' lives by reflecting upon what they learned.
(2) Explain that throughout the last series of MI activities a variety of learner objectives were targeted. Rather than expressing them in the customary pre-lesson way (i.e. 'Learners will...'), include the following 'I hope you have' wishes in a handout delivered to each learner:
'I HOPE YOU HAVE...'
  (a) gained valuable insight about how nonverbal behavior influences the whole communication process;

(b) discovered a myriad of ways in which different cultures non-verbally express emotion;

(c) boosted your awe at the complexity of intercultural communi-cation (which hopefully heightened your passion to engage in it even more!);

(d) deepened your self-awareness of your own MI strengths and weaknesses;

(e) strengthened your preferred intelligence(s) by experimenting with your personally chosen one(s);

(f) explored your self-perceived 'weaker' intelligence(s) by interact-ing with others who exhibited strengths in it (those);

(g) re-evaluated the status you had originally given your 'weaker' intelligence(s) by experimenting with activities that tapped into it (them);

(h) increased your *interpersonal* intelligence by interacting with others of similar and dissimilar intelligence complexes through task-based group work, peer feedback and whole group interaction;

(i) improved your *intrapersonal* intelligence by entertaining new strategies for accomplishing self-defined goals and by exploring your self-awareness, your strengths and weaknesses, and the triggers to your emotional well-being.

(j) THROUGH ALL OF THIS, IMPROVED YOUR LANGUAGE SKILLS!!!

(3) Ask learners to silently read through the 'hopes' , then write the letters *a* through *j* on a piece of paper and respond to each of the 'wishes' on a scale of 1 to 5 evaluating how well teachers' wishes were granted. (5 = Definitely true of me; 4 = True of me; 3 = Neither true nor untrue of me; 2 = Not true of me; 1 = Definitely not true of me).

(4) Learners keep the 'wish list.' Collect responses for personal teacher self-reflection.

MODIFICATIONS:

Emergent learners: Re-write the 'wish list' items to simplify the syntax and vocabulary

Technology: Although this 'wish list' is not much more than a disguised list of learner objectives, masking it with the emotional appeal of 'I hope you have...' transforms it from the students' perspective of 'just one more likert-type questionnaire in an endless stream of 'what I can do' assessments' into a meaningful and personal inquiry into what students have learned by a teacher who cares. Call us sentimental, but we like the special touch that receiving a 'personal' wish list hand-delivered by the teacher implies. Although modifying the technology from a photocopied handout to an individually addressed hand-written letter would most optimally communicate the sentiment we are trying to amass, that technology modification is a bit impractical and time-consuming. However, it is at your own peril that you technologically modify what was meant to be a printed and personally delivered wish list (albeit mass produced and photocopied) into an electronic version of an online 'what I can do' Likert-type questionnaire.

4   Motivation

From Premise...

Why do individuals decide to pursue the challenges they do? What keeps them doggedly engaged in the long haul, even in the face of failure? What drives individuals to stay absorbed with the moment to moment minutia and tediousness that complex challenges demand?

The story is told of Sir Edmund Hillary, the first man who on May 29, 1953, reached the summit of Mount Everest, the highest mountain then known. His book, *High Adventure,* gives readers a glimpse of the origins of his success. His 1953 attempt to scale the giant was not his first. He had tried and failed to climb the 29,000 foot mountain in 1952. Several weeks after this failure, he was invited to speak to a group in England. While walking on stage to thunderous applause by people who recognized his *attempt* at greatness, Hillary felt himself a failure. Rather than walking up to the microphone, he walked to the edge of the platform, made a fist while pointing at a photo of Mount Everest and exclaimed loudly, 'Mount Everest, you beat me the first time, but I'll beat you the next time because you've grown all you are going to grow... but I'm still growing!' (Cavanaugh & Cavanaugh, 2004).

Motivations for language learning and mountain climbing have a lot in common.

There is little doubt *THAT* motivation contributes to successful language learning, but there is some question about *HOW* motivation does so, and from *WHERE* does language learning motivation come? In general terms, motivation gives behavior its energy and direction (Reeve, 2005). Flowing from this definition are the many forces that push or pull us toward certain actions and away from others. A challenge in the literature on motivation in second language acquisition (SLA) has been the framework in which to conceptualize it. Definitions of motivation change depending upon the researcher's theoretical approach: social psychologists, cognitivists, sociolinguists and others each highlight different concepts and processes. Although the terminology differs across different theories, Gardner and Clément (1990) astutely observed that, for all their differences, the various motivational models generate very similar predictions; no theory contradicts any other. That is, rather than reflecting confusion or conflicting approaches, different models choose to focus on different centerpiece concepts, different processes and different timescales. For the purposes of this chapter, we will not delve into the theoretical nuances of the models but rather lay out key concepts from different perspectives.

To orient readers our plan is to review:

(1) seminal social psychological theories that targeted why language learners are initially motivated to pursue language learning;
(2) cognitive models that aligned views of language learning motivation with popular educational tenets and situated it in a classroom context; and
(3) process-oriented, dynamic models that suggest that motivation is a dynamic variable in an ever-changing system influenced by the social nature of learning, including identity, self and the learner's imagination.

Our activities primarily target motivation as described by the process-oriented and self/identity paradigms.

Exploring Motivation, Its Origins and Its Significance

Social psychological and cognitive language learning motivation models

One of the most enduring SLA motivation models is Gardner and Lambert's (1959, 1972) social psychological approach (see Gardner, 2010 for the most recent updates). For Gardner (2010), a motivated student must possess three characteristics: generally positive attitudes toward language and the people who speak it, positive emotional engagement, and effort directed toward learning. Two key supports for motivation lay in what Gardner (1985) calls integrative and instrumental orientations. An integrative orientation is focused upon learning language to meet and communicate with people who speak it, and to take on their desirable characteristics – including the language they speak. An instrumental orientation is focused on more pragmatic benefits that come from language learning, such as good grades or job opportunities. The two orientations are not exhaustive nor are they mutually exclusive; students can endorse simultaneously both integrative and instrumental reasons for learning. It must be emphasized that merely being oriented toward these goals, however, is not enough to generate motivation. The orientations merely give motivation its color or flavor. If we think of an integrative orientation as an apple and an instrumental orientation as a cherry, either can be one of the ingredients in a motivational pie.

The Social Psychological Approach adequately addresses *why* an individual might want to initiate and persist at learning another language, but it does not focus specifically on classroom tasks and theory from educational psychology. Thus, after two full decades of almost uncontested appeal, the social psychological macro approach was supplemented by researchers focused on classroom processes and the cognitive notions that were taking educational psychology by storm. Among those having an important impact in SLA were:

- Self-determination theory: a macro-theory that links a continuum of extrinsic and intrinsic motives with three key psychological needs relevant in educational contexts – autonomy, competence and relatedness.
- Clément's social context model: a macro-theory that expanded on Gardner's model to propose a tension between approaching new languages as an opportunity for growth with a fear of losing one's native language and identity. Clément also proposed a secondary motivation process called *self-confidence* based on integrating perceptions of competence and anxiety.
- Foraging theory: John Schumann presented a neurolinguistic approach that emphasized structures in the brain that evolved to facilitate language learning as a way to adapt to the environment and for relationships with con-specifics (i.e. other people).
- Task motivation: a micro-perspective that focuses on the qualities of specific language tasks that increase or decrease students' motivation (Julkunen, 2001). Different tasks motivate learners in different ways and can be classified under a variety of rubrics, such as open vs. closed tasks, individual vs. group tasks, form vs. meaning-focused tasks.

The richness of motivational concepts provides ample food for thought as we consider what gives language learners their energy and direction. Languages are learned in order to form relationships, create competencies, adapt to new surroundings and develop as a person. But language learning also can be demotivating because it is difficult, takes a long time and it can be frustrating, anxiety-provoking and boring. Yet for all the rich concepts available from SLA approaches to motivation, one of the persistent problems that theories faced was describing the sometimes rapid process of change in motivational states. None of the models described so far center on motivational changes over time, whether time be measured in the span of a class or over a lifetime. Teachers often asked questions such as:

- Why do students sign up for a language class and then refuse to speak?
- Why are some learners in the classroom highly motivated at one moment and bored out of their minds the next?
- Why does a task or activity work in one class but not the next?

As these questions persisted, it became clear that a different conceptual paradigm was needed to study the dynamics of change.

Dynamic motivation – identity, self and the imagination

Motivation as a process

Questions concerning the dynamic character of motivation and its temporal variation were targeted when Dörnyei and Otto (1998) constructed their process model. The process model focused on processes that take place before, during and after a language-related event. At the pre-actional stage, three events take place: goal setting, intention formation and the initiation of intention enactment. These processes prepare the person to act, but remain in the cognitive domain until the individual 'crosses the Rubicon' into action. Once action begins, three additional processes kick in: subtask generation and implementation, a complex ongoing appraisal process and the application of a variety of action control mechanisms. These processes control the activity of the learner as it is taking place, much as a gas pedal and brake regulate a vehicle's speed by making adjustments on the fly. The post-actional phase is focused on attributions or explanations for positive and negative outcomes and the initial preparation for the next action.

The process model includes motivational concepts such as goal setting, action control and attributions but uses a very brief timescale to capture processes of motivation and adjustment. In one sense, the model is highly cognitive in portraying people as rational decision-makers implementing and evaluating plans. The prominent role of affective and emotional processes of Gardner's model is not the focus of the process model. Emotion is a powerful motivator (MacIntyre & Gregersen, 2012a) with a significant interaction with cognition, so this is a notable omission. However, the process model's main strength is that it describes ways in which motivational adjustments are made on a continuous basis.

Negotiating motivational processes in an ongoing fashion is a highly specific process, but it is contextualized within the learner's psychological system, and the learner is embedded within a social system. Even as we look at the micro-processes involved in language learning, other theories emphasize the context in which these processes take place. Sociolinguists have traditionally been uncomfortable discussing individual differences, including motivation, without contextualizing them in a social context.

Motivation as influenced by identity, self and the imagination

Social context has a wide range of effects on learners whose identity can shift markedly among different contexts, something that Clément and Noels (1992) call *situated identity*. Bonny Norton, a sociolinguist interested in identity, argued that TL motivation theories had trouble accounting for the diverse experiences faced by language learners and the sometimes erratic performances within the same individual. Rather than asking traditional questions concerning motivation and personality, she questioned why a learner was at times 'motivated, extroverted and confident' and at others 'unmotivated, introverted and anxious' (Norton, 1995: 11). She wanted to know why in one place social distance existed between a specific group of language learners and the target language (TL) community, but in another, it was minimal. She wondered why a language learner spoke on certain occasions but not on others. Norton's focus on change that learners experience differs from previous motivation models that emphasize stability. No doubt we experience both stability and change, and theories differ considerably in their emphasis on each.

Norton's key concept is *investment*, 'the socially and historically constructed relationship of learners to the target language and their sometimes ambivalent desire to learn and practice it' (Norton, 1997: 411). For her, a learner's investment in the TL is connected to their ever-changing identity, for when learners invest in their TL, they expect to receive symbolic and material resources in return, which ultimately makes their cultural capital worth more (Norton, 2010). The social conceptualization of investment emphasizes that a learner's complex identity changes across time and space and is *reproduced in social interaction* (Dörnyei, 2001), dynamically re-adjusting as the learner struggles to adapt and change (Norton, 2010). As language learners interact in their TLs, they are engaged in ongoing identity construction.

In a socially constructed view of motivation, power is an influential variable in learners' quests for identity. When an individual speaks, his or her goal is not only to be understood, but also to be given credibility. Individuals interact in the world, unconsciously aware of their social place, attempting to meet linguistic expectations and being well-received at the same time. Bourdieu (1977: 648) proposes that when evaluating language competence, learners' efficacy in demanding their 'right to speak' and their 'power to impose reception' must also be included. Power relations can generate frustration for the language learner who feels encouraged and valued in one context (such as a classroom) but feels marginalized in another context (such as talking with native speakers in a market). Viewed through the lens of power differentials, language learners who struggle within an identity position can be helped to reframe the relationship with those interlocutors and claim alternative, more powerful identities. That is, learners who create 'counter-discourses' (i.e. re-stated identities that demand greater respect and increased value for their resources) enhance the opportunities for language interaction in the social networks of their learning communities (Norton & Toohey, 2001: 318).

The concept of investment works with the notion of *communities of practice,* which are real or imagined groups of people who share a concern or passion for something they do and learn how to do it better as they interact regularly; they may be 'as broad as a society or culture, or as narrow as a particular language classroom' (Lantolf & Pavlenko, 2001: 148; Norton, 2001). Learners must be favorably situated as participants within these communities and invested in ongoing practice for learning identities to evolve. Full members of their communities have access to a variety of ongoing activity, other community members, information resources and opportunities for participation. An understanding of those imagined communities with which learners would like to be affiliated and cognizance of the social structures in learners' real communities will help teachers facilitate learners' access to those communities and spark learners to vividly imagine them.

'Imagined communities refer to groups of people, not immediately tangible and accessible, with whom we connect through the power of imagination' (Kanno & Norton, 2003: 241). The concept of imagined communities was developed as an extension of investment and creates a way to better appreciate the connection between language and identity (Pavlenko & Norton, 2007). According to Norton (1996: 355), '[i]n many language classrooms, the community may be, to some extent, a reconstruction of past communities and historically constituted relationships, but also a community of the imagination – a desired community that offers possibilities for an enhanced range of identity options in the future.' Pavlenko and Norton (2007: 669) argue that both the learners' current and aspired to connections in imagined communities influence their language learning through their capacity to act, their motivation and investment, and maybe even their resistance to language learning. Language learners see not only the four walls of their classrooms, but they also envision a community that transcends time and space and extends to an imagined world outside the classroom (Norton, 2001).

Motivation as international posture

An example of one of these envisioned communities involves *international posture*. There is little doubt that, in the early 21st century world, English has become the international lingua franca. The imagined community of international English speakers has members who are global citizens and maintain a world identity, not tied to a specific English-speaking country. Yashima (2009) describes an international posture that draws upon the motivational qualities of integrativeness, combined with conceptualizations of motivation as dynamic and influenced by an imagined future. International posture reflects the degree to which a learner values and is open to the identity associated with the imagined foreign community. An individual with an interest in international issues, who is willing to work or live overseas, desires to interact with international associates, and demonstrates cultural competency with low ethnocentrism is better positioned to learn other languages.

Lamb (2004) used the term 'bicultural identity' to characterize a person whose identity is rooted in local culture, while another part feels connected with the global culture. He argues that the media, including television and the internet, give people from all over the world a sense of belonging to a global culture without having to leave their own borders. Authors writing from this perspective argue that the idea of integrating with an identifiable group or nation-state generally is less prominent than a desire to invest in a global community of speakers. Dörnyei (2005: 97) notes specifically that 'in the absence of a salient group in the learner's environment, identification can be generalized to the cultural and intellectual value associated with the language, as well as to the actual target language.' This approach serves to emphasize the power of the imagination as a motivational tool.

Motivation as a self-system
The power of the imagination in pursuit of self and identity in language learning is also featured in Dörnyei's construction of the *L2 Self Model*, fashioned from Markus and Ruvolo's *Possible Selves* work in personality psychology and Higgins' work in social psychology. In the Possible Selves paradigm, learners create specific, vivid representations of what they might become, what they would like to become, and what they are afraid of becoming. 'Possible selves are specific representations of one's self in future states, involving thoughts, images and senses, and are in many ways the manifestations or personalized carriers, of one's goals and aspirations (and fears, of course)'(Dörnyei, 2005: 99). 'Imagined 'possible selves' must be a present reality for the individual, and must frame future goals through creating vivid self-images' (Markus & Ruvolo, 1986: 954). Through embellishing one's possible selves, an individual creates a dynamic forward-propelling future guide by hoping, wishing and fantasizing, with detailed imagery integrating the various elements of the self. Goals are set and translated into action. 'Thus, possible selves give form, meaning, structure, and direction to one's hopes and threats, thereby inciting and directing purposeful behavior. The more vivid and elaborate the possible self, the more motivationally effective it is expected to be' (Dörnyei, 2005: 100). Increased motivational force results from juxtaposing positive future images with potential negative or feared outcomes, creating a dynamic balance between what one hopes for and what one fears (Markus & Ruvolo, 1989).

Motivation as influenced by emotion
Generally speaking, emotion is one of the most reliable indicators of motivation. From an evolutionary perspective, the function of emotion is to generate the motivation to act. Intense emotion produces a strong urge to act immediately. Strong emotions are fundamentally motivating, taking over the individual's state of mind and focusing attention exclusively on dealing with the source of the emotion and/or the emotional reaction itself. Like physical pain, a state of high anxiety, intense anger, or profound sadness will predispose people to certain types of actions. But language learning is a

long-term process, the emotions often are less intense, more subtle in their effects, and often can be ambivalent (see Chapter 7).

Baumgartner *et al.* (2008) offer an important distinction between anticipatory emotion and anticipated emotion that specifies the link between imagination and emotion.

> 'On the one hand, a person may currently experience an emotion due to the prospect of a desirable or undesirable future event (i.e. hope or fear). These affective reactions are **anticipatory** emotions, because they are currently experienced due to something that could happen in the future. On the other hand, a person may imagine experiencing certain emotions in the future once certain desirable or undesirable future events have occurred (e.g. anticipated joy or regret). These affective reactions are **anticipated** emotions.' (p. 685, emphasis added)

Baumgartner *et al.* (2008) highlight two categories of emotion as prototypes: positive (e.g. hope) and negative (e.g. fear) anticipatory emotions. These are the same categories used in Possible Selves research: the hoped-for and feared future self (Markus & Nurius, 1986; MacIntyre *et al.*, 2009), strengthening the ability of the learner's imagination to motivate.

One of the key developments in the literature on emotion has been mapping out the ways in which positive emotions and negative emotions are qualitatively different. They should not be seen as opposite ends of the same continuum; instead, they represent two different continua. MacIntyre and Gregersen (2012a) argue that positive emotions have the effect of broadening a person's focus, allowing him or her to take in new information that might not be noticed otherwise. Positive emotions such as pride, joy and happiness can be associated with a wide variety of actions and efficient ways of learning. Negative emotions, such as fear, anger or disgust narrow a person's focus and predispose individuals to a specific course of action (e.g. disgust leads to rejection and avoidance) that often is at odds with language learning, especially in classroom contexts.

Capitalizing on Motivation: An Action Plan

Social identity

'Going beyond the possible to what is desirable' is a fitting mantra for language teachers attempting to capitalize on learner identity (Norton, 2010). Transformative classrooms are spaces where language transcends being exclusively a linguistic system and becomes a social practice that organizes experiences and negotiates identities. Integrativeness means that learners are genuinely interested in participating in the TL group. Investment means that learners take ownership over their meaning-making and re-imagine an expanded range of identities for the future. Possible selves captures the vision of oneself in the future, participating in the activities unlocked when one uses another language. These concepts tap into a wellspring of motivation.

The first six activities help provide social spaces where individuals develop motivation through imagination, construct their identities in imagined communities, foster integrativeness and expand their linguistic skills. Classroom practices are enhanced with multi-modal resources and authentic materials that transform language into a means of communication and identity construction while exploring issues of power. A combination of linguistic, bodily and sensory modes foster learner engagement in meaning-making and offer the strongest possibility of tapping into the imaginations of as many students as possible. Systematically integrated multimodal pedagogies including drawing, photography and drama can be a novel means of inspiring new possible selves and validating learners' cultural experiences.

The motivational goal is to transform the TL into a viable means of communication, expression, and meaning ownership, with an open posture toward TL speakers. 'Educators and researchers should utilize the cultural experiences and embedded bodily knowledge of their students as starting points, not for bemoaning the failures and inadequacies of their charges, but to render more conscious for them what is unconsciously rendered in their cultural practices' (Willis, 2003: 413). Furthermore, authentic materials, when subjected to learners' critical thinking, provide opportunities for learners to question and reshape the powerful discourses that control the social milieu. Text-focused activities using popular media like newspaper and magazine articles and advertisements encourage learners to explore how meaning and power is encoded in texts (Wallace, 2003). Norton's (1995: 26) 'Classroom-Based Social Research' (CBSR) extends learners' participation beyond the classroom by encouraging them to 'claim the right to speak outside the classroom.' The incorporation of learners' lived experiences and social identities into the language curriculum encourages learners to pursue interaction with TL speakers to increase their language skills by eliminating the boundaries between their classrooms and their communities.

Awareness of task motivation processes

For many students, motivation seems to just happen, as if its presence or absence was beyond their control. Similarly, the goals that a language learner has might be vague, implicit, or mismatched with the task at hand. We believe that an explicit awareness of the motivation process that unfolds during specific tasks can lead to students noticing both their own unique sources of motivation, and those shared with other learners. If greater awareness is achieved through a learner's self-analysis, greater autonomy can be possible in their own learning. Activity 7, Performers and Reporters, asks students to take turns monitoring the task motivation of their partner, using Dörnyei and Otto's process model. The intent of this activity is to make explicit what is often an implicit process of goal setting and monitoring.

Entity versus mastery orientations when aptitude meets motivation

Carol Dweck, in a classic paper, outlined the differences between a mastery and an entity orientation with respect to beliefs about intelligence; we can extend this same distinction to beliefs about learning a new language. On the one hand, for those who hold an entity orientation, language acquisition is a matter of innate ability that cannot be changed – a natural ear for language. It stands to reason that those who struggle to learn, who must exert effort, must be lacking this ability. One can easily imagine the difficulty caused by any perspective in which exerting effort is a bad thing. On the other hand a mastery orientation holds that language learning ability is adaptable, it changes over time, and each new language learned makes it easier to learn the next. If language ability is changeable and can be improved, then the meaning of effort is reversed – effort will lead to success, it's just a matter of time and perseverance. Activity 8 presents learners with an opportunity to consider their personal views on the relative contributions of innate ability and effort, and to learn about an admired person who had to struggle to achieve.

International posture

Learning a language, any language, builds bridges across cultures, allowing individuals access to new and exciting people and places. English in particular allows learners to link themselves with global concerns. Tapping into an openness to all things international, Yashima (2009: 159) suggests that learners can expand their sense of multiple selves by creating new images of themselves and 'find meaning in learning English while learning to use the language.' In her educational initiatives, Yashima offers an approach that solicits the creation of situations in which task-related Possible Selves are connected to the learner's Ideal English Self. Learning another language transforms a learner's relationship to the world as well as their self-conceptualizations. In view of this, language learning will 'allow learners to take a global outlook, enhance critical thinking and enable multiple perspectives, because a fundamental goal of TL learning is to empower learners to deal with an increasingly more complex globalizing world' (p. 159). Activities 9 and 10 will encourage learners in pursuit of their bicultural and international identities.

L2 self system

Dörnyei (2009: 18) lists six specific conditions that enrich or thwart the motivational force of the ideal and ought selves: accessibility, plausibility, harmony, activation, procedural strategies, and a juxtaposed Feared Self. With the combination of ideal and feared selves, the imagined future takes on maximum motivational effectiveness because it energizes approach and avoidance motives toward the same goal. Dörnyei (2009: 33) also provides strategic implications that function as the premises for several classroom activities in this chapter:

- Creating the vision: Awareness raising; Guided selection of previous aspirations, dreams, desires, etc.; Intensifying consciousness about the importance of ideal selves.
- Strengthening the vision. Imagery enhancement through the invocation of creative or guided imagery; Boost controllability of the image.
- Substantiating the vision: Build realistic expectations on the premise that the greater the prospect of goal achievement, the higher the degree of positive motivation.
- Activating the vision: Provide a framework to maintain engagement
- Operationalizing the vision: Supply a set of concrete action plans and continual self-evaluation; Modify ineffective plans/Celebrate successful plans.
- Counterbalancing the vision: Contemplate the repercussions of failure. Activate 'dreaded' selves.

Learners will explore a series of activities leading to the creation, strengthening, substantiating, activating, operationalizing and counterbalancing of their possible selves in Activities 11 through 17.

In the same vein, caveats with pedagogical implications were added to the Possible Selves model by MacIntyre and his team (2009) when they attempted to develop a scale to measure possible selves. Research suggests that in order to be effective, the creation of possible selves must be easily brought to mind and frequently invoked, including two important considerations:

(1) are the possible selves actually potentially viable in the future, and
(2) does the possible self describe the learner presently?

On the one hand, elements of the present self that are perceived as being relevant in the future will facilitate ongoing development, especially if some factors are not currently part of the self concept, but could conceivably be added. On the other hand, thinking that a present self is not desirable in the future or is not expected to continue will be demotivating. For possible selves to be productive, the imaginer must have a plan of action to achieve the goals and not just a 'feel good' strategy. 'Thus, it is important to find out how likely participants consider a possible self to be; a highly unlikely possible self probably will have little relation to motivation' (MacIntyre et al., 2009: 197). Activity 18 gives space for students to explore their anticipatory/anticipated balance.

In sum, we want to highlight how important it is for teachers to view motivation through a process-oriented lens and to see how the self and identity dynamically interact in each learner. A contemporary view of motivation assigns a pivotal role to both the social nature of learning and the learner's imagination. The sociolinguistic notions of self and identity are key components in a dynamic motivational paradigm where individual learners, interacting in a variety of social milieus and drawing upon their imaginations, are continually re-conceptualizing their imagined communities and possible selves. Furthermore, the power of the imagination can be captured by language learners who simultaneously invest in their TL and develop their social identities through developing imagined communities, assuming an international posture, and visualizing possible selves. These processes evoke positive and negative emotion, occasionally at the same time, that are intimately tied to the ongoing motivation process.

To conclude this Premise section on motivation, let's return to our opening vignette and draw some parallels with language learning. Sir Edmund Hillary decided to climb mountains – Mount Everest in particular. He maintained a positive attitude toward mountain climbing, consistent positive emotional engagement, **used anger to drive the motivation to overcome the mountainous obstacle** and exerted a concerted effort toward conquering mountains. He set goals and made decisions. However, this did not account fully for the moment to moment emotional and physical energy he had to muster to reach one hand above the other to heave his body up the 28,000 feet inch by inch. That is the same kind of tenacity that language learners need as they tap into the positive-broadening energy required to conjure up their willingness to communicate, dive into TL communicative events, and stay engaged in the language learning process even when negative-narrowing emotion may sometimes arise in the face of failed attempts.

...To Practice

Motivation Activities

Although teachers do not have a lot of control over *why* language learners decide to pursue language learning in general and their TL in particular, they do have some influence on the classroom process, how interaction transpires, and the tasks that keep learners engaged (or not). They can also encourage learners to approach their social contexts with greater confidence and sense of personal empowerment. Teachers who positively impact learner motivation are attuned to learners' changing emotional dynamics and inspire them to imagine their best possible selves. The activities in continuation provide a starting point to heightened motivation.

Motivation Activity 1: Speak Up and Be Heard Lest the Wagon Leave Without You

The most common way people give up their power is by thinking they don't have any – Alice Walker

Level: Intermediate/Advanced

In preparation:

(1) Randomly divide learners into two equal groups: the powerful and the powerless – those who bestow the right to speak (usually members of the dominant culture) and those that want it (usually the language learner). Create an equal number of identities for each group. We have started a list for you:

Those Who Bestow the Right	Those Who Need to Claim the Right
a. Store owner	a. Language learner who is lost
b. Police officer	b. Language learner who just got robbed
c. Lawyer	c. Language learner whose car broke down
d. Doctor	d. Language learner who feels ill
e. Restaurant owner	e. Language learner who needs something to eat
f. Teacher	f. Language learner who just wants to practice speaking

(2) Place chairs in two concentric circles with the inner circle chairs facing outward and the outer circle chairs facing inward, creating pairs of chairs.

Procedure:

(1) Preface this activity by explaining to learners that motivation is not a fixed personality trait but that it must be understood and acted upon considering social relations that create (or not) the possibilities for language learners to speak (Norton, 1995).
(2) Invite learners to take a chair in either of the concentric circles. Assign a role from the chart to each learner: those in the inside circle will be members of the dominant culture (those who bestow the right to speak); and those in the outside circle will be the language learners (those who need to claim the right to speak).
(3) Ask learners to talk about their lived, out-of-the-classroom experiences and social identities concerning their claiming the right to

speak to frame their role plays. Give learners three minutes to spontaneously act out a role play where the language learner must claim
the right to speak.

(4)   Invite learners on the outside circle to rotate one seat to the right. Tell
learners to maintain the same invented identity and engage again in
conversation with their new interlocutor. Rotate seats as many times
as necessary for all pairs to have the opportunity to interact.

(5)   Debrief this activity in a whole group discussion, asking learners in
the outer circle which strategies seemed to work the best in claiming their right to speak. Question the students in the inner circle
about how it felt to have the roles reversed: what did it feel like to
be the one granting access to the language?

MODIFICATIONS:

Large groups: Divide the students into groups to form several pairs of
concentric circles

Technology: Especially for large groups and reticent learners, instruct
learners to post their de-briefing responses to a discussion board and to
respond to at least two of their classmates' posts (Step 5).

Motivation Activity 2: The Fourth Student
(Adapted from Judy Sharkey and Carolyn Layzer
[Sharkey *et al.*, 2003: 58])

Imagination is the beginning of creation. You imagine what you
desire, you will what you imagine and at last you create what you
will – George Bernard Shaw

Level: Intermediate/Advanced

In preparation:

(1)   With clear mental images of your learners' purposes for and attitudes toward learning their TL, create three fictitious profiles of
'Any Learner' where learners can glimpse fragments of themselves
and their classmates within the characters you describe. For each
profile, write on separate color-coded post-it notes (or scraps of
paper with adhesive) information on the following that will later be
displayed for your students:
(a)   Head (What dreams or goals does each of your fictitious learners have to use their TL?)

    (b) Ears (What things does each fictitious learner like to listen to in the TL?)

    (c) Eyes (How does each fictitious learner like others to see him or her in the classroom and outside?)

    (d) Shoulders (What problems does each fictitious learner have to face both inside and outside the classroom?)

    (e) Hands (What things does each fictitious learner like to do or make with the TL?)

    (f) Heart (What things does each fictitious learner feel strongly about concerning the TL?)

    (g) Feet (What places does each fictitious learner want to go?)

(2) Trace an outline of a human body on a large piece of newsprint, list the anatomical parts along with the questions listed above, and hang it on the wall.

Procedure:

(1) Preface this activity by explaining that its purpose is for learners to explore the similarities and differences between their TL and native language identities and how these perceptions of identity influence their desire to self-disclose.

(2) Introduce learners to the three profiles of the fictitious 'Any Learner' that were prepared in advance. As each fictitious learner is discussed, attach the post-it note with the answer to the questions to the corresponding body part on the newsprint.

(3) Distribute seven post-it notes to each student with these instructions: 'Imagine that you are the 'fourth student'. Think about your purposes for and attitudes toward learning and using (TL) both inside and outside the classroom. Write a profile of yourself to share with the class using a post-it note to answer each question.'

(4) Have learners complete their post-it notes. Starting with the head and working down the outline of the human body, invite learners to share their vision of the 'fourth student' while sticking their post-it notes to the drawing.

(5) Debrief this activity by discussing how learners feel about using their TL in different contexts and social interactions. Work into the conversation the topic of how learners identify themselves in relation to their interlocutor.

MODIFICATIONS:

Technology:

(1) Create a Googledoc. Register all learners as collaborators to grant access and posting rights to the site (Preparation).

(2) Rather than providing an outline of the human body using a poster, ask learners to each post a full-body picture of themselves as the 'fourth student' to the Googledoc.

(3) Instead of post-it notes, instruct learners to post answers next to their photos to the same profile questions as those in Step 3 above, starting with the head and working their way down, thus sharing their vision of the 'fourth student.'

(4) Debrief using a prompt on the class discussion board (Step 5).

Motivation Activity 3: Media Manipulation – Media's Daily Impact on Me and My Imagined Communities
(Adapted from Judy Sharkey and Carolyn Layzer [Sharkey *et al.*, 2003: 58])

All media exist to invest our lives with artificial perceptions and arbitrary values – Marshal McLuhan

Level: Intermediate/Advanced

In preparation:

(1) Find media (newspaper, magazine, advertisements, etc.) that are obvious attempts to manipulate consumers by targeting specific, potential 'imagined communities' that your learners have well-developed ideas about. Gender roles and occupations are easy targets. Bring them to class and use them as models to exemplify how attitudes are influenced.

(2) Invite learners to bring in old magazines, newspapers, advertisements and the like that can be cut up.

Procedure:

(1) Preface this activity by explaining that its purpose is for learners to negotiate the meaning of what they see and hear in the media and to actively contest conflictive images and messages through the creation of their own media artifact. Explain that identity is often shaped by broader societal practices, including the media in all its forms by highlighting the role of cultural values and opinions that are inherently communicated in the ideological messages of the media as they shape individual identities (Sharkey *et al.*, 2003). Show the class your examples.

(2) Define the idea of 'imagined communities' that was presented in the earlier part of this chapter as groups of people with whom one

would like to affiliate, not immediately tangible and accessible, with whom one can connect through the power of imagination. Explain how the media attempts to influence individuals into wanting into some communities and not into others.

(3) Show the following internationally recognized signs for 'permitted' and 'not permitted':

(4) Ask learners to create a T-chart graphic organizer on a piece of paper with the title, 'My Desired Imagined Communities' on one side, and 'My Undesired Imagined Communities' on the other. Invite learners to work with a partner to fill in their charts, but because every individual has their own desired and undesired imagined communities, each learner must complete his or her own.

(5) Instruct learners to find images and words in magazines, newspapers, advertisements or other media that symbolize the desired and undesired community groups that are written on their T-Charts. Tell them to: (a) cut the images and words out; (b) glue them to a large piece of paper or cardboard in two distinct collage groups with the images within each group overlapping a bit; and (c) use the two symbols above (either cut out of heavier paper and placed over the collage or with heavy markers drawn around and through the collage) to pictorially indicate the 'Desired Imagined Communities' and the 'Undesired Imagined Communities.'

(6) Place learners in small groups to present their work and discuss why they chose the communities in their collages.

(7) De-brief this activity by discussing the positive impact that creating 'imagined communities' can have as a motivational tool. Also, talk about how the media influences their identity choices through its dominant images.

MODIFICATIONS:

Emergent learners: The visual nature of this activity lends itself well to emergent learners. If necessary, scaffold the creation of their T-Charts with a list of possible imagined communities from which they may choose (Step 4).

Technology:

(1) Instruct learners to make a T-Chart in the table making function in their word processing system and fill in an electronic copy (Step 4).

(2) Give learners the option of making a 'video collage' by searching YouTube for videos of their 'Desired' and 'Undesired Imagined Communities'. Ask them to copy their chosen links into an electronic document, separating them into two separate categories to present in and discuss with their small groups (Steps 5 and 6).

Motivation Activity 4: Language Learning Map
(Adapted from Norton's 1995 Classroom-Based Social Research [CBSR] model: Objectives One and Two)

Committing yourself is a way of finding out who you are. A man finds his identity by identifying. A man's identity is not best thought of as the way in which he is separated from his fellows but the way in which he is united with them – Robert Terwilliger

Level: All

Procedure:

(1) Preface this activity by explaining that its purpose is for learners to 'collapse the boundaries between their classrooms and their communities' by focusing on 'aspects of their social lives with a view to enhancing language learning and social interaction' (Norton, 1995: 26).
(2) Instruct learners to draw a map of their language learning journey from its beginning, noting whatever events, people, or places they think are important.
(3) Ask for volunteers to share their creations with the group.
(4) Invite learners to reflect back upon the previous week, and in the style of the first map where learners chronicled their entire language journey, create a second map that systematically accounts for the opportunities they had to interact with TL speakers, whether at home, at work, at school, or in the community.
(5) Invite learners to share with the group the one most productive interaction with a TL speaker that they experienced in the past week by answering the following questions:
    (a) Under which conditions did you have this conversation?
    (b) How and why did this interaction take place?
    (c) What results followed?
(6) De-brief this activity by discussing the socially structured nature of these conversations and how social relations might be implicated.

MODIFICATIONS:

Technology: Rather than create the two pencil and paper maps outlined above, place learners in pairs to chronicle each other's language journeys through video recording (Steps 2 and 4) for subsequent sharing (Steps 3 and 5). The sophistication of the videos will depend upon whether they can get out-of-class footage or keep it to a simpler 'video diary' mainly oral recording.

Motivation Activity 5: Teacher/Learner Dialogue Identity Journals
(Adapted from Norton's 1995 Classroom-Based Social Research [CBSR]
model: Objectives Three, Four and Five)

The greatest explorer on this earth never takes voyages as long as those of the man who descends in the depth of his heart – Julien Green

Level: All

Procedure:

(1) Preface this activity by explaining that its purpose is for learners to 'converse' with you through their dialogue journals to critically reflect on their 'opportunities to practice the target language outside the classroom, their investments in the target language, and their social identities' (Norton, 1995: 27).

(2) Invite learners to periodically (frequency at teacher's discretion) make observations in their dialogue journals that:
   (a) Critically examine any communication breakdowns that occurred with TL speakers.
   (b) Report any occurrences, actions, or events that surprise them or strike them as unusual and discuss the differences between the social practices in their native countries and the TL community.

(3) Collect learners' journals regularly and make personal comments in them to encourage learners to initiate new experiences from a position of strength rather than weakness.

(4) At regular intervals (weekly or monthly), use a circulating diaries technique where all the diaries are collected, randomly shuffled, and passed back. Instruct learners to read designated entries and write some helpful feedback or provide a reaction to the original writer.

(5) Tell learners to read, write and exchange diaries until everyone has read and written a response to several diaries.
(6) De-brief this activity by asking learners how it felt to compare their observations. Was this a meaningful exchange of information that made them feel like a community of learners who are invested with others in the class?

MODIFICATIONS:

Technology:

(1) Invite learners to write their dialogue journal entries electronically in a Googledoc (Step 2).
(2) Ask learners to send you their Googledoc at regular intervals. Use the 'comment' function to respond to their writing (Step 3).
(3) To circulate the diaries among learners, instruct the writer of the Googledoc to hit the blue 'share' button in the top right corner. In the box that appears, type in the name of the recipient, hit 'share and save' and then in the drop menu that appears hit 'can comment.' Continue circulating the diaries (Steps 4 and 5).

Motivation Activity 6: Fostering Integrativeness through Rolestorming

Hear me, four quarters of the world — a relative I am! Give me the strength to walk the soft earth, a relative to all that is! Give me the eyes to see and the strength to understand, that I may be like you. With your power only can I face the winds – Black Elk

Level: All

Procedure:

(1) Preface this activity by explaining that when language learners have integrative motivation, they want to communicate with people who speak their TL and take on their desirable characteristics. Explain that this Rolestorming activity (i.e. taking on the identity of another to remove the embarrassment of sharing unusual ideas, lowering inhibitions, and stimulating ideas that may not have otherwise been considered) will provide an opportunity to explore the attributes of the TL group that they currently share and those that they would like to share in the future by actually taking on the

identity of a TL group member to uninhibitedly brainstorm their desirable characteristics (Griggs, 1985).

(2) Tell learners to individually imagine themselves as a member of their TL community and invent a specific identity.

(3) Divide the class into small groups. Invite each learner to assume his or her imagined identity and finish the following sentence: 'One thing that other people admire about me is…' Instruct one member of each group to record the answers as the 'incognito' group members share their responses.

(4) Reconvene the whole class and ask reporters to share the small group responses. Write them on the board.

(5) Have learners divide a piece of paper into three columns and label them: (1) Attributes that I currently share; (2) Attributes I that I would like to share; and (3) Attributes that do not interest me.

(6) Tell learners to work alone and place each item from the list of Rolestormed attributes into one of the three columns.

(7) De-brief this activity by discussing possible strategies that would move attributes from the 'what I would like to share' column to the 'what I currently share' column.

MODIFICATIONS:

Large groups: Rather than reconvening the whole class, combine three small groups and assign the role of 'recorder' to one person who will create the joint list from the three reporters.

Technology:

(1) Without dividing learners into small groups, instruct learners to contribute to an electronic brainstorming exercise, making sure to include in the prompt that the answers learners provide originate from their assumed TL identities (Step 3).

(2) Using the table making function in a word processing program, have learners create the three columns and complete the exercise electronically (Steps 5 and 6).

Motivation Activity 7: A Process-oriented Approach: Performers and Reporters

There are only two rules for being successful. One, figure out exactly what you want to do, and two, do it – Mario Cuomo

Level: Intermediate/Advanced

Preparation:

(1) Choose an up-coming classroom exercise that will demand learners to exert a concerted effort. Use the activity in continuation as an immediate follow-up.

Procedure:

(1) Preface this activity by explaining that as students continue learning their TL, they are making motivational adjustments on a continual basis. They begin by preparing (setting goals and forming intentions); followed by performing (where action is controlled); and finally by appraising (where learners attribute or explain their positive and negative outcomes and prepare for the next action).

(2) Place learners in pairs. Assign one to be the 'performer' and the other the 'reporter.' Tell the reporter to interview the performer and write answers to the following three questions:

 (a) Frame 1: Prepare. What did you do to prepare for the classroom exercise we just completed? (i.e. What goals did you set or what intentions did you form? What made you want to begin?)

 (b) Frame 2: Perform. While you were involved in the activity, what did you do to maintain your motivation? (i.e. What did you do to eliminate off-task distractions, negative emotions, or physical difficulties?)

 (c) Frame 3: Appraise. When you finished the exercise, how did you evaluate the experience? (i.e. Did you attribute your success or failure to anything specific? Did you think about other strategies you might use in the future? Did this evaluation have any influence on how you will proceed next time?

(3) Switch roles and repeat the activity.

(4) De-brief this activity by asking learners to share ways in which making their implicit motivations to prepare, perform and appraise explicit will help them to generate more task motivation for the next time.

MODIFICATIONS:

Technology: Rather than reporting the results of the interviews in writing, have learners videotape the oral exchange.

Motivation Activity 8: Aptitude Meets Motivation

The winner's edge is not in a gifted birth, a high IQ, or in talent. The winner's edge is all in the attitude, not aptitude. Attitude is the criterion for success – Denis Waitley

Level: Intermediate/Advanced

Procedure:

(1)   Preface this activity by explaining that success more often accompanies highly motivated and hard-working individuals than those who depend solely on innate ability and that through this activity, they will explore their attitudes toward this balance.

(2)   Ask learners to assign a percentage (0%–100%, totaling 100% for each item) for the relative contributions of innate vs. effort for each of the following activities.

	% innate	% effort
(a) Playing piano		
(b) Running fast		
(c) Solving puzzles		
(d) Singing		
(e) Solving complicated mathematical equations		
(f) Writing a book		
(g) Climbing mountains		
(h) Creating new inventions		
(i) Making friends		
(j) Understanding yourself		
(k) Learning a language		

(3)   In small groups, have learners justify and discuss their responses.

(4)   As individuals, have learners brainstorm a list of people, past and present, whose success they admire (gifted performers, athletes, scientists, etc.).

(5)   Tell them to choose one. Instruct them to use as many sources as possible (interviewing, reading, etc.) to discover how hard they have to work to make things seem so easy.

(6)   Ask learners to share their findings with the class.

(7) De-brief this activity by drawing the connection between what learners discovered and their attitudes and motivation toward language learning.

MODIFICATIONS:

Technology:

(1) Create the five-point Likert-type survey using free web-based software like that found at www.surveymonkey.com This will combine learners' results in one place for easier discussion (Step 2).
(2) Invite learners to use internet sources to research their admired person (Step 5).
(3) Tell learners to share their findings via a PowerPoint or Prezi presentation and to consider incorporating YouTube video of their chosen personality into it.

Motivation Activity 9: Developing a Bicultural Identity Through a Trip to the Global Village

We travel to learn, and I have never been in any country where they did not do something better than we do it, think some thoughts better than we think, and catch some inspiration from heights above our own – Maria Mitchell

Level: Intermediate/Advanced

Note: Although this activity explicitly targets English language learners, it can be modified to guide learners to a bi-cultural identity – not of local plus global – but of the L1 and TL cultures of their specific group of learners.

Procedure:

(1) Preface this activity by introducing learners to the concept of 'bicultural identity' (Lamb, 2004) which characterizes language learners as rooted in their local culture but aware of their relationship to the global culture where the use of English gives them in-group status in a world-wide culture. Explain also the related notions of 'international posture' (Yashima, 2009) and 'imagined communities' (Norton, 2001), which allow learners to envision themselves using English and participating in an 'imagined international community.'

(2) Invite learners to arrange themselves in a circle, get comfortable, relax, close their eyes and visualize going on a trip with you. Use the following guided imagery script:

You are about to embark upon a long journey from your country of origin to a place called the 'Global Village' where everyone speaks different varieties of English and all are celebrated and understood. There is a very unique custom in this global village that is always respected: when you arrive, you must bring both a gift and a burden that is specific to your country of origin and leave it there. The gift and the burden must be something with which you identify greatly. Upon leaving, you must choose a gift and a burden from the global village to take away with you. These gifts and burdens are not necessarily material objects, even though they could be. They may also be conceptual gifts or burdens like a firmly-held value or norm. The road to this Global Village is long and arduous because it necessitates the learning of English to gain access and be accepted there, but you have done it and you have achieved great fluency. You are now at the gate. What gift and what burden did you bring to leave, and why?

(3) Allow learners time to reflect. Go around the circle and invite each learner to share his or her gift and burden one by one.
(4) Continue the guided imagery:

It is now time for you to make the journey back to your country of origin. You loved every minute of the time spent in this 'imagined international community', but now you find yourself at the gate with the all-important decision of which gift and which burden you will take away with you. Reflect a minute and choose carefully.

(5) Allow learners a few moments to reflect and repeat the step of sharing which burden and gift they have selected to carry away with them and why that special gift and that particular burden were chosen.
(6) De-brief this activity by asking volunteers to share what events they interacted in while in the Global Village.

MODIFICATIONS:

Emergent learners:

(1) Simplify the guided imagery script to align with learners' proficiency level (Step 2)
(2) Ask learners to mime their gifts and burdens (Steps 3 and 5).

Motivation Activity 10: Stretching Your International Posture

For a community to be whole and healthy, it must be based on people's love and concern for each other – Millard Fuller

Level: Intermediate/Advanced

Procedure:

(1) Preface this activity by highlighting the importance of being knowledgeable about the current events and international affairs of learners' TL culture to increase integrative motivation via learners' international posture (Yashima, 2012).
(2) On a weekly basis, have learners research news sources to discover something new that is happening in one of their TL cultures and write a brief entry in their language learning journals.
(3) Provide frequent opportunities for learners to share what they have found:
  (a) through short informal student presentations in whole or small group format; or
  (b) through the periodic combining of what learners have found to produce a class 'newspaper'; or
  (c) through small group interaction where learners discuss what they have found and are encouraged to give their opinions; or
  (d) through informal debates where one issue of the many presented are targeted, researched, and argued from various positions.
(4) De-brief these frequent and continual activities by soliciting learner feedback on whether being informed increases their desire to integrate and know more.

MODIFICATIONS:

Technology:

(1) Invite learners to research the current events of their TL cultures through electronic news sources (Step 2 and 3d).
(2) Ask learners to create a PowerPoint or Prezi presentation to accompany their talk (Step 3a).
(3) Produce the class newspaper using an online newspaper creation program (Step 3b).
(4) Place learners in groups for online 'chats' about their current events research (Step 3c).

Motivation Activity 11: Creating the Vision of the Ideal Self through Miming Gifts

People often say that this or that person has not yet found himself. But the self is not something one finds, it is something one creates – Thomas Szasz

Level: All

Procedure:

(1) Preface this activity by telling your learners that in order to create a vision of their ideal TL self, they must have their awareness raised and choose from among the aspirations, dreams and desires that they most likely have entertained in the past (Dörnyei, 2009).

(2) To model this idea, tell students the story of Perseus, a legendary character in Greek mythology who aspired to great things by challenging and killing Medusa. In order to pursue his vision, Perseus was given a series of gifts from the gods: Hesperides gave him a rucksack to securely hold Medusa's head; Zeus presented him with a sword and Hades' helmet of darkness to hide; Hermes provided winged sandals to fly; and Athena gave him a polished shield. Without these gifts Perseus could never have proceeded to the Gorgons' cave to defeat Medusa. Perseus had a clear, ideal vision of who he needed to be and what he needed to do in order to meet his defined challenge and he also had the tools with which to carry it out.

(3) Instruct students to get into pairs to conduct interviews of each other using the following prompt, 'What possible selves – representing the language user that you would like to become – have you entertained in the past?' Explain that these visions could come from views held by others such as parents, peer groups or the media. While one person talks, the other takes notes. After several minutes, have learners switch roles.

(4) Instruct learners to use this information to create personalized 'mimed' gifts for their partner that would allow their partner's vision to be realized. (For example, if Learner A told Learner B that his vision of his ideal TL self contained the ability to go to any English speaking country in the world and be able to interact effectively in all of them, then Learner B might mime the gift on an airplane and say, 'Here is an airplane [mime an airplane – arms spread wide, flying through the air] so you can take it to experience any cultures in the world that you dream about.' Ask learners to write on a Post-it note a brief description of their partner's envisioned TL ideal self. Collect these to use in Activity 14 (Guided Imagery).

(5) Stage the gift-giving ceremony, allowing each pair of partners to bestow their gifts upon each other in front of the rest of the class.
(6) De-brief this activity by explaining that this was a creative TL ideal-self-generating activity that drew upon their pasts in order to create a vision for their future. Ask for feedback as to whether it helped learners explore potential identity alternatives without committing to one in particular.

MODIFICATIONS:

Large groups: Carry out the gift-giving ceremony in small groups.

Technology:

(1) In preparation, create a presentation in Google on to which students can upload images. In Google, instead of creating a 'document,' hit 'presentation.' Give it a name and save. This way, images will appear one by one rather than as a collage so that learners may present their gifts.
(2) Rather than miming a gift, invite students to find pictures on the internet that represent the gift they would like to give to their partner and have them upload them into a class-created Google presentation. To do this, have each learner find an image and save it on to the computer. Enter the Google presentation, hit 'insert', then find 'image' in the drop menu. Hit 'choose image' and upload (Step 4).
(3) Stage the gift-giving ceremony using images.

Motivation Activity 12: Creating the Vision of the Ideal Self (Part II) through Capitalizing on Existing Strengths and Avoiding Weaknesses
(Adapted from an activity found at www.rider.edu)

The thing that is really hard, and really amazing, is giving up on being perfect and beginning to work on becoming yourself – Anna Quindlen

Level: All

In preparation:

(1) Using your understanding of your particular learners and who they might ideally like to become (from the previous activity and your teacher intuition), choose as many pairs from the following list that are the most appropriate for your select group.
(a) Hammer or nail
(b) Racket or ball

(c) Picasso or DeVinci
(d) Jeans or a suit
(e) Egg white or egg yolk
(f) Sun or moon
(g) Cube or ball
(h) Rock group or string quartet
(i) Yes or no
(j) Mountain or valley
(k) Question or answer
(l) Leather jacket or Harris tweed
(m) Leaf or wind
(n) Pencil or eraser
(o) Earthquake or typhoon
(p) Tortoise or hare
(q) City or country
(r) Dictionary or novel
(s) Agape or Eros
(t) Cat or mouse
(u) TV or radio

Procedure:

(1) Preface this activity by explaining that it is a mental exercise in abstract thinking in which learners are to use their imaginations to think of themselves in non-concrete terms.
(2) Read the entire list of paired alternatives and tell learners to silently choose the option from each pair that best describes them *at this moment in their language learning journey.*
(3) Read the first pair of alternatives again, this time telling learners to raise their hands to indicate their choice. (For example, 'Who is the pencil? Who is the eraser?') Ask learners to turn to their partners for a moment to share the reason(s) for their choice.
(4) Reading the same two alternatives, ask learners to indicate by raising their hands the alternative which would best describe the *language learner they would ideally like to become.* Again, in dyads, have learners discuss why they chose this alternative and why it is the same or different from the previous response that included ideas of their 'present' selves.
(5) Ask learners to write a paragraph that summarizes the interaction with their partner and hand it in.
(6) De-brief this activity by explaining that its purpose was for learners to compare the images of what they know about themselves presently in order to capitalize on their current strengths and avoid

problems as they project into the future. Ask learners to comment on the paragraphs they turned in.

MODIFICATIONS:

Technology:

(1) Change this from a listening/speaking exercise to a reading and writing one by posting the list of alternatives on a class discussion board.
(2) Provide two separate prompts, one that asks them to consider themselves at this point in their journey and another that asks them about what they would ideally like to become, and instruct them to respond to both (Steps 2 and 4).
(3) Tell learners to respond to two of their peers' responses (Step 5).
(4) Add a third de-briefing prompt to the discussion board that addresses the question in Step 6.

Learner Identity Activity 13: Creating the Vision of the Ideal Self (Part III) through Invoking Role Models
(Adapted from: http://www.flyingsolo.com.au/working-smarter/professional-development

The most single important influence in the life of a person is another person... who is worthy of emulation – Paul D. Shafer

Level: All

In preparation:

(1) Reproduce the graphic organizer found below by either asking students to copy it from the board or by photocopying and distributing it.

Procedure:

(1) Preface this activity by suggesting that individuals choose role models who are inspirational and whose actions are worthy of emulation. In the context of this activity, they can project an individual's vision of his or her ideal TL self.
(2) Instruct learners to reflect on their strengths and weaknesses in learning their TL. Tell them to choose three key qualities of their ideal TL selves to work on in areas they feel are not naturally strengths. Their qualities might be something linguistically related like pronunciation

or affectively related like feeling more confident when speaking the TL in a social setting. Ask them to fill in the first part of the graphic organizer.

(3) Next, tell learners to seek someone who effectively capitalizes on each quality. Although some learners may be inspired by people who are publicly successful or have celebrity status, others may find that they are more motivated to model TL users they have had the opportunity to get to know.

(4) Explain that they need not try to find one person who displays all of the character traits in their TL ideal self but rather to choose three role models by selecting three different qualities they desire from a number of inspiring individuals. Instruct learners to write their weaknesses along with the names of the people they would like to emulate in the graphic organizer.

(5) Describe modeling as adopting someone else's behavior. To model successfully, learners must fine tune their observation skills and watch for the small details. While selecting the right role model is important, learners must also discern which *attainable* behaviors they desire to adopt. Explain that they will be more successful finely honing their skills in areas that are a more natural fit (i.e. naturally shy and quiet learners might want to reconsider extroverted exuberance). Instruct learners to clearly and vividly detail these TL ideal self behaviors in their graphic organizer.

(6) Instruct learners to create a plan to practice their targeted behavior as frequently as they can and to add this information to the graphic organizer.

(7) Debrief this activity by inviting learners to share their ideal TL selves visions. Remind individuals to use positive self-talk, drawing on the strengths of his or her 'Self,' adding the qualities of their role model to enforce these new behaviors as your own.

Role model graphic organizer

Brainstorm Strengths		Brainstorm Weaknesses	
1.		1.	
2.		2.	
3.		3.	
Quality to work on:	My role model:	Behaviors to emulate (Clear, vivid description):	Plan to practice these behaviors:
1.	1.	1.	1.
2.	2.	2.	2.
3.	3.	3.	3.

MODIFICATIONS:

Technology:

(1) Reproduce the graphic organizer as an electronic document. Have learners fill it in on their computers.
(2) If learners chose a famous person who has videos posted to YouTube, invite those learners to watch the footage to spark further ideas about what they would like to emulate from that person.

Motivation Activity 14: Strengthening the Vision of the Ideal Self through Guided Imagery
(Adapted from http://www.guidedimagerydownloads.com/guided_imagery/script.html)

To bring anything into your life, imagine that it's already there –
Richard Bach

Level: Intermediate/Advanced

In preparation:

(1) This activity will be done in two phases. For the first phase, learners will need the 'Post-it Notes' from Activity 11 where they briefly described their partner's envisioned TL Ideal Self.
(2) For the second phase, learners will need to have the Role Model Graphic Organizer that they filled out in Activity 13.

Procedure:

(1) Preface this activity by explaining that guided imagery is a strategy that capitalizes on students' active imaginations and triggers visualization. Explain that the purpose of this activity is to bring to life learners' ideal TL selves and to make their visions more meaningful (Dörnyei, 2009).
(2) Phase 1: Stick learners' 'Post-It Notes' that contain a brief description of their envisioned TL ideal selves to a large surface (i.e. the floor or wall). Instruct learners to remain silent, and through communicating non-verbally, ask them to organize the notes into what they perceive as 'natural' categories. For example, groupings might be based on 'linguistic' or 'affective' notions; or 'pronunciation' or 'fluency.' Let students decide how to group the notes and then come up with a title for each group.

(3) Ask learners to find their 'Post-It Note' and along with the other learners in that category, form a small group. (If some learners' ideal TL self traits did not have matches with others, allow the individual to choose a group with which he or she feels affinity.)

(4) Instruct groups to collaboratively compose their own 'Guided Imagery Scripts' using their combined 'TL ideal selves' to direct their visualization. Here are a few guidelines:

 (a) Begin your script with some basic instructions about getting comfortable, relaxing and looking inward.

 (b) Include messages about being open to new input, suggestions, and ideas and to prepare to discard old patterns, behaviors and ideas.

 (c) When you begin to address your goals, try to incorporate all of the senses: What and how will learners see, hear, and feel as they experience the positive outcomes found in their ideal TL selves? Keep the message positive and refrain from words, phrases, or images that might trigger a downbeat reaction.

(5) Give each group the opportunity to lead the class through their Guided Imagery Script, allowing learners to get comfortable on the floor, close their eyes, and visualize.

(6) Phase 2: Recreate this activity, but this time use the 'Role Model Graphic Organizer' as the catalyst around which to form the groups. Ask learners to find the natural categories inherent in the role models selected by the learners and, with the other students having similar visions, create another Guided Imagery Script, focusing on the small details that this TL Ideal person exudes: the presence this person has as they walk into a room, their body language, the words they use, how they pronounce them, how others respond to him or her.

(7) Give each group the opportunity to lead the class through their scripts.

(8) De-brief this activity by discussing whether the use of guided imagery was a helpful tool in strengthening each individual's vision of their ideal TL self.

MODIFICATIONS:

Technology: For students who found YouTube videos to reinforce their choice of role models, invite them to project the video(s) silently while they lead the class through a 'voice over' guided imagery script (Steps 6 and 7).

Motivation Activity 15: Who Am I?: Substantiating the Vision of the Ideal Self

To desire is to obtain; to aspire is to achieve – James Allen

Level: All

Procedure:

(1) Preface this activity by explaining that learners' ideal self-images must be anchored in reality and that individuals must believe that his or her ideal self is indeed attainable (Dörnyei, 2009).
(2) Tell learners they will respond in writing to ten questions. Next, ask them ten consecutive times to respond to the question: 'Who is my ideal TL self?'
(3) Instruct learners to keep in mind the attainability of each response and cross off three of the items. Wait a minute and then ask them to eliminate three more.
(4) In small groups, have learners discuss the types of responses they wrote for their TL ideal self identity. Ask the following questions:
    (a) How did it feel to cross off items?
    (b) Why are the first ones you crossed off less attainable than those remaining? Do the obstacles and difficulties found in the first crossed off items deter your resolve to proceed?
    (c) Do you believe that the remaining items are achievable?
(5) De-brief this activity by asking learners whether their perception of the likelihood of attaining their goals has increased and whether this perception heightens their motivation to pursue their ideal TL selves with greater fervor.

Motivation Activity 16: Operationalizing the Vision of the Ideal Self through Developing an Action Plan

The value of identity of course is that so often with it comes purpose – Richard Grant

Level: Intermediate/Advanced

Preparation:

(1) Reproduce the graphic organizer found below by either asking students to copy it from the board or by photocopying and distributing it.

Procedure:

(1) Preface this activity by reminding learners that the more vividly they can imagine and articulate their 'selves' the more likely the images will be drawn upon for inspiration and motivation. Explain that future self-guides are most successful when they are accompanied by a well-defined plan of action that channels their energies in a specific direction (Dörnyei, 2009).

(2) Invite learners to fill out the following tables; one table for each TL ideal self attribute that they want to attain. Learners can choose between traits taken from previous activities in this chapter or develop new ones now.

(3) In the first row, the 'ideal self' represents a learner's identity goals and aspirations of the 'Self' he or she would ideally like to attain.

In the second row, the 'ought-to self' represents a learner's ideas about his or her responsibilities and obligations with regard to that 'Self'; it may involve the expectations of teachers, parents or peers.

In the third row, the 'feared self' represents a learner's ideas about what he or she could become if either the ideals or perceived obligations and responsibilities are not attained (Kubanyiova, 2009).

In the first column, invite learners to use vivid adjectives and adverbs to clearly articulate a description of what their imagined three selves look like.

In the second column, ask them to use specific language to articulate the role they chose for each of the 'selves.'

In the third column, tell learners to write particular activities for acting upon each 'self.'

Self Trait #1: _____

	Description (Use vivid modifiers)	What things do I say?	What things do I do?
ideal self			
ought-to self			
feared self			

Self Trait #2: _____

	Description (Use vivid modifiers)	What things do I say?	What things do I do?
ideal self			
ought-to self			
feared self			

Self Trait #3: _____

	Description (Use vivid modifiers)	What things do I say?	What things do I do?
ideal self			
ought-to self			
feared self			

(4) Direct learners to fill out the following table using the traits they defined in Step 2, and to set up their own individual action plan.

Goal chart

	Trait 1: (Write it here)	Trait 2: (Write it here)	Trait 3: (Write it here)
To reach my goal, I will: This week: This month: This year:			
I know I have reached my goal when: This week: This month: This year:			
Measures that will help me maintain my dedication: This week: This month: This year:			

(5) De-brief this activity by reminding learners to continually review this grid, to re-examine their goals, modifying those that need revision and celebrating the accomplished ones.

MODIFICATIONS:

Emergent learners: Provide a list of options from which learners may choose. Use the opportunity to increase their vocabularies.

Technology: Provide the graphic organizers in an electronic format. This allows easier modification when learners re-examine their goals.

Motivation Activity 17: Counterbalancing the Vision of the Ideal Self through Activation of the Dreaded Self

A man is fortunate if he encounters living examples of vice, as well as of virtue, to inspire him – Brendan Francis

Level: All

Procedure:

(1) Preface this activity by explaining to learners that their 'Possible Selves' are stronger if they exploit the collective power of both approach and avoidance desires; that is to say, that the ideal self will be more active when compared with the self that is feared (Dörnyei, 2009).
(2) Invite learners to complete this sentence on a piece of paper: 'When considering all my 'possible selves', the one I fear most is….'
(3) Collect the pieces of paper, shuffle them, and put them in a box or a hat. Invite learners one at a time to select a paper and read aloud the feared self of another classmate. Allow the reader to comment on it briefly and then move to the next reader.
(4) De-brief this activity by asking whether learners found a tendency in what the group feared and suggest that regular activation of the 'dreaded' self may be an effective deterrent of it becoming an 'actual' self.

Motivation Activity 18: Finding the Anticipatory/Anticipated Balance

An intense anticipation itself transforms possibility into reality; our desires being often but precursors of the things which we are capable of performing – Samuel Smiles

Level: All

Procedure:

(1) Preface this activity by explaining that its purpose is to explore and celebrate the rich diversity of anticipated and anticipatory feelings that learners bring to language learning by tapping into the energizing effects of positive-broadening expectations and investigate alternative forms of thinking for negative-narrowing emotion. Explain that if they anticipate good things to come in the future, they feel good about it today; but if they anticipate bad things to come, they may experience a sense of dread in the present.

(2) Distribute six post-it notes to each learner, three of one color and three of another. On the first set of three, tell them to respond to the prompt: 'What are all the exciting events I am anticipating from this language class?' Give them an opportunity to brainstorm their ideas by writing one idea per post-it note. On the second set of three, give them the following prompt, 'What are the events that cause me discomfort when I think about my future in this language class?' Tell them to respond with one thought per note. Collect the six responses from each learner, keeping them in color-coded groups.

(3) Stick the two groups of notes to a large open space and ask learners to read and then organize them by 'natural' categories, giving each category a title.

(4) Tell learners to form a large open circle around the room. Explain that you will be calling out the learner-generated positive-broadening category titles from the first group of colored post-it notes but that the positive anticipation felt by some may or may not be felt by everyone. Instruct learners that if the item applies to them, to run into the middle of the circle and do a 'high five' with anyone else who runs in. Call out the category titles. Repeat the process as many times as you have different ideas/category titles.

(5) Call out the category titles of the other group of negative-narrowing post-it notes. Tell learners to choose the category which most concerns him or her. Form groups based upon these responses.

(6) Tell groups – each dedicated to one type of negative anticipated concern – to brainstorm strategies to deal with it. Explain that

these are not supposed to be 'feel good strategies', but rather a purposeful plan of action . (For example, if a group is negatively anticipating a grammar test next week, they might brainstorm ideas such as 'set aside twenty minutes each evening to study' or 'form a study group.')

(7) Reconvene the whole group and share responses.
(8) De-brief this activity with a class discussion on how individuals feel in the moment when they anticipate a future event positively or negatively.

5 Language Learning Strategies

From Premise...

The familiar parable about a farmer's donkey falling into a well illustrates the effectiveness of taking purposeful and deliberate action in plotting a course for language learning.

> In the story, the captive fallen donkey sobs wretchedly as his owner contemplates his options and finally decides that the animal is old and that the hole needs to be covered anyway, coming to the conclusion that extricating the beast holds little merit. So with his collaborating neighbors, everyone grabs shovels and begins heaping dirt into the hole. Realizing his fate, the beleaguered donkey bawls dreadfully. Within seconds however the diggers hear nothing but the scooping of their own dirt – the donkey had ceased bleating! A few shovel loads later, the farmer finally peers into the well and is astonished by the vision. With every shovel-load of earth that thumps his back, the donkey shakes it off and takes a step up. As the farmer's neighbors continue to heap dirt on top of the animal, he intentionally persists in his purposeful task to survive and be free. Within minutes, to everyone's amazement, the donkey leaps up over the rim of the well and trots off!

The language learning pathway is strewn with holes of varying proportions that can cause obstacles to the unwitting learner. Whether making a detour to avoid them or an extraction plan to pull themselves out, language learners must be able to navigate the path and continue forward in their journeys. Strategizing is critical.

The inconsistent conceptualizations and conflicting results found in the research supporting language strategy pedagogy somewhat hampers our quest for a consensual definition and a workable taxonomy. Even amid the theoretical dissent, however, the pedagogical notion that language learning strategies help foster increased foreign language proficiency, learner autonomy, and self-regulation retains widespread support (Dörnyei, 2005). Our challenge as authors is to do justice to the expansive body of complex research without be-fuddling classroom teachers with the intricacies of the controversies. With this in mind, we humbly attempt in this chapter to harmonize some of the contradictions found in the language learning strategy literature and bring as much clarity as possible to the ambiguity therein by providing broad, comprehensive conceptualizations and categorizations so that through strategy instruction, teachers can encourage their language learners to be more 'proactive and informed' contributors to their own learning (Dörnyei, 2005: 195). If we err by simplifying some of the theoretical shortcomings in the strategy literature, it is for the sake of providing a workable framework for teachers to help language learners pursue more active and conscious learning.

We begin the chapter by defining what language learning strategies are and how they can be classified. Although a precise definition and paradigm is elusive, there is general agreement that their efficacy is not measured by their quantity or frequency of use, but rather by a learner's personal orchestration of the strategies available (Macaro, 2006), taking into account a learner's individual differences, the learning task and the learning environment. This reveals two things that effective teachers do: (a) they raise learners' awareness – through presentation, modeling and peer input – of a variety of potential strategies so that learners have a stock from which to choose; and (b) they show learners how to assess and continually monitor their own strategy use and its relationship to their individual differences (i.e. age, gender, prior knowledge and all of the variables covered in this text), the task at hand (i.e. complexity or difficulty) and the environment (i.e. culture, richness of and possibilities for interaction) in order to employ the most effective strategy or combination of strategies (Cohen, 2007). To this end, this chapter provides an initial list of broadly defined cognitive, metacognitive, social and affective strategies generated from different taxonomies to widen the scope of teachers' strategy instruction. The 'Premise' section concludes by providing strategy instruction guidelines that directly connect research to the activities in the 'Practice' section that follows.

Exploring Language Learning Strategies, Their Origins and Their Significance

What language learning strategies are

Language learning strategies have been characterized as *attempts, actions, steps* (Cohen, 1996, 2012; Oxford, 2012) *thoughts and behaviors* (Cohen, 2003, 2012) *methods and techniques* (O'Malley & Chamot, 1994) and as *learner's contributions* (Dörnyei & Skehan, 2003) among others. Although these portrayals contain seemingly contrasting behavioral and cognitive learner manifestations, all of them contain one thing in common: They are what learners DO (Rubin, 1975) – whether that 'doing' is a mental activity such as using visual images to activate knowledge or a physical one such as making a chart or table to remember something (Griffiths, 2008). To 'give learners' strategic behaviors the rightful place they deserve in a theory of learning,' Gu (2007: vii) states, '... what learners choose to *do* also makes a difference in the learning process' (italics added). This inclusiveness is embraced in Macaro's (2006: 332) framework when he states that a strategy '... comprises a goal, a situation *and* a mental action' (italics added).

This expansive list of nouns used to define language learning strategies is accompanied by an equally wide-ranging inventory of descriptors that modify them: *deliberate, intentional, goal-directed, chosen, teachable* (Cohen, 2007, 2012; Griffiths, 2008; Oxford, 2012; Weinstein *et al.*, 2000), *conscious or semi-conscious* (Cohen, 2003), *purposeful, at times automatic* (Griffiths, 2008). In an attempt to coalesce these elements, we propose: Strategies, either consciously or semi-consciously chosen by a language learner, operate somewhere on a continuum between being intentionally deliberate and fully automatic, are purposeful and goal-directed and can be enhanced through instruction.

For us, strategies are about doing something out of the ordinary for the purpose of meeting a goal or objective. The notion of *intention* is key. For example, breathing helps us speak but it is not strategic until we decide to take a deep breath as a way to finish a sentence uninterrupted or take a breath as an anxiety-reduction strategy. If we are breathing automatically, then it is not strategic (albeit it is always healthy to keep breathing!). There may be a distinction to be made between strategic actions and facilitating actions, with the former often being a sub-category of the latter. Instruction in strategy use is what initially draws the strategy out as an intentional act even though it may become more automatic with experience.

Although not extremely precise, our inclusive formulation harmonizes enigmatic areas where the literature is still somewhat riddled with dissent: Are strategies behavioral or mental? Are strategies different from skills, tactics or techniques? How conscious and intentional does the 'doing' of the learner have to be for that 'doing' to be called a strategy? At this point in our quest for a definition, the question arises: 'For what purpose?'

With its origins in mainstream educational psychology, the description of learning strategies as being *self-regulatory*, is now commonly observed in SLA literature (Cohen, 2007; Dörnyei & Skehan, 2003; Griffiths, 2008; Oxford, 2012). It refers to 'the learner's conscious and proactive contribution to the enhancement of her or his own learning process' (Dörnyei & Skehan, 2003: 611) which allows learners to 'regulate or control their own learning, thus making it easier and more effective' (Oxford, 2012: 12), and to become more autonomous and self-motivated success-seekers outside the language classroom (Cohen, 2007). The aggregation of self-regulation to our strategy discussion shifts attention from product to process (Dörnyei & Skehan, 2003) and bestows a more active role upon learners for the management and control of their own learning processes and as a consequence maximizes their learning outcomes (Gu, 2010, as cited in Oxford, 2012).

Beyond self-regulation, language strategies also serve the purpose of enhancing or facilitating learning (Cohen, 2007; Griffiths, 2008; Oxford, 2012) by increasing its depth, productivity and longevity (Cohen, 2007). Utilizing effective strategies, either alone or in combination (often called *strategy chains*) allows learners to perform specified tasks or to solve particular problems, and as an end result, strategies can '... make learning easier, faster, and more enjoyable' (Cohen, 2007: 39; Oxford, 2012: 14).

The significance of strategies in language learning

This litany of purposes also speaks to the importance of strategies in the language learning process, with one necessary caveat: Although strategy use has been related to language learning success on a variety of levels (Macaro, 2006), language strategies are not inherently effective with a one-size-fits-all pattern. Evaluating the effectiveness of language learning strategies necessitates that they be contextualized within a learning context that includes the individual learner, the task at hand and the environment into which learning is inserted. In an ideal world, there would be a single strategy suitable for all learners for all tasks, but as individual learners may apply the very same strategies in different ways and because of the myriad of individual differences that make each learner unique (Cohen, 2003), learners need to be purposefully determined to choose and then pursue that strategy or chain of strategies that are *appropriate* for them in specific learning situations to enhance their individual learning efficacy (Riding & Rayner, 1998). Some learners require and appreciate more direction from teachers, whereas others are more autonomous. The desirability of autonomy itself may fluctuate with the learning situation and the task at hand.

Categorizing language learning strategies

In this section, we expand the definition and purposes of language learning strategies by presenting the most prominent taxonomies and specific strategies. One polemic question for theoreticians in creating a classification system to conceptualize language learning strategies is the relationship between language *learning* and language *use* strategies. Few would contest the notion that target language (TL) use promotes acquisition; however, some researchers (Cohen, 1998; Ellis, 1994; Selinker, 1972) – for argumentation purposes we shall call them the 'Separatists' – propose that the two processes are functionally and psycholinguistically deserving of theoretical separation, whereas others (O'Malley & Chamot, 1990a; Oxford, 1990a, 2012) – the 'Amalgamators' – propose that TL learning cannot be separated from its use. The Separatists propose that 'some strategies contribute directly to learning ..., whereas other strategies have as their main goal that of using the language' (Cohen, 1996: 7). Although the former have the overt aim of advancing a learner's knowledge and understanding of a TL, the latter are invoked by learners once the necessary language material is at least minimally accessible. Even as both may well lead to learning, language *use* strategies primarily focus on utilizing language already existent in a learner's interlanguage (Cohen, 1996; Cohen *et al.*, 1996). The Amalgamators, on the other hand, reject any clear-cut dichotomy between language learning and use as they perceive them as fluidly interactive and mutually influential (Oxford, 2012), citing SLA research and general learning theory that, among other principles, states that learning transpires through experience and that it relies crucially on using what is being learned.

Operationally speaking, after tweaking for 'relatively minor' discrepancies (i.e. separating or combining categories) among the most prominent taxonomies (Cohen, 2009; O'Malley & Chamot, 1994: Oxford, 1990a, 2012), the Separatists and the Amalgamators converge on the basic components of *learning* strategies as being composed of:

(a) Cognitive strategies (allowing learners to manipulate or transform the TL through identification, retention, storage and/or retrieval). These include: *Using the senses to understand and remember; Activating knowledge; Reasoning; Conceptualizing with details; Conceptualizing broadly,* and *Going beyond immediate data* (Oxford, 2012: 46).
(b) Social strategies (allowing learners to increase TL communication and practice). These include: *Interacting to learn and communicate; Overcoming knowledge gaps in communicating;* and *Dealing with sociocultural contexts and identities* (Oxford, 2012: 88).
(c) Affective strategies (allowing learners to regulate their emotional conditions and experiences). These include: *Activating supportive emotions, beliefs and attitudes,* and *Generating and maintaining motivation* (Oxford, 2012: 64).
(d) Metacognitive strategies (allowing learners to invoke higher order control functions to analyze, monitor, evaluate, plan and/or organize TL performance). These include: *Paying attention; Planning; Obtaining and using resources; Organizing; Implementing plans; Orchestrating strategy use; Monitoring;* and *Evaluating.*

Of further interest in Oxford's (2012) recent taxonomy is her expansion of the notion of 'meta' to the affective and sociocultural interactive (expanded from the social dimension to include context, communication and culture) strategy categories. She has consistently touted the importance of metacognitive strategies as a general management mechanism for cognitive strategies throughout the years, but her new paradigm recognizes that these executive, higher-order functions are also important in managing affective and social domains:

Metastrategies, by virtue of their executive-control and management function, help the learner know whether and how to deploy a given strategy and aid in determining whether the strategy is working or has worked as intended. Strategies and metastrategies in the model are highly dynamic, because they respond to changing needs of the learner for varying purposes in different sociocultural contexts (p. 19).

Thus, she exhorts learners to manage their language learning cognition, affect and sociocultural interaction by applying the metastrategies of paying attention, planning, obtaining and using resources, organizing, implementing plans, orchestrating, monitoring and evaluating in each dimension. That is to say, effective language learning strategists will not only pay attention (and all the other 'meta' actions just mentioned) for enhanced cognition, but will also do it for improved affect and more salient social contexts, communication and culture.

Whereas a general consensus among experts was found concerning language *learning* strategy categories, the impasse on language *use* strategies continues with Cohen (2009, 2012) leading the Separatists' charge and including in his taxonomy the following language use categories:

(a) Communication strategies (allowing learners to express meaningful information). These include: Avoidance or reduction strategies; Achievement or compensatory strategies; Stalling or time-gaining strategies; and Interactional strategies (Cohen, 2009).
(b) Retrieval and rehearsal strategies (allowing learners to call up TL information from storage and practice TL structures).
(c) Cover strategies (allowing learners to project a positive image). This includes creating an appearance of TL ability.

Consistent with the Amalgamators' philosophy of language learning/use inextricableness, Oxford melds communication strategies directly into the 'social' category of the *learning* strategy template mentioned above (Oxford, 2012), and retrieval and rehearsal strategies into the 'cognitive' category (Oxford, 1990a).

Notice that we included an initial list of broadly defined examples of strategies within each category. We call it 'initial' because it is a starting point from which learners add their own successful strategies. We also broadly define the strategies so as to avoid pigeon-holing learners into one 'correct; way of doing their learning. For example, by choosing to broadly articulate the affective strategy, 'activating supportive emotions, beliefs, and attitudes' (Oxford, 2012), we give learners the space to choose what works for them under that umbrella, whether their tactic includes setting low expectations so that when they do better they can feel good about themselves, or using positive imagery for expectations so that they can envisage performing well. Both are valid but largely incongruent tactics whose implementation depends upon the individual learner.

Capitalizing on Language Learning Strategies: An Action Plan

The central goal in language strategy instruction is to transform learners into self-managers and self-regulators so they can select strategies that will accomplish a defined task, skill, or goal and ultimately become more self-directed in their learning (Oxford, 2012; Rubin *et al.*, 2007). Although research demonstrates that all strategy instruction in not universally success-ful (McDonough, 1999), its value can be augmented if it focuses on metacog-nition, is carried out over lengthy periods of time as a regular feature of instruction that is incorporated into the teacher's normal classroom behav-ior, and if it is adjusted for students' learning styles (Cohen, 1996; Ehrman *et al.*, 2003; Macaro, 2006; McDonough, 1999). If strategies are taught effec-tively, learners become more aware of the ways in which they learn best, increase their capacity to manage cognitive and affective strategies, improve their motivation and performance, and enhance their knowledge and skills to continue learning on their own (Cohen, 1996; Rubin *et al.*, 2007).

Effective strategy instruction requires that teachers heed two recommen-dations: (a) embed strategies into daily class materials and tasks; and (b) explicitly instruct learners on how, when and why strategies can be used to accomplish those language tasks. To integrate strategies into classroom tasks, teachers can choose to begin with a set of targeted strategies and devise activities to introduce and/or reinforce them, or they can use established course materials and then define strategies which might prove helpful. Another possibility is spontaneously inserting appropriate strategies along the way (Cohen, 1996).

Concerning the second recommendation, research suggests that whereas levels of instructional explicitness can vary, the more overt the instruction, the more successful it will be (Oxford, 2012). Most direct strategy instruc-tion models concur that training should begin with teacher scaffolding that progressively tapers into learners taking responsibility for using their self-selected strategies independently (Chamot *et al.*, 1999).

Raise learners' awareness

Teachers begin by raising learners' awareness (see Activities 1A and 2A) of the strategies they currently use in familiar tasks (Chamot, 2004, 2005; Chamot *et al.*, 1999; O'Malley & Chamot, 1990; Oxford, 1990a, 2012; Rubin *et al.*, 2007). Oxford (2012) suggests the use of games, questionnaires and open discussions. Chamot (2004) highlights the value of the instructional applica-tions of research tools such as retrospective interviews, stimulated recall inter-views, questionnaires, written diaries and journals and think-aloud protocols by teachers who wish to discover their students' current learning strategies before initiating instruction in learning strategies. Rubin *et al.* (2007) have a variety of recommendations that outline each technique's pros and cons. They suggest using: (1) Questionnaires (highly practical but the relationship between the chosen strategy(s) and specific task or problem is imprecise); (2) Focus groups (topics can be directly related to learners' goals, problems and/or tasks, but they are time intensive and demand teacher familiarity with a wide range of strategies for de-briefing); (3) Asking a question (can be used anytime but learners may need encouragement to access strategies); (4) Journals (personalized consciousness-raising technique for assisting learners to consider alternatives, but if learners are low proficient, language might be problematic); and (5) Reading about process (individualized and can be done out-of-class but language ability of beginning groups might be an issue).

Deepen learners' awareness

Some classroom researchers (Grenfell & Harris, 1999; Macaro, 2001; Oxford, 2012) recommend deepening awareness-raising (See Activities 1B and 2B) through performing 'cold' tasks without any strategy instruction followed by an exploration into possible strategies available and brainstorming/sharing what works and what does not. This is a discovery-based phase which elicits learner interaction.

Present and model strategies

The next phase in the instructional cycle is teacher and/or strategic peer presentation and modeling of strategies (see Activities 3A and 3B) to explain new strategies and highlight potential benefits (Chamot, 2004, 2005; Chamot *et al.*, 1999; O'Malley & Chamot, 1990; Oxford, 1990a, 2012; Rubin *et al.*, 2007). Adaptations include asking students if and how they have used a strategy (Chamot, 2004, 2005; Chamot *et al.*, 1999) and drawing up a checklist of strategies for subsequent use (Grenfell & Harris, 1999). One important caveat is that effective strategy instruction needs to be contextualized and related directly to learners' specific problems. Learners must recognize their habitual errors and be ready to work on them. If strategies are presented on a 'need to know' basis when learners are feeling overwhelmed by the material, they will be primed to readily accept assistance. Think-alouds, focused journal writing and focus groups that target a particular skill and/or function arouse learners' appreciation that they might need help and that focusing on the learning process is beneficial. Because strategy use differs by learner, task and goal, the effective presentation of strategies depends upon highlighting their usefulness and refraining from presenting them as recommendations, emphasizing that there is no 'right' or 'wrong' strategy but rather one that works for the particular learner for the particular task and goal (Rubin *et al.*, 2007).

Provide opportunities to practice strategies

Subsequently, learners need a large range of practice opportunities (see activities 4A and 4B) through which they can deploy their new strategies or combinations of strategies and move toward greater autonomy with the gradual removal of teacher scaffolding (Chamot, 2004, 2005; Chamot *et al.*, 1999; Grenfell & Harris, 1999; Macaro, 2001; O'Malley & Chamot, 1990; Oxford, 1990a, 2012; Rubin *et al.*, 2007). Some self-directed learners might also begin monitoring their strategy use at this stage by determining whether they are capitalizing on the strength of a strategy as it was demonstrated (Oxford, 2012). 'Just in time' practice opportunities provided by teachers when a learner runs into immediate difficulty while carrying out an activity are very powerful because these strategies meet a learner's immediate need and take on concrete form (Rubin *et al.*, 2007).

Self-evaluate strategy efficacy

Afterward, learners self-evaluate (see Activities 5A and 5B) the effectiveness of the strategies used (Chamot, 2004, 2005; Chamot *et al.*, 1999; Macaro, 2001; Oxford, 1990a, 2012; Rubin *et al.*, 2007). Armed with the awareness of whether a strategy works for them, learners can perceive the advantages of using it, thus making this instructional step vital. Learners must generate their own reservoir of strategy knowledge, personal learning style insight, appreciation of which strategies work best for them, and an awareness of how to connect strategies to their task and goals. Discernment about past strategic successes will help the cause. One possible technique is to promote goal-setting prior to a particular task, ask learners to identify which strategies might effectively serve them, establish their measure for success and then examine the relative efficacy of those strategies upon task completion (Rubin *et al.*, 2007).

Transfer strategies to new tasks

The next step contains techniques for learners to transfer (see Activities 6A and 6B) the strategies to fresh tasks, making choices on which to use, considering how to cluster them into strategy chains, and generating a repertoire of favored strategies – all the while teachers are releasing control and removing scaffolding (Chamot, 2004, 2005; Chamot *et al.*, 1999; Grenfell & Harris, 1999; Macaro, 2001; Oxford, 1990a, 2012; Rubin *et al.*, 2007).

Continue to evaluate and monitor strategy use

The final step in the cycle includes evaluation and continued monitoring (see Activities 7A and 7B) both by teachers and learners, whether formally or informally, to assess the impact on performance (Chamot, 2004, 2005; Chamot *et al.*, 1999; Grenfell & Harris, 1999; Macaro, 2001; O'Malley & Chamot, 1990; Oxford, 1990a, 2012; Rubin *et al.*, 2007). Teachers can increase learner ownership through discussions, bulletin boards and/or think-pair share (Oxford, 2012), encouraging learners to set new goals for themselves (Grenfell & Harris, 1999) and rewarding effort (Macaro, 2001).

The story with which we began this chapter's 'Premise' section compared the language learning journey to a hole-strewn road that is often difficult to navigate. Bringing that metaphor back full circle, we would like to conclude this section by sharing a very wise person's five short chapters on change (author unknown):

- Chapter 1: I walk down the street and there's a deep hole in the sidewalk. I fall in. It takes forever to get out. It's my fault.
- Chapter 2: I walk down the same street. I fall in the hole again. It still takes a long time to get out. It's not my fault.
- Chapter 3: I walk down the same street. I fall in the hole again. It's becoming a habit. It is my fault. I get out immediately.
- Chapter 4: I walk down the same street and see the deep hole in the sidewalk. I walk around it.
- Chapter 5: I walk down a different street.

. . . To Practice

Strategy Activities

The main goal of the following activities is to increase learner self-regulation, and to this end, two sets of seven sequential tasks are provided that consist of: (1) raising learners' awareness; (2) deepening awareness-raising; (3) presentation and modeling; (4) practice; (5) self-evaluation; (6) transfer; and (7) evaluation. The activities are meant to be done in order and learner responses should be carefully recorded as information from previous activities is used in subsequent ones. They are embedded in a socio-cultural model of self-regulation using Vygotsky's 'dialogic model' that suggests that learning is best mediated through interaction with a more knowledgeable peer or teacher (Oxford & Schramm, 2007); hence, the activities incorporate numerous occasions for dialogue among language class participants so that learners can discover for themselves the strategies that they are presently using and self-assess them against other potential strategies that are modeled or presented by others. Through continued interaction, learners practice alternative strategy options, self-evaluate the strategy's efficacy, and when deemed useful, they contemplate and put into action how the strategy can be transferred to other language tasks. Continued monitoring and evaluation of strategies by the learner makes the self-regulation process a cyclical one. The 'magic' of the two series of activities, with each activity building upon the previous one, is that the results are completely learner-generated and are therefore entirely unique to each classroom of individuals working together, hopefully giving learners a deep sense of ownership over the process.

Strategy Activity 1A (First Series): Raising Learners' Strategy Awareness through Focus Groups

Until you make the unconscious conscious, it will direct your life and you will call it fate. – C.G. Jung

Level: All

Preparation:

(1) As focus group discussion moderators, teachers might find the following guidelines useful (Costigan-Lederman, 2009):
  (a) Pause the conversation, if necessary, to draw out the full range of learner opinions and to see if it is shared by others by asking questions like, 'This person said this … what do others think?' or 'Does anyone think differently?'
  (b) Remain neutral and make it safe for opinions to be expressed freely by keeping personal comments to a minimum and by dissuading learners from passing judgment on the interventions of others.
  (c) Create another space for quieter focus group participants to respond and for learners to think by allowing at least 15 seconds before using a prompt.
  (d) Ask one question at a time. Start with general questions and use the prompts to be more specific. To stimulate discussion, offer alternative ideas on any strategies that come up; for example, 'Some learners think that setting low expectations so that they are pleasantly surprised when they are surpassed is a good affective strategy, but others think that setting high goals is better. What do you think?'

Procedure:

(1) Preface this activity by explaining that its purpose is raise learners' awareness of the strategies they currently use in familiar language tasks by participating in a focus group – a moderated conversation about a precise topic. Clarify that there are no 'right' or 'wrong' strategies so learners should feel comfortable sharing without fear of judgment.
(2) Ask for a volunteer to be the note-taker to record comments on the whiteboard or on a sheet of chart paper to enable learners to see and reflect on what they have said.
(3) Begin with the following question: What strategies do you use when carrying out familiar *speaking* and *listening* tasks?

Prompts (use as needed):
(a) Is there anything special you do to seek out opportunities to speak and/or listen in (TL)?
(b) What do you do to control your emotions or attitudes when speaking and/or listening?
(c) Do you have special things you do to analyze, monitor, evaluate, plan or organize your learning when speaking and/or listening?
(d) Tell me what you do to retrieve language you have already learned in order to produce or comprehend (TL).
(e) What do you do when you have something you want to say but don't know how to say it?
(f) Is there anything special you do to make others think you know more (TL) than you actually do?

(4) Next ask: What strategies do you use when carrying out familiar *reading* and *writing* tasks?

Prompts (use as needed):
(a) Is there anything special you do to seek out opportunities to read and/or write in (TL)?
(b) What do you do to control your emotions or attitudes when reading and/or writing?
(c) Do you have special things you do to analyze, monitor, evaluate, plan or organize your learning when reading and/or writing?
(d) Tell me what you do to retrieve language you have already learned in order to write or read (TL).

(5) De-brief this activity by explaining to learners that this activity and the ones that follow are meant to proactively involve them in enhancing their own learning, and that as there are no one-size-fits-all strategies, only the individual learner can assess whether a strategy will be effective for him/her for a specific task in a particular context. Keep a record of learners' input for subsequent activities.

MODIFICATION:

Technology: Because the benefits of focus groups are found in their synchronicity and the idea that one respondent feeds off of another, any technology modifications must be in 'real' (synchronous) time. Try an online chat session.

Strategy Activity 2A (First Series): Deeping Learners' Strategy Awareness through Think-Aloud Protocols

As you become more clear about who you really are, you'll be better able to decide what is best for you – the first time around. – Oprah Winfrey

Level: All

Preparation:

(1) Choose two language tasks that are commiserate with your learners' level of proficiency that will evoke the potential strategies or chain of strategies that need most urgent attention.

Procedure:

(1) Preface this activity by explaining that, similarly to the previous focus group tasks, the purpose of this activity is make learners conscious about the strategies they presently use; but unlike the focus group, learners will 'think aloud' as they carry out a 'cold' language task, without any strategy instruction, to illuminate their dynamic, moment-by-moment strategy use.
(2) Place learners in pairs. Instruct Learner A to carry out the first task, all the while explaining aloud his/her method of attempting to complete it. This should also illuminate any difficulties the learner encounters in the process. Learner B takes extensive notes – everything that Learner A says or does is relevant. Learner B remains silent except for, if necessary, prompting Learner A to keep talking.
(3) Present the first of the two tasks from the Preparation Phase above – describe its goals, but not the steps required to complete it – and ask Learner A to begin.
(4) Upon completion of the first task, tell the partners to switch roles. Explain the second task and ask Learner B to complete the task while Learner A takes detailed notes.
(5) Invite pairs to compare and contrast the strategies they each used to complete the tasks. Tell learners that they will need the transcripts to participate in the next activity.
(6) De-brief this activity by initiating a class exploration of the possible strategies that were available to complete the task and sharing what worked and what did not. Keep a record of learners' input for subsequent activities.

MODIFICATION:

Technology:

(1) Invite learners to videotape each other rather than observe and take notes. Have pairs view the videos, comparing and contrasting their strategy use.

Strategy Activity 3A (First Series): Strategy Presentation and Modeling Using Guided Imagery

Teach and practice, practice and teach – that is all we have; that is all we are good for; that is all we ever ought to do. – Ernest Holmes

Level: All

Preparation:

(1) Review the information generated during the focus groups and think-aloud procedures from Activities 1A and 2A and the list of strategies from the Premise section of this chapter. Select several strategies and reflect upon what tasks and language learning contexts might necessitate the implementation of those chosen. Pay attention to those strategies whose instruction will target learners' specific problems and/or habitual errors.

(2) Create a guided imagery script for each selected strategy that evokes learners' imaginations about specific language learning tasks and contexts where the strategies could be used effectively. Here are some examples:

    (a) If 'activating supportive emotions, beliefs and attitudes' is chosen from the focus group and/or think-alouds transcripts or from the chapter's list, a guided imagery scrip might sound something like this: 'Imagine that you are five minutes away from having to give an oral presentation in front of the class. Your heart is racing, your palms are sweating and your mouth tastes like cotton ...'

    (b) Likewise if 'overcoming knowledge gaps in communicating' is selected, a guided imagery script might sound like this: 'Imagine you are in a country where (TL is spoken) and you initiate a conversation with a stranger in order to get directions to the nearest post office. You introduce yourself as a guest to this country. You thank the stranger for stopping to help. The conversation is going well, your conversant is understanding everything you say ... (pause) ... until you forget the word for "post office"...'

Procedure:

(1) Preface this activity by explaining that by having participated in a focus group and a think-aloud interview, they should now have a clearer idea of the strategies they already use. Explain that the objective of the next activity is to share and explore new language learning strategies and highlight their potential benefits – not to present them as recommendations, but to draw attention to their usefulness.

(2) Tell learners that you will begin a guided imagery script, but one of them must take it up where you leave off in order to finish it with a successful ending. Invite learners to listen for tasks or contexts that lend themselves to using strategies that they have explored in the previous focus group and think aloud activities and to volunteer to participate in the game.

(3) Invite learners to get comfortable, relax, close their eyes and to vividly imagine the scenarios they are about to hear. Begin the first script using a soothing and engaging voice. Let your voice trail off to signal where you want a learner to take over the image and insert his/her own ending thereby creating a space for learners to present and model effective strategy use. Allow all volunteers to share their 'happy endings.' Record their answers for subsequent activities.

(4) Begin recitation of a new prepared guided imagery script after all volunteers have had the chance to finish the first one in their own ways.

(5) De-brief this activity by asking learners to imagine their own current language learning struggles and to visualize using the strategies presented and modeled by their classmates.

MODIFICATION:

Large groups: Divide learners into small groups. Recite the beginning of the guided imagery and ask someone in each small group to finish it.

Strategy Activity 4A (First Series): Accounting for Strategy Practice through Checklists

An ounce of practice is worth more than tons of preaching. – Mahatma Gandhi

Level: All

Preparation:
(1) From the strategies learners presented and modeled during the guided imagery activity, create a 'Language Learning Strategy Checklist' (with a place to tick off items as well as a larger space for comments) that lists all of the strategies mentioned by learners.

Procedure:
(1) Preface this activity by explaining that it is important for learners to monitor their strategy use so that when needed for specific language tasks and contexts, concrete strategies can be invoked to meet their immediate needs.
(2) Place learners in small groups and tell them that the class is about to participate in 'friendly group competition,' and that group members are to encourage and hold their teammates responsible for practicing each strategy on the checklist. Hand out the checklist and invite individuals for the next week to keep track of whether/how often each strategy was practiced, explaining that the 'comment section' is for describing the context in which each was used.
(3) At the end of the week, groups tabulate the individual scores to calculate a group tally.
(4) De-brief this activity by asking whether group accountability for practicing the strategies was helpful. Remind learners that, although they were keeping track of the frequency of each strategy's use, it is more important to use them appropriately. Invite learners to comment on the tasks and contexts where each strategy was most effectual.

MODIFICATION:

Technology: Create a Google document at www.doc.google.com so learners can keep track of the strategies they use. Click 'Create' and then 'Form'. When prompted, fill in each question box with a different strategy and then 'Check Box' as the 'Question Type' thus producing an electronic checklist.

Strategy Activity 5A (First Series): Self-Evaluating Strategy Use through Self-Rated Efficacy Scales

Ask yourself the secret of your success. Listen to your answer, and practice it. – Richard Bach

Level: All

Preparation:

(1) Repeating the same items from the checklist used in Activity 4A, create an 'Efficacy of Individual Strategy Use Survey' using a five-point Likert Scale for learners to self-report each strategy's efficacy by circling one of the five options. Include an option '6' ('not applicable) for learners to respond that they did not choose to practice the strategy. For example:

'Overcoming knowledge gaps in communicating by using mime and gesture'

(1) Completely ineffective
(2) Somewhat ineffective
(3) Neither effective nor ineffective
(4) Somewhat effective
(5) Completely effective
(6) Not applicable (I did not choose to practice this strategy)

Procedure:

(1) Preface this activity by emphasizing that what works for one person might not be effective for another, thus demonstrating the importance of self-evaluation in strategy selection.
(2) Hand out the 'Efficacy of Individual Strategy Use Survey.' Invite learners to complete it recalling their own experience and consulting their checklists from Activity 4A, if necessary, to remember specific tasks or contexts in which a strategy was used during the previous week. Underscore that choosing not to practice one of the strategies is as valid as other options as the particular strategy under question may not have matched their learner profile.
(3) Debrief this activity by re-iterating the principle that individuals accumulate their own awareness of which strategies work best for them based upon their own individuality.

MODIFICATION:

Technology: Create another Google document with the procedures outlined in Activity 4A, but instead of creating boxes to be checked, click 'Multiple Choice' as the 'Question Type.'

Strategy Activity 6A (First Series): Line Up for Strategy Transfer

Observe, record, tabulate, communicate. Use your five senses. Learn to see, learn to hear, learn to feel, learn to smell, and know that by practice alone you can become an expert. – William Osler

Level: All

Preparation:

(1)   Extend a piece of masking tape from one side of the room to the other.

Procedure:

(1)   Preface this activity by explaining that its purpose is to have learners contemplate how to transfer the strategies they have been exploring to new tasks, how to cluster them into combinations and to generate a repertoire of preferred strategies.

(2)   Tell learners that the tape placed on the floor represents the five point continuum of the five point scale that they used in Activity 5A to measure the effectiveness of the strategies they have practiced. Indicate the ends that represent 'completely ineffective' and 'completely effective.'

(3)   Choose one of the items listed on the 'Efficacy of Individual Strategy Use Survey', and ask learners to consult and stand at the point in the line that represents their opinion. To do this, they need to talk to their neighbor about his/her rating and truly understand their own.

(4)   Instruct learners to turn to the person next to them. Invite learners who found the strategy in question to be 'effective' to brainstorm the following questions:

(a)   How can this strategy be effectively transferred to other language learning tasks?

(b)   How can this strategy be clustered or combined with others?

For those learners who found the strategy ineffective, collaborate to answer the following:

(a)   Why did it not work well?

(b)   What strategies do you think can replace it and function more successfully?

(5)   Repeat the lining up process and brainstorming until learners have had a chance to discuss their transfer options for all of the strategies on the survey.

(6)   De-brief this activity by asking learners to share the results of their conversations.

Strategy Activity 7A (First Series): 'I Will ...' Continue to Monitor and Evaluate Strategy Use (Adapted from Oxford, 2012, metastrategies)

To know that we know what we know, and to know that we do not know what we do not know, that is true knowledge. – Copernicus

Level: All

Procedure:

(1) Preface this activity by explaining that its purpose is to help learners determine whether given strategies continue to be useful or have worked as intended by increasing learners' integration of 'metastrategies' for cognition, affect and sociocultural interaction. Explain that metastrategies help learners become more self-regulated by providing management tools for their learning. Highlight the importance for continued monitoring and evaluation of strategies as they are highly dynamic and need to respond to the fluctuating needs of learners (Oxford, 2012).

(2) Either provide the 'Metastrategies "I will ..."' template as a photocopy or show it to learners to copy into their language diaries. Instruct learners to finish the 'I will ...' items in each of the three dimensions listed across the top of the chart. Invite learners to fill it out considering that:
    (a) the cognitive dimension helps the learner construct, transform and apply TL knowledge;
    (b) the affective dimension helps the learner create positive emotions and attitudes and stay motivated; and
    (c) the sociocultural interactive dimension helps the learner interact to learn and communicate and deal effectively with culture.

(3) De-brief this activity by encouraging learners to continue up-dating this chart as it will serve for metastrategic goal-setting and allow them to revise their plans as their language needs change.

Metastrategies 'I Will ...'

'I will ...'	Cognition	Affect	Sociocultural Interactive
Pay attention to ...			
Plan ...			

(Continued)

Obtain and use resources ...			
Organize ...			
Implement plans ...			
Orchestrate ...			
Monitor ...			
Evaluate ...			

Strategy Activity 1B (Second Series): Raising Learners' Strategy Awareness through Gallery Walking

Perception is strong and sight weak. In strategy it is important to see distant things as if they were close and to take a distanced view of close things. – Miyamoto Musashi

Level: All

Preparation:

(1) Hang four large sheets of poster-sized paper around the room with the following headings: 'Speaking Strategies,' 'Listening Strategies', 'Reading Strategies' and 'Writing Strategies.'

Procedure:

(1) Preface this activity by explaining that it is meant to develop learners' metacognitive awareness of their own learning and to practice the self-reflection necessary to become aware of the current strategies they use with familiar language tasks.
(2) Assign learners randomly to one of the posters and instruct them to converse among themselves and to write any actions they take to enhance their own learning for the skill under question.
(3) Invite each group to move to the next poster and repeat the exercise.
(4) De-brief this activity by asking for a volunteer to read the strategies written on each poster. Allow learners to comment.

MODIFICATION:

Technology: Invite learners to take a 'gallery walk,' sharing their strategies through an electronic wiki with four different 'strategy nodes': Speaking, Listening, Reading and Writing.

Strategy Activity 2B (Second Series): Deeping Learners' Strategy Awareness through Retrospective Interviews (Newell, 1996)

Study the past if you would define the future. – Confucius

Level: Intermediate/Advanced

Preparation:

(1) Carefully choose a familiar language task commiserate with learners' proficiency level and whose completion would demand using a wide array of strategies.

Procedure:

(1) Preface this activity by explaining that it is meant to expand learners' self-awareness of the their strategy repertoires by participating in a retrospective interview, a procedure that will interrupt learners' performance before, during and after participating in a language task to ask them to interpret the task, to specify their plans for the next phase and to evaluate their finished product.

(2) Place students in pairs. Give the instructions for the language task, asking them to carry it out the way they usually do without trying to do anything special.

(3) Before beginning the task, invite learners to interview each other and record the responses using the following questions:
    (a) Explain in your own words what the task is asking you to do. Why do you think the teacher assigned it?
    (b) What are some of the ideas that come to mind about his task that you might want to consider?
    (c) How are you going to get started?

(4) Instruct learners to begin the task. When they are half way through, pause the task execution and have learners interview each other again, using the following questions and recording each other's answers:
    (a) Tell me what you have done so far.
    (b) What do you plan to do next?

(5) Direct learners to continue the task to completion. At the end of the procedure, tell learners to interview and record responses using the following prompts:
    (a) Now that you are finished, what do you think of your work?
    (b) Did you have any new ideas about how to approach the task as you were doing it?

(6) De-brief this activity by asking the dyad members to collaborate on creating a list of strategies that were embedded in their

performances by using the interview transcripts. Remind learners that this process is meant to make individuals more self-directed and that this begins with greater self-awareness of what strategies are currently used with familiar language tasks so that this repertoire can be added to through future interaction with other learners.

MODIFICATION:

Technology: Ask pairs to post their strategies to a wiki, inviting them to add any strategies they used to the list so that a whole class list is available.

Strategy Activity 3B (Second Series): Strategy Presentation and Modeling through the Glass of a Fishbowl

Tell me and I'll forget; show me and I may remember; involve me and I'll understand. – Chinese proverb

Level: Intermediate/Advanced

Preparation:
(1) Place four chairs facing one another in the center of the room. Take the remaining seats and form a large circle around the inner ones.

Procedure:
(1) Preface this activity by explaining that its purpose is to have strategic learners explain and demonstrate potential new language strategies.
(2) Instruct learners that the small group in the center will carry on a conversation about a strategy of their choice while the outside group listens and prepares questions and comments for the discussants. The empty chair is meant to be occupied by a learner in the large circle who wants to contribute to the discussion. When someone occupies the empty seat, a different member of the inner circle quietly switches places.
(3) Based on your observation of the 'Gallery Walk' in Activity 1B and the 'Retrospective Interviews' in Activity 2B, choose three students who you perceive as the most 'strategic.' Invite them to take three of the four seats in the center.

(4) Read the lists of strategies from Activities 1B and 2B. Ask one of the inner circle participants to choose one of the strategies. Among the three seated participants, invite them to collaborate to explain the strategy, stress the potential benefits and demonstrate an example of how it can be used. Remind learners that they may join the inner circle and give their input to the discussion at any time by occupying the empty chair.
(5) When the inner circle conversation winds down, allow participants in the large outer circle to ask questions of the discussants.
(6) Repeat this procedure for each of the strategies from Activities 1B and 2B.
(7) De-brief this activity by reminding learners that there are no 'right' or 'wrong' strategies – that learners must find what works most effectively for them for a given task taking into account their individual differences and their language learning purposes/goals.

MODIFICATION:

Technology: Post the strategies from Activities 1A and 1B as different threads on Voicethread. Ask learners to post their own ideas on the potential benefits and uses of each strategy, inviting them to comment on the responses posted by others. To make this an oral activity, use webcams, computer microphones or telephones to contribute ideas.

Strategy Activity 4B (Second Series): Wagon Wheel Strategy Practice for Specific Tasks

Knowledge is of no value unless you put it into practice. – Anton Chekhov

Level: Intermediate/Advanced

In preparation:
(1) Place eight chairs in two concentric circles. The four inner circle chairs face outward, whereas the four outer circle chairs face inward, creating pairs of chairs.
(2) From the information generated on learners strategy use in Activities 1B, 2B and 3B, create two sets of cards. On each card of Set A, write a strategy from the student-generated lists, articulating each

strategy in a general enough way so that it could be applied to numerous language tasks; for example, 'interacting to learn and communicate'. For Set B, present a language learning task/situation that could benefit from the implementation of any of the strategies in the first set; for example, 'Use the words from the vocabulary lesson in original sentences'.

Procedure:
(1) Preface this activity by explaining to learners that it provides them with numerous opportunities to practice the strategies that the class has generated through their previous gallery walks and retrospective interviews and which were modeled and explained by classmates in the fishbowl.
(2) As students file in, ask them to take a chair in either of the concentric circles. Distribute Set A cards to learners in the inner circle and Set B cards to the outer circle. When everyone is seated, with each pair facing the other, tell them that they will have five minutes to deploy the strategy (Set A) to perform the task (Set B). Invite them to try out a variety of activities related to the general strategy category on their cards and if necessary, to specify language situations that will allow them to imagine a hypothetical situation.
(3) At the end of the allotted time, learners on the outside circle rotate one seat to the right. Repeat the procedure.
(4) Debrief this activity by asking the class whether any of these strategies arrived 'just in time' for any immediate difficulties they are currently experiencing. Making this connection increases learners' readiness to work on them.

MODIFICATION:

Technology: Use Skype. To practice spontaneous oral language, follow the format above, using the videoconferencing function. To practice writing, use the chat function. To facilitate the exchange of partners, have the four pair combinations prepared in advance with one partner assigned to 'Set A' and the other to 'Set B', so that when 'time' is called, the partner with the 'A' card calls the individual with the 'B' card with no confusion over who makes and receives the call.

Strategy Activity 5B (Second Series): Self-Evaluating Strategy Use through an Action Plan of Personal Goal Setting and Self-Assessed Objectives Completion

Knowing is not enough; we must apply. Willing is not enough; we must do. – Johan Wolfgang Von Goethe

Level: Intermediate/Advanced

Procedure:
(1) Preface this activity by explaining that learners will complete an action plan that guides their application of specific strategies to defined problems and/or tasks and provide accountability for its execution.
(2) Either provide the 'Action Plan for Strategy Use' template as a photocopy or show it to learners to copy into their language diaries.
(3) Invite learners to fill it out using the following instructions:
   (a) In the first column, learners define a language task or a problem that they would like to address in their learning. Inform them that they can include as many as they would like.
   (b) Under 'Strategy Ideas,' learners identify a strategy or combination of strategies for addressing the specific task or problem.
   (c) 'Action Steps' refer to the identification of steps learners will take to implement the strategies they desire to use.
   (d) For 'Success Indicators,' learners define signs they will use to indicate whether they have overcome their language problems or accomplished their task as the result of the action steps they took for strategy implementation.
   (e) At predetermined intervals, learners review their action plans and reflect on their progress: Have they executed their action steps? If so, have they mitigated their original problem or improved the performance of the defined language task? How do they know? If they are not making progress, what do they need to do so?
   (f) 'Outcomes' refer to what has happened as a result of learners taking these action steps in pursuit of overcoming language learning problems or achieving specified tasks.
(4) In collaboration with learners, determine time intervals for their 'progress reviews.'
(5) De-brief this activity by putting learners in small groups to discuss their advancement at the appointed 'progress review' times. Discuss the advantages of using 'Action Plans' to improve strategy use.

Action plan for strategy use

	Strategy Ideas	Action Steps	Success Indicators	Progress Review	Outcomes
Learning Task/Problem 1:_____					
Learning Task/Problem 2:_____					
Learning Task/Problem 3:_____					

Strategy Activity 6B (Second Series): Transferring Strategies through Think/Pair/Share and Journaling

Find out who you are and do it on purpose. – Dolly Parton

Level: Intermediate/Advanced

Procedure:

(1) Preface this activity by explaining that its purpose is to broaden learners' use of strategies from the specific contexts in which they were first learned to other language tasks.

(2) Place learners in pairs. Instruct them to review the first column in their 'Action Plan for Strategy Use' that they filled out in Activity 5B where they defined language learning tasks or problems to work on. Invite them to discuss and take notes on how each strategy might be used in other contexts beyond the ones they have already tried.

(3) Encourage learners over the next few weeks to try each strategy in a new way, making a journal entry in their language learning diaries reflecting upon its success.

(4) De-brief this activity by allowing learners to share which strategies they were able to transfer successfully to other tasks. Ask learners for 'personal experience tips' on how ineffective strategy use could be modified for greater success.

MODIFICATION:

Technology: Invite learners to contribute their ideas to a Discussion Board thread.

Strategy Activity 7B (Second Series): Evaluation and Continued Monitoring

It is necessary ... for a man to go away by himself ... to sit on a rock ... and ask, 'Who am I, where have I been, and where am I going?' – Carl Sandburg

Level: All

Procedure:

(1) Preface this activity by reminding learners that they must be continually monitoring and evaluating the strategies they use in light of their performance – that a strategy used successfully at one time for one task may not be the most effective forever and always.

(2) To exemplify this idea, guide your readers through the following imagery (Covey, 2004). Ask them to close their eyes, get comfortable and listen as you read.

'Once upon a time a very strong woodcutter asked for a job from a timber merchant, and got it. The pay was really good and so were the working conditions. For these reasons, the woodcutter was determined to do his best.

His boss gave him an axe and showed him the area where he was supposed to work.

The first day, the woodcutter brought 18 trees.

'Congratulations,' the boss said. 'Continue on!'

Very motivated by the boss' words, the woodcutter tried harder the next day, but he only could bring 15 trees. The third day he tried even harder, but he only could bring 10 trees. Day after day he was bringing fewer and fewer trees.

'I must be losing my strength', the woodcutter thought. He went to the boss and apologized, saying that he could not understand what was going on.

'When was the last time you sharpened your axe?' the boss asked.

'Sharpen? I had no time to sharpen my axe. I have been very busy trying to cut trees ...'

(3) In pairs, invite learners to discuss the parallels between this story and their language learning journey, asking them in particular to

define what skills/strategies they have failed to sharpen and what task has drawn their attention away from them.

(4) Maintaining their dyads, have learners brainstorm the tasks on which they would like to re-focus their energies and a list of potential strategies to strengthen their performance.

(5) De-brief this activity by reminding learners to continually keep their sights set on sharpening their metaphorical axes.

6 Language Learning Styles

From Premise...

After arguing with our parents, our teachers, our boss or our spouse, it's likely that at some point we all have been told 'it's just the way things are done.' There often are numerous ways in which things can be done, and we often carry a sense of how they *should* be done. This reflects a style preference. More than beliefs, styles reflect how people approach what they do.

> A boy found a butterfly's cocoon and every day he observed it for any changes. One day his patience paid off and a small opening appeared. He sat for several hours and watched as the butterfly struggled to force its body through the tiny hole. Then it seemed to stop making any progress, appearing as if it had gotten as far as it could and could go no further. So the boy decided to 'help' the butterfly. Taking a pair of scissors, he snipped off the remaining bit of the cocoon allowing the butterfly to emerge easily. But much to the boy's dismay, it had a swollen body and small, shriveled wings. He continued to watch the butterfly expecting that, at any moment, the wings would enlarge and expand to support the body, which would shrink in time. However, neither occurred! In fact, the butterfly spent the rest of its life crawling around with a swollen body and shriveled wings, never once being able to take flight.
>
> What the boy in his kindness and haste did not understand was that the restricting cocoon and the struggle required for the butterfly to get through the tiny opening were nature's way of forcing fluid from the body of the butterfly into its wings, so that it would be ready for flight once it achieved its freedom from the cocoon.

Like well-intentioned teachers who strive to match learning styles to accommodate learners' comfort zones, the boy's seemingly helpful actions ultimately stunted the butterfly's development. Research shows that style matching has benefits but sometimes style stretching is exactly what language learners need to equip them for future struggles, prepare them for those moments when they find themselves outside their comfort zones and build their confidence to stretch their wings. 'Styles' reflect an appealing concept to both teachers and learners, offering insight into each other's ways of doing things. But the multiplicity of styles also can be a difficult concept with which to work.

This is because we all have comfort zones – those places where we seem to flourish and find the positive-broadening energy to meet challenges and accomplish goals. In language learning, certain zones are comfortable because they allow individuals to approach tasks and activities that draw upon their preferences and habits. Some may be more stable, somewhat genetically pre-determined dispositions like those found in cognitive styles or personality preferences. Others are more malleable, having been shaped and formed by previous learning experience like those found in learning styles and sensory preferences (Cohen & Dörnyei, 2002; Reid, 1987).

Both teachers and learners have these 'go to' places, and while in an ideal world, everyone would be able to flourish in their zones by matching up their styles, the number and variability of styles makes this unfeasible. For example, certain teachers may prefer presenting information visually, while some learners may have auditory or kinesthetic preferences. What is a teacher to do when half of her class is composed of introverts who enjoy working alone and the other half are extroverts who flourish in social interaction through group work? Teachers who deliver step-by-step directions might tap into the strengths of concrete-sequential learners, but send random-intuitive learners over the edge. Deadline-seeking closure-oriented students would be able to plan ahead with teachers who gave specific time limits but the open, relaxed learner types would cease to enjoy their discovery learning. How would detail-oriented analytic learners fare with a teacher who continually pre-sented information globally and persistently pushed learners to communi-cate even if they didn't have a firm grasp on all the language concepts? At some point, although matching styles might seem the ideal solution, stretch-ing learners' preferences and approaches to learning will inevitably be the only recourse. Furthermore, when evaluating the current cost of stretching learners beyond their existing preference with the future benefit of their growth owing to exposure to new approaches, the cost–benefit ratio might just come out on the side of stretching.

Exploring Language Learning Styles, Their Origins and Their Significance

What they are and where they come from

A precise consensual definition of learning styles has suffered a fate simi-lar to other conceptualizations of individual differences variables (e.g. lan-guage learning strategies and aptitude) in that detractors criticize that the loose bandying about of labels causes problems with measurement and the inability to formulate clear distinctions between notions like learning and cognitive styles, making it difficult to separate them from variables such as personality and intelligence (Dörnyei, 2005; Ehrman *et al.*, 2003).

How can sense be made of what Dörnyei (2005) and Griffiths (2012) call a conceptual 'quagmire?' First, *cognitive* styles and *learning* styles are dynamically interrelated. The former are partially biologically determined; encompass how the learner remembers, organizes, processes and represents information; and act as precursors to learning styles. The latter consist of how the learner perceives, interacts with and responds to the learning environment; come into play in specific educational milieus; and tend to be molded by previous learning experience (Dörnyei, 2005). Sensory preferences, the perceptual modes through which students take in information visually, aurally and/or kinesthetically, are also included here. Second, adding the notion of personality preferences to the mix further complicates pinning down a precise definition. Whereas Ehrman (1996) frames personality constructs such as extroversion/introversion that appear in both learning style and personality taxonomies as 'personality-based styles,' Griffiths (2012) is unwavering in her position that these variables do not belong in a discussion on learning styles. Because of the preponderance of personality dimensions in the learning styles taxonomies and their strength in interacting with and determining learning preferences, we purposefully chose a paradigm to guide our activities which includes them. Although the notion of learning styles is conceptually challenging on several planes, most agree that learners' diverse styles exist and we can capitalize upon style preferences through designing effective instruction. Styles might appear to be highly stable, but none are completely fixed or immune to change (Dörnyei & Skehan, 2003; Reid, 1987). A variety of style preferences exist within most classrooms and learners can be flexible in their style preference day-to-day. These are important considerations for teachers who try to match styles and struggle with the awareness that they cannot please every learner all the time.

Categorizing Language Learning Styles

Although quarrels persist over what elements and dimensions constitute learning styles, there is clear overlap concerning their expression as value-neutral preferences that are typically represented on a continuum with bipolar extremes. A myriad of learning style paradigms and accompanying measuring instruments – some devoted to general learning preferences and others specifically created for ESL contexts – have been developed throughout the past quarter century with many related terms and definitions among them. The most commonly cited inventories in the language teaching arena follow a self-report format in which respondents indicate their answers by marking one of the options on a rating scale. Among them are the Perceptual

Learning Style Preference Questionnaire (PLSPQ), which rates visual, auditory, kinesthetic, tactile, group and individual preferences (Reid, 1987); the Style Analysis Survey (SAS), which targets sensory preferences (visual, auditory and hands-on), dealing with other people (extroversion vs. introversion), handling possibilities (intuitive vs. concrete-sequential), approaching tasks (closure-oriented vs. open) and dealing with ideas (global vs. analytic) (Oxford, 1999); and the Ehrman and Leaver Learning Styles Questionnaire, which uses 10 subscales that, in combination, create the superordinate ectasis vs. synopsis style dimension that considers the variable of how much conscious control learners need or want over their learning processes (Ehrman & Leaver, 2003).

The paradigm that we ultimately chose to guide the activities in this chapter is the Learning Style Survey (LSS) created by Cohen *et al.* (2001). Although teachers do not administer this questionnaire directly in our practice section, the eleven-faceted LSS is used to provide a framework for a variety of activities that will help teachers assemble a multifaceted sketch of their learners' style profiles. The LSS builds upon the strengths of other similar instruments by including a number of additional language-related style dimensions beyond those provided in the PLSPQ and SAS, while at the same time draws upon the solid theoretical construct found in Ehrman and Leaver's (2003) model (Dörnyei, 2005). A closer look at the theoretical underpinnings of the dimensions found in the LSS will provide insight into the nature of learning styles as well as lay out the framework that guided the selection and organization of the activities that follow.

According to its creators (Cohen *et al.*, 2001: 151–152), the LSS is intended to appraise learners' 'general approach to learning' – not to predict behavior – but to present a clear tendency in learners' preferences, helping them 'recognize their strengths' and 'stretch beyond their ordinary comfort zone, expanding their potential to adapt to different learning and working situations' through 'style stretching.' Table 6.1 summarizes the eleven dimensions. The labels are value-neutral and define opposite ends of a continuum (with the exception of sensory perceptions, the first dimension, which has three). Examples of behaviors are provided to give a sense of how learners on each side of the continuum might respond.

The LSS incorporates a variety of options for heightened self-awareness in a multiplicity of dimensions that could be conceptualized under the rubrics of learning and cognitive styles, sensory preferences and field independence/field dependence. It enables language teachers to compile multidimensional profiles of students' learning styles so that they can plan, and where necessary, modify their teaching according to their students' preferences. For learners, the activities based on the LSS will heighten self-awareness and empower them to maximize their learning opportunities, at the same time showing learners the variety of styles that are possible.

Table 6.1 Summary description of the learning style survey (Cohen *et al.*, 2001)

---

1) HOW I USE MY PHYSICAL SENSES

Visual: Prefer learning through sense of sight (You write things down, take detailed notes, need written directions)	**Auditory:** Prefer learning through listening and speaking (You prefer listening to lectures to reading, like music while studying, need oral directions)	**Tactile/Kinesthetic:** Prefer learning through projects, working with objects and moving around (You think better when you are moving, draw lots of pictures during lectures)

---

2) HOW I EXPOSE MYSELF TO LEARNING SITUATIONS

Extroverted: Prefer social interaction (You work better with others than by yourself, meet people easily, experience first and understand later)	**Introverted:** Prefer independent work (You are energized by your inner world, enjoy individual work, understand before trying)

---

3) HOW I HANDLE POSSIBILITIES

Random-Intuitive: Future-oriented, prefer speculation/abstraction (You have a creative imagination, plan for the future and are open-minded to new ideas)	**Concrete-Sequential:** Present-oriented, prefer step-by-step activities (You focus on what is – not what could be, you trust facts and follow directions)

---

4) HOW I DEAL WITH AMBIGUITY AND DEADLINES

Closure-oriented: Prefer to focus, meet deadlines, plan ahead (You plan study sessions, carefully organize materials, want to know what things mean in the TL, want to understand rules)	**Open:** Prefer discovery learning, no deadline concerns (You let deadlines pass, are not bothered by unorganized piles and are not worried about comprehending everything)

---

5) HOW I RECEIVE INFORMATION

Global: Prefer getting the gist or main idea (You like short answers, ignore details and see the big picture)	**Particular:** Prefer to focus on detail and remember specifics (You pay attention to specific facts, catch new phrases and enjoy filling in missing blanks)

---

6) HOW I FURTHER PROCESS INFORMATION

Synthesizing: Summarize well, enjoy guessing meanings and predicting outcomes, notice similarities (You can paraphrase quickly, consider key points and pull ideas together)	**Analytic:** Prefer logical analysis, pull ideas apart, focus on rules (You want to know every word, are good at solving puzzles and notice details

Table 6.1 (*Continued*)

7) HOW I COMMIT MATERIAL TO MEMORY	
Sharpener: Notice differences and seek distinctions. Separate current from prior memories (You store new material separately for retrieval and pay attention to all the features of new material)	**Leveler:** Clump material together to reduce differences. Focus on similarities (You ignore language differences that might make you more accurate and merge new and previous memories)
8) HOW I DEAL WITH LANGUAGE RULES	
Deductive: Go from general to specific – rules to examples (You pay attention to patterns)	**Inductive:** Go from specific to general – examples to the rule (You like indirect learning through exposure)
9) HOW I DEAL WITH MULTIPLE INPUTS	
Field-Independent: Prefer to separate material from context (You check grammar for agreement and assess appropriate formality and politeness)	**Field-Dependent:** Prefer to manage information holistically (You pay more attention to content than grammar, and neglect grammar and style issues)
10) HOW I DEAL WITH RESPONSE TIME	
Impulsive: React quickly (You go with your instincts and jump in)	**Reflective:** Prefer to think before taking action (You need validation before trusting your gut)
11) HOW LITERALLY I TAKE REALITY	
Metaphoric: Conceptualize material in metaphoric terms (You learn best through stories and examples)	**Literal:** Represent material literally (You take things at face value)

Capitalizing on Language Learning Styles: An Action Plan

Conceptually, the notion of 'learning styles' can be thought of as a multitude of intersecting individual approaches to learning, including cognitive styles, learning preferences, sensory perceptions and/or personality. Although the innumerable combinations of dynamic intersecting learning style variables make it impossible for teachers to accommodate all learners at all times, there are still benefits to greater learner and teacher styles awareness.

To capitalize on the diversity of language learners' styles and to celebrate what teachers and learners *can* do rather than what they *cannot*, we suggest a *'Mixed and Many'* approach to promote teacher/learner exploration of balance and choice. The five basic principles outlined below are the foundation for activities that: (1) promote teachers' discovery of their own teaching preferences; (2) encourage learners' exploration and definition of their favored learning approaches; (3) foster teacher–learner teamwork in the pursuit of balance; (4) juxtapose tasks that expose learners to both style matching and stretching; and (5) provide opportunities for learners to reflect and gain insight into their strategies, linguistic progress and affective response under matching and stretching conditions. We believe that styles, however defined, should not be treated as immutable characteristics of the teacher or learner, but as expressions of preferences that can be accommodated or ignored as part of the learning and growth process.

Principle 1: *Effective teachers are aware of their own instructional styles*

Teachers' instructional decisions are heavily influenced by previous teaching and learning experience. That is, teachers teach as they prefer to learn or as they themselves have been taught (Oxford, 1990b; Peacock, 2001b). Running the gamut from choices concerning presentation modalities, to interactional processes, to task and materials selection, to syllabus organization, the decisions that teachers make can either harmonize or collide with students' preferential approaches to learning. Here is the dilemma: Researchers suggest that a mismatch between teaching and learning approaches sometimes results in learning failure and frustration (Peacock, 2001b; Reid, 1987). Yet, the variability in learners' styles makes it impossible for teachers to meet every need of each learner all the time. The style mismatches that occur among the teachers and learners in a given classroom make it imperative to share classroom decision-making and empower learners to occasionally stretch their learning styles to match those of their teachers and other fellow learners.

Principle 2: *Self-aware learners identify their preferred approaches to language learning for themselves and for their teachers*

Individuals approach learning differently – whether referring to partially biologically determined ways of responding to information and situations, personality-based 'comfort zones' (Ehrman, 1996), sensory processing preferences, or learning contextualized within an educational environment fused with affective, physiological and behavioral factors (Brown, 2000) – the point is that each learner is unique in his or her preferred way of personally interacting and responding to the learning environment. Empowering learners with the self-knowledge afforded through the identification of their own learning styles and arming teachers with this knowledge make learning more effective (Oxford & Anderson, 1995) by contributing to an understanding of how learning transpires. Learners who recognize their preferred and habitual learning approaches, as well as the range of acceptable style variations, are attentive to available alternatives and how to capitalize on their own strengths and limit their weaknesses (Reid, 1998). Teachers who are aware of their learners' preferences can more deliberately and successfully orient their instruction to match or stretch learners' style preferences (Oxford, 2003). The effort to accommodate stylistic differences leads teachers toward providing more variety and choice (Nel, 2008).

Principle 3: *Through a 'mixed and many' approach, teachers and learners together can explore ways to balance their styles*

In tandem, Principles One and Two buttress Dörnyei's (2005: 158) suggestion that 'the heterogeneous nature of style distribution and the complex interference of several coexisting learning styles might make style-based instruction a far too complex issue for ordinary teachers to handle.' This seems most likely to happen when teachers try to match styles in a fairly rigid fashion. Whether considered explicitly or implicitly, the challenge remains for teachers to design and deliver language instruction relevant to a multiplicity of learning styles (Nel, 2008). We propose that rather than attempting to accommodate learners' styles by seeking robotic, in-step everyone-embrace-the-same-approaches teaching, that as a team, all classroom participants are involved in lesson planning (Peacock, 2001b) that includes: (a) material presentation and language input modalities; (b) interaction processes; (c) time constraints; and (d) the selection of tasks (both in-class and outside-the- class naturalistic activities). Together teacher–learner teams can adopt the 'mixed and many' mantra by seeking variety in learning styles that does not excessively favor one over another (Peacock, 2001b) and that gives learners various options from which to choose. That is to say, individual learners inserted in a classroom context benefit from alternative (and sometimes simultaneous) presentation and practice routines that allow them to capitalize on both variety and choice. For example, while presenting a new grammatical form, teachers using a 'mixed and many' approach might accommodate sensory preferences by multi-modally imparting new information to the whole group through input that is both visual (i.e. show how the phrase looks written on the board) and auditory (demonstrate its use through a variety of oral samples). This could be followed by the practice phase of the lesson where learners' introvert/extrovert personality preferences are considered by offering the option of communicative activities in cooperative groups that energize participants 'in the outer world of people' or in individual tasks that tap into the 'inner world of ideas and experiences' (Dörnyei, 2005: 19).

For learners, heightening their cognizance of their individual learning styles as a self-reflection tool is a step toward building autonomy. For teachers, this translates into the construction of a composite picture of learners as both a product of their pasts and as individuals with potential to be flexible and adaptable to an unknown future (Ely & Pease-Alvarez, 1996).

Principle 4: *By agreeing to occasionally 'stretch' and sometimes 'match', teachers and learners together can resolve learning style conflicts*

Even if teachers and learners are team players in balancing and planning instruction, mismatches are still bound to occur. When they do, teachers and learners must continue to share the responsibility for resolving difficulties, understanding that there is not one 'best' style that works all the time. Just as an instructor's preferred teaching styles will not benefit all of his or her learners under all conditions, so is it also true that a learner's preferred style will not always help him or her solve every problem in all learning situations.

For teachers, fostering language learning success not only requires awareness of learners' individual approaches, but also a willingness to vary teaching styles. Some experts recommend that teachers modify their styles to accommodate the needs of the greatest number of learners (Cheng & Banya, 1998). We recommend an approach that includes sufficient eclecticism to take into account the variety of approaches that enable learners to achieve at least a modicum of success (Cohen, 2003). In practice, this means that some learners' styles are being stretched even as others are being matched and vice versa. Advocates of matching propose that it leads to more uniform success than providing a single type of instruction to a diverse group (Tight, 2010), and that dissatisfaction and burnout may arise if learners are subjected to teaching styles inconsistent with their learning style preferences over extended time (Smith & Renzulli, 1984). Others, however, propose stretching as a better option suggesting that exposure to a variety of educational situations better prepares students to be more effective life-long learners and provides opportunities to experiment with extending their preferred styles. 'Stretching' advocates argue that learners will inescapably need to cope with problems and challenges that demand the use of their less preferred modes, and so should repeatedly practice using those modes (Felder & Henriques, 1995). Given the complexity of the language learning process, and the diversity among language learners, it seems likely that matching and stretching are likely to occur at every turn. This is not a bad thing; variety is the spice of life.

Routinely providing a learner-centered 'mixed and many' approach guarantees broader learner satisfaction (Oxford, 2003). Integrating a balance and variety of approaches begins with noticing learners' preferences and providing instruction that touches each individual's favored style sometime during each lesson. In doing this, teachers are not only offering activities that *match* a given learner's style, but they are also providing tasks that *stretch* the learner's style, thus enhancing learning flexibility (Oxford, 1999). A balanced approach places learners, the most knowledgeable experts concerning their own habits and preferences, front and center in meeting their own needs – on both sides of the classroom door (Peacock, 2001b). By offering an extensive variety of presentation and practice options that cater to different learning styles, teachers encourage learners to develop beyond the comfort zone implied by their usual style preferences.

Principle 5: *Reflective learners consider how their beliefs, strategies and abilities connect to their individual learning styles*

Besides style mismatches between teachers' instructional decisions and learners' preferences and habits, a disconnect can also exist between a learner's style and other individual variables like his or her own beliefs, strategies or abilities (Dörnyei, 2005). For example, internal conflict may result within a learner who defines his or her learning styles as global and inductive yet *believes* that a form-focused approach is the most effective means to language learning; or *strategizes* using bottom-up reading techniques; or who does not have a natural disposition toward grammatical sensitivity. Learners often experience a state of ambivalence – being of two minds simultaneously as when an anxious learner wants to speak but holds herself back (MacIntyre, 2007). Providing opportunities for learners to explore their internal conflicts head-on through reflection and interaction with both peers and teacher is the first step to reconciling conflicting tendencies.

... To Practice

Language Learning Styles Activities

The activities in this chapter, guided by the dimensions found in the LSS, focus on capitalizing on the diversity of language learning styles in the classroom. The purpose of the first activity is for teachers to become cognizant of their own teaching styles. The remaining activities are presented in pairs with a series of tasks within each set for learners to explore their individual preferences and experiment with matching and stretching different style dimensions. In general, there are two ways in which classroom participants can become explicitly aware of their style preferences: by either relying on self-reports that elicit their perceptions of their own cognitive functioning or by executing tasks that are followed up by making inferences from those performances (Dörnyei, 2005). Our paired learner activities are accompanied by a task or series of tasks that use an alternative means (i.e. not established self-report surveys) for learner self-identification of their style preferences. Although there are many effective style instruments that do a 'reasonably good job' at measuring learning styles (Dörnyei, 2005: 129), we decided to heed Skehan's (1991: 285) recommendation to 'go beyond questionnaires' to adopt 'more open-ended and ethnographic techniques.' At times, we include qualitative interview-based activities, and in others, we provide tasks where students write about or discuss their learning styles and observe each other (Ehrman, 1996; Reid, 1998). The tasks were created under the assumption that learners are usually able to report quite reliably on their own typical learning preferences, and that those learning preferences can be categorized quite simply (Tyacke, 1998).

Throughout the styles self-identification tasks, we attempt to carefully consider the unique requirements of the language learning context and the purpose of collecting the data (James & Gardner, 1995). Usually, our purpose is not necessarily the pursuit of the level of scientific rigor demanded by research, but rather the accrual of teacher and learner self-awareness. Advocates of learner styles awareness emphasize that the essential purpose of assessment is self-knowledge (Young, 2010). Furthermore, when appropriate, we add specific examples to the questions/tasks to mitigate the ambiguity found in self-report measures that do not provide specific scenarios to exemplify each style (Peacock, 2001b). Additionally, we view each learning style not as a category but rather on a continuum that is dynamically interacting with a myriad of other factors in the learning process. Most of the style self-identification tasks we include require learners to state a preference for one end of the continuum or the other. We concur with Tudor (1996) that a teacher's main purpose for style measurement is to help choose among a limited number of options by grouping learners' preferences and responding to learners' needs in an informed manner. Hence, we simplify the task by exploring one dimension at a time and provide multiple opportunities for teachers and learners to investigate and identify their place on each dimension's continuum. This will, we hope, lead teachers to explore different approaches, asking which is most effective in specific learning situations and for particular learning purposes (Cheng & Banya, 1998). In the case that learners have flexibility in their styles, or categorize themselves 'incorrectly,' our pairing of tasks offers an opportunity for learners to interact in the classroom from opposing positions. In the end, neither the theoretical vagueness of the learning styles construct nor limitations in its measurement eliminate the value of self-reflection in the development of learner autonomy. Ultimately a learner can accept or reject any attempt to categorize his or her style (Young, 2010).

The activities in this chapter ask learners to identify their position on a specific learning style continuum, then participate in groups to carry out two series of tasks: one set that will match their self-reported style and one set that will stretch it. This juxtaposition is designed to give learners insight into their affective and linguistic progress under both conditions. Adaptable teachers and learners understand that style extremes are not always bad, nor is flexibility always good. Therefore, our activities promote 'productive flexibility,' encouraging learners to discriminate between styles that can be adopted successfully in particular situations (Tyacke, 1998: 44). Whereas one of the activity sets is designed to match the learner's preference, the more interesting experience might be the other set of tasks. By stretching themselves, we hope that learners become more empowered in an array of language learning contexts and expand their comfort zones to embrace a larger style repertoire (Cheng & Banya, 1998). Stretching styles might incorporate approaches to learning that individuals have resisted in the past (Cohen & Dörnyei, 2002). Furthermore, grouping learners together is a step in the direction of what Dörnyei (2005: 157) calls 'streaming learners according to their learning style preferences.' We should note that rather than developing different syllabi to accommodate group tracks, we provide special tasks that allow learners to flex and relax under both stretching and matching conditions. Felder and Henriques (1995: 27) hypothesize that 'language instructors who adapt their instruction to address both poles of each of the ... dimensions should come close to providing an optimal learning environment for most (if not all) students in a class.' Through these activities, teacher–learner teams will test that hypothesis.

Each activity ends in a 'de-briefing' wherein an opportunity is provided for reflection and learner-teacher communication. Through the juxtaposition of activities that stretch and match styles, participants are encouraged to contemplate the strategies they used and then communicate their deliberations. The de-briefings provide a constructive avenue for learners to inform their teachers when approaches and/or activities do not meet their needs. Completing the stretching activity can help to increase tolerance of ambiguity. 'Such tolerance will serve (learners) well in adjusting to different learning styles and will allow them to work to strengthen their weaker learning style preferences' (Cheng & Banya, 1998: 83). According to Tyacke (1998: 43), '... understanding the individual and encouraging individual reflection on and implementation of preferred learning styles is more important than trying to impose "good" habits or styles.'

Teacher Styles Activity 1: Knowing your own preferences

The teacher who is indeed wise does not bid you to enter the house of his wisdom but rather leads you to the threshold of your mind – Khalil Gibran

Procedure:
Collecting the data for this activity can be carried out in one of two ways:

- Option 1: An activity of retrospection. Gather your lesson plans from the last two weeks, read them for evidence of the eleven items (codify if desired) found in the statements below, and provide a frequency count in the spaces provided.
- Option 2: A keeping-a-tally activity. After carrying out each language lesson during the next two weeks, keep a tally in the spaces provided of how often you implemented the behaviors found in the eleven statements below.

Each set of the behaviors found below (eleven total) corresponds to the subsequent 11 learner activities. The dimensions have been simplified into straightforward easily observable behaviors to facilitate their identification and later comparison to learner outcomes.

(1) Count up the number of times you presented information or asked learners to practice...

Visually _____ (i.e. used books, videos, charts, pictures etc.)
Aurally _____ (i.e. used discussions lectures, role plays etc.)
Kinesthetically _____ (i.e. moving around, projects, experiments etc.)

Using social interaction _____ (i.e. games, conversations, discussions etc.)
Using independent work _____ (i.e. studying, reading alone, computer etc.)

Giving step-by-step instructions _____ (i.e. present oriented)
Giving open-ended loose parameters _____ (i.e. future oriented)

With strict deadlines and explicit directions _____
Without concern for deadlines, allowing learner discovery _____

Using and/or seeking main ideas _____
Using and/or seeking specific information _____

Summarizing and guessing _____
Analyzing and focusing on rules _____

Memorization through noticing differences and seeking distinctions
_____

Memorization through eliminating differences and chunking material _____

Starting with the general and going to the specific _____ (rules then examples)
Starting with the specific and going to the general _____ (examples then rules)

Separating information from its context _____ (seeing more trees than forest)
Dealing with information holistically _____ (seeing more forest than trees)

Giving and expecting quick reactions _____
Giving and expecting reflection   _____

Expressing ideas metaphorically and encouraging students to do the same _____
Expressing ideas literally and encouraging students to do the same
_____

(2) Compare the numbers from each set. Identify those sets with the greatest variability between the numbers. These are the teaching styles where you need to seek greater balance for the benefit of those learners who have dissimilar learning styles.
(3) Throughout the next eleven Learner Style activities, keep in mind the results from this Teaching Style activity to actively compare how your results fare with those of your language learners.

Learner Styles Activity 1: Seer? Listener? Toucher? – Exploring your Physical Senses

Magic is really only the utilization of the entire spectrum of the senses. Humans have cut themselves off from their senses. Now they see only a tiny portion of the visible spectrum, hear only the loudest of sounds, their sense of smell is shockingly poor and they can only distinguish the sweetest and sourest of tastes. – Michael Scott

Level: All

Preparation:

(1) Hang nine pieces of three different colored posters around the room (or use blackboard or whiteboard space if available) leaving space for students to write their names and brief commentaries below each phrase.

On three of the same color (identifying your 'visual learners'), title each one separately:

(a) 'I remember something better if I write it down;'
(b) 'I need written directions for tasks;' and
(c) 'Charts, diagrams and maps help me better understand what someone says.'

On three of another color (identifying your 'auditory learners'), title each one separately:

(a) 'I remember things better if I discuss them with someone;'
(b) 'I need oral directions for tasks;' and
(c) 'Background music helps me think.'

On the final three (identifying your 'kinesthetic/tactile learners'), title each one separately:

(a) 'Manipulating objects helps me to remember what someone says;'
(b) 'I think better when I move around;'
(c) 'I prefer to start doing things rather than checking the directions first.'

Procedure:

(1) Preface this activity by explaining that the next series of tasks will require learners to reflect upon which physical senses they prefer when learning language. They will participate in two sets of activities; the first set will accommodate their preferences while the second set will encourage learners to explore outside their comfort zones.
(2) Instruct learners to walk around the room, look at the different posters, sign their names on any of the sheets that are true of them and, if they want, invite them to write a brief commentary that expands their thoughts.
(3) Ask a learner representative from each color group to read the names of the people who accompany him on the lists and any comments that learners expressed. Tell learners to join the group where their

names appeared most often. If some learners' names appear the same number of times on different colored groups of posters, allow them to choose which group they feel most comfortable with. If numbers are unmanageable, sub-divide the groups (this being most likely with the 'visual' learners). At this point, learners are in groups with others of similar learning style preferences.

(4) Considering language material that you are currently working on in class, modify the 'practice phase' of any lesson by simultaneously doing the following:

   (a) Give 'visual' learners written directions to activity. Provide handouts and/or a video. Encourage members of this group to take notes and color code information while reading.

   (b) Give 'auditory' learners oral directions to the activity. Provide them with the opportunity to discuss the topic at hand and to pair up for peer tutoring. Encourage members of this group to agree on some background music and allow them to play it softly as they work.

   (c) Give 'kinesthetic/tactile' learners a problem-solving activity using objects they can manipulate and demands active participation, like a role play or drama.

(5) After learners have completed their assigned activities in their 'preferred groups', explain that they will now re-group, but instead of forming groups by considering the high frequency with which their names appeared on the posters, they will now become participants in the group where their names appeared the least!

(6) Re-cycle the activities from 4 above, but in this phase, explain that learners will participate in activities that 'stretch' their style preferences.

(7) De-brief this activity by inviting learners to share their 'matching' and 'stretching' experiences while working on tasks that juxtaposed their most and least preferred sensory learning styles. Ask for learners' input on how they think language classes could be more balanced for ALL learners.

Learner Styles Activity 2: Independent Introvert or Experienced Extrovert?

If introversion is a disease, then can I please get a disability so I don't have to work with extroverts all the time¿¿¿ – Anonymous

Level: This set of tasks can incorporate a variety of target language (TL) material of diverse proficiency levels, themes and/or functions. The important caveat is that the tasks are juxtaposed so that extroverts and introverts are given the opportunity to 'stretch' themselves through one of them and feel 'matched' through the other. Although we offer a specific example that provides beginning learners with practice asking and answering questions in the simple present tense, language opportunities are limitless so long as the first task encourages learners to talk to one another and form groups through social 'game-like' interaction and the second task uses the same linguistic/functional features from the first task in independent work.

Procedure:

(1) Preface this set of activities by explaining that, in tandem, the tasks will help learners explore and clarify their source of energy – whether their force originates in the inner world of ideas and experiences or whether it is invigorated in the outer world of people – and to develop strategies for making the most of both learning situations. They will have the opportunity to use the TL while exploring conflicting strategies and attitudes.

(2) Explain that this game-like activity is about forming and reforming groups quickly and that one of its main goals is to speak to as many people as possible by heeding the TL cues called out by the teacher. In order to form groups, learners will need to ask and answer questions posed by each other.

(3) Begin by calling out: 'Form a group of people with the same number of siblings as you … Go!' (For example, this might encourage question forms like, 'How many brothers and sisters do you have?' and answers like, 'I have two sisters.') Do not worry if the first groups are not formed by the time the next cue is called: 'Think of the first vowel in your first name. Find others with the same letter.' Again, before learners are all placed, keep them moving by calling out: 'Find everyone born in the same month as you.' As new criteria for group formation are called out, learners continue to ask and answer questions of each other. Continue re-grouping with criteria pertinent to the group of learners.

(4) Next, ask learners to take a seat and take out a pencil and paper. Instruct them to independently write a dialogue between two strangers who have just struck up a conversation at a bus stop using question and answer forms similar to the ones used in the previous grouping activity.

(5) When complete, invite learners to choose a person they know well and exchange their dialogues. Allow partners to first read each other's dialogues silently before asking them to take a role and read them together aloud.

(6) De-brief this activity by asking for a show of hands indicating whether learners preferred the first or second task. Group learners according to their preferences.

(a) For those learners who preferred the first 're-grouping' task (i.e. those tending toward 'extroversion'), assign a 'recorder' to write down responses and ask them to brainstorm the different strategies that they used to complete each of the two tasks. Ask them to compare the two lists and discuss their conflicting attitudes toward doing group activities versus seated independent/pair work.

(b) For those learners who preferred the second 'seated independent/pair work' (i.e. those tending toward 'introversion'), ask them to independently brainstorm their strategies for the two tasks and to write a journal response focusing on their contradictory attitudes.

Learner Styles Activity 3: Speculation Specialist or Fact Finder?

Reality is a question of perspective; the further you get from the past, the more concrete and plausible it seems – but as you approach the present, it inevitably seems incredible. – Salman Rushdie

Level: Intermediate/Advanced

Procedure:

(1) Preface this activity by explaining that this set of tasks will allow learners to explore their preferences concerning how they handle possibilities – whether they tend to be future-oriented speculators and abstract thinkers or whether they favor present-oriented

one-step-at-a-time learning. Learners will have the opportunity to raise their learning style self-awareness by comparing their attitudes and strategies under both matching and stretching conditions and share what they learned with classmates and their teacher.

(2) This activity can be done as an in-class writing assignment or as homework. Provide learners with the following two sets of instructions for a five paragraph essay and ask them to select one:

    (a) For concrete-sequential learners:

        (i) For your 5-paragraph essay complete the following sentence – which will ultimately be your thesis statement and located at the end of your introduction: 'Speaking more than one language is important in our world today because...'

        (ii) Before beginning to compose, list three reasons in outline format to support your thesis.

        (iii) Write an introduction of at least three sentences to introduce the topic, adding your thesis statement at the end.

        (iv) Develop your three points, using one paragraph for each. Make sure that your topic sentence is clearly supported by all the ensuing information. Pay attention to the transitions between ideas.

        (v) Write a conclusion that re-states your thesis and summarizes your three main points. Compose a final remark that encourages everyone to pursue bi/multi-lingualism.

    (b) For random-intuitive learners:

        (i) For this writing assignment follow your passions and create a piece that answers the question, 'Why will it be important for future generations to speak more than one language?'

(3) Upon completion of the writing task, place learners who chose the same instructions in dyads and provide the following peer-editing guidelines:

    (a) For the concrete-sequential learners who chose the step-by-step instructions in (a):

        (i) Exchange papers. On a separate blank sheet, give your partner feedback that focuses on what they should maintain in future writing endeavors and what they might consider changing.

    (b) For the random-intuitive learners who chose to follow their passions and focus on future speculations:

        (i) Exchange papers. On a separate blank sheet, respond to the following:

(ii)   In one sentence each, write out the main reasons your partner discussed as important. Is there cohesion and coherence
among the ideas? If not, how can it be improved?

(iii) For each main point of your partner's paper, write a brief
sentence that summarizes his/her justification for that
point. Is that justification reasonable? If not, how can it
be improved?

(iv) Does the introduction clearly present the main thrust of
the paper? Does it create audience interest?

(v)   Now re-read the body of the paper one paragraph at a
time. Underline the topic sentences. Do all of the sentences in each paragraph support the topic sentence? If
there is deviating information, draw a line through it.

(vi) For what purpose did your partner use his/her conclusion?
In your opinion, was this effective?

(vii) With a different colored pen, correct all of the grammar
and spelling errors you can find.

(4)   De-brief this activity by pointing out that the instructions for the
writing task, because they had a choice, probably matched their
favored approach to learning, but that the peer editing task most likely
stretched their learning style. Ask learners to compare the two experiences and share how their attitudes toward the tasks were different.
What strategies did they use that were successful under matching and
stretching conditions?

MODIFICATION:

Emergent learners: Simplify the two sets of activity instructions
keeping in mind that one set should be written in a concrete step-by-
step format that orients learners to the present, while the other should
orient learners to the future and allow them the space to be speculative
and abstract.

Technology: Tell learners to write their assignments using a word
processor. Allow them to peer review using the editing function.

Learning Styles Activity 4: Fanatic for Focus or Diva for Discovery?

Man cannot discover new oceans unless he has the courage to lose sight of the shore. – Andre Gide

Level: Intermediate/Advanced

Preparation:

(1) Reproduce the following lists of ambiguous sentences (from: www. gray-area.org, compiled by Jeff Gray) on two separate sheets of paper. On the first, put the following:
- We must polish(a) the Polish(b) furniture.
- He could lead(a) if he would get the lead(b) out.
- The farm was used to produce(a) produce(b).
- The dump was so full that it had to refuse(a) more refuse(b).
- The soldier decided to desert(a) in the desert(b).
- This was a good time to present(a) the present(b).
- A bass(a) was painted on the head of the bass drum(b).
- When shot at, the dove(a) dove into the bushes(b).
- I did not object(a) to the object(b).
- The insurance was invalid(a) for the invalid(b).

On the other, reproduce these:

- The bandage was wound(a) around the wound(b).
- There was a row(a) among the oarsmen about how to row(b).
- They were too close(a) to the door to close(b) it.
- The buck does(a) funny things when the does(b) are present.
- They sent a sewer(a) down to stitch the tear in the sewer(b) line.
- To help with planting, the farmer taught his sow(a) to sow(b).
- The wind(a) was too strong to wind(b) the sail.
- After a number(a) of injections my jaw got number(b).
- Upon seeing the tear(a) in my clothes, I shed a tear(b).
- I had to subject(b) the subject to a series of tests(b).

(2) On two separate sheets of paper, reproduce the following lists of signs (from: www.gray-area.org, compiled by Jeff Gray) found posted in non-English-speaking countries. On the first:
- Because of the impropriety of entertaining guests of the opposite sex in the bedroom, it is suggested that the lobby be used for this purpose (posted in a Zurich hotel).
- Ladies are requested not to have children at the bar (posted in a Norway cocktail bar).

- You are welcome to visit the cemetery where famous Russian and Soviet composers, artists and writers are buried except for Thursday (posted in a Moscow hotel).
- The lift is being fixed for the next day. During that time we regret that you will be unbearable (posted in a Bucharest hotel).
- Ladies may have a fit upstairs (posted in a Hong Kong tailor shop).
- Please do not feed the animals. If you have any suitable food, give it to the guard on duty (posted in the Budapest Zoo).
- We will take your bags and send them in all directions (posted in a Copenhagen airline office).
- Fur coats made for ladies from their own skin (posted in a Swedish furrier).

On the other, reproduce these:

- Roasted duck let loose and beef rashers beaten up in the country people's fashion (posted in a Polish menu).
- Our wines leave you nothing to hope for (posted in a Swiss eatery).
- Teeth extracted by the latest methodists (posted in a Hong Kong dentist office).
- Dresses for street walking (posted in a Paris shop).
- Order summer suits early. In a big rush we will execute customers in strict rotation (posted in a tailor's shop in Rhodes).
- Drop your trousers here for best results (posted in a Bangkok dry cleaners).
- Ladies, leave your clothes here and spend the afternoon having a good time (posted in a Rome laundry mat).
- Please leave your values at the front desk (posted in a Paris hotel).
- You are invited to take advantage of the chambermaid (posted in a Japanese hotel).

Procedure:

(1) Preface this activity by explaining that learners will be exploring their ability to accept ambiguity – to deal with unknown language, partially understood information and/or unfamiliar situations. Learners who have developed a high tolerance of ambiguity will more likely remain calm and employ useful strategies to communicate successfully; however, an excess of tolerance could indicate a lack of noticing and self-monitoring resulting in inaccuracy and fossilization. The following activities juxtapose tasks that will

both stretch and match learners on both sides of the tolerance of ambiguity scale.

(2) Explain that besides having different approaches to language processing, 'Closure-oriented' learners are organized planners and work well with deadlines, while 'Open' learners are not as attentive to organization and planning for deadlines. Ask learners to take out their language learning diaries, leaf through them and rate them on a scale from one to ten; one meaning totally disorganized and ten meaning extremely organized. Next, have them reflect upon their study plans for the next week and also rate their planning on a scale from one to ten; one meaning they have no plans thought out and ten meaning they have every day planned. Looking at these two numbers, tell learners to self-place themselves as either 'closure-oriented' or 'open.'

(3) To match tasks to the learners' styles, give the first list of ambiguous sentences to the 'closure-oriented' learners and tell them to provide a written definition on a piece of paper of the words labeled 'a' and 'b' in each sentence, using a dictionary if necessary. Also, hand out the first list of signs posted in non-English speaking countries to the 'open' learners and ask them to form pairs and discuss what the signs mean. Ask dyads to take notes of their conversation.

(4) To stretch learners' styles to meet the task, switch the assignments. Hand out the second list of signs to the 'closure-oriented' learners and the second list of ambiguous sentences to the 'open' learners and repeat the instructions.

(5) To de-brief this activity, have a class discussion about learners' responses to ambiguity. Ask the closure-oriented learners how they felt and what strategies they used when trying to clarify the ambiguity of the signs. Was it more difficult without a dictionary and a clear cut answer? Ask the open learners which activity they enjoyed more. Did their strategies differ from those of their 'closure-oriented' counterparts?

Learning Styles Activity 5: Spotlight on Specifics or Jumping to the Gist?

> It is the harmony of the diverse parts, their symmetry, their happy balance; in a word it is all that introduces order, all that gives unity, that permits us to see clearly and to comprehend at once both the ensemble and the details. – Henri Poincare

Level: All

Preparation:

(1) For the first part of this activity, select an interesting medium-length proficiency-appropriate text to read aloud.
(2) For the second part of this activity, choose two separate paragraphs corresponding to learners' proficiency level and eliminate every seventh word in each, replacing it with a blank.

Procedure:

(1) Preface this activity by explaining that the tasks will stretch and match learners' preferences concerning how they receive language information. Do they focus on details or main ideas?
(2) Introduce your selected text by telling learners that when you are finished reading it, that they will need to write down what they remember about it. Read it. Allow adequate time for learners to write.
(3) In pairs, have learners exchange their papers and: (a) Count the number of details that were included; and (b) Count the number of phrases that act as summaries of information.
(4) Next, re-arrange learners in homogeneous pairs based upon whether they included more details (i.e. those tending to be more 'particular) or more summaries (i.e. those tending to be more 'global').
(5) Provide a copy of the first pre-selected paragraph with every seventh word deleted to each pair. Instruct the 'particular' learners to fill in the blanks and the 'global' learners to express the main idea (without filling in the blanks).
(6) Hand out a copy of the second paragraph that has been similarly modified to each pair, but this time, tell the 'particular' learners to express the main idea and the 'global' learners to fill in the blanks.
(7) De-brief this activity by asking about how this activity may have increased learners' self-awareness of their learning preferences concerning details and main ideas. Pair a 'particular' learner with a 'global' learner and have them discuss the strategies they used in approaching both tasks.

MODIFICATIONS:

Technology: Post the reading passages and paragraphs with every seventh word deleted on the computer and allow learners to read the passage and fill in the blanks from their screens.

Learning Styles Activity 6: Penchant for Predicting or Prowess for Puzzles

Too rigid specialization is almost as bad for a historian's mind, and for his ultimate reputation, as too early an indulgence in broad generalization and synthesis. – Samuel E. Morison

Level: Intermediate/Advanced

Preparation:

(1) For each group of four learners appraised as 'Analyzers', provide a copy of the following mystery puzzle and on a separate piece of paper, the solution to it.
   The Mystery: 'On a dark and dreary night as the cold of winter began permeating their city and November was coming to a close, the evening commute home of a group of New Yorkers was interrupted by a blood-curdling scream. Police raced to the scene but were unable to gather enough evidence to discover who had done the murderous deed. Several months passed and still no suspects. Until one day, police got word through one of their informants that Edward Stewart had been bragging about being the culprit. They interviewed him but he claimed to have an alibi. They let him go but told him that the next day they would return and he must produce proof of his whereabouts at the time of the crime. The detectives returned the following day. Edward showed a sales receipt for a $18.50 gas purchase at 6:00 pm on November 31 at a gas station 300 miles away from the crime scene. He was immediately placed under arrest. What was Edward's big mistake?'
   Solution: 'There are only 30 days in November. Edward's proof of an alibi must have been fabricated.'
(2) For each group of four learners appraised as 'Synthesizers,' provide a copy of the following 'Story-Without-an-End':
   The Story (adapted from **Smithsonian**, 1980): 'Jim Lewis and Jim Springer first met February 9, 1979, after 39 years of estrangement.

They are identical twins that had been separated at birth. Both were very nervous at first, but now consider the reunion 'the most important day of my life.' Amid the euphoria over their rediscovery of each other, they came across astonishing similarities in their lives and behavior. Both had been adopted by separate families in Ohio (USA) and had grown up within 45 miles of each other. Both had been named James by their adoptive parents and both had married twice; first to women named Linda and second to women named Betty. Both had children, including sons named James Allan. Both had at one time owned dogs named Toy. The story of how they found one another again is truly amazing...'

Procedure:

(1) Preface this activity by explaining that learners will participate in tasks that will tap into their predilections concerning guessing/predicting and pulling apart/analyzing. Highlight that while some learners might favor summarizing, paraphrasing and predicting outcomes, others tend toward noticing details and solving complex mysteries and puzzles.

(2) Pair learners and ask them to interview each other asking the following questions about their classroom behavior:
   (a) When you write an outline, do you begin with the big ideas first or with the fine points you want to make?
   (b) When you take notes, do you paraphrase what the speaker says or do you write details?
   (c) When you tell a story, can you summarize your information quickly and easily or does it take you a long time?
   (d) When you approach language in this class, do you focus on grammar rules or the communicative context?

(3) Based on this information, have the interviewer distinguish whether the interviewee is an analyzer (one who likes the fine points, details, takes a relatively long time to tell a story and focuses on grammar rules) or a synthesizer (one who prefers big ideas, paraphrasing, summarizing and focuses on context). Place learners in homogeneous groups of four based upon this appraisal.

(4) To 'match' the learners' preferences, the 'Analyzers' will scrutinize details to solve a puzzle while the 'Synthesizers' will use their summarizing and paraphrasing skills to get a big picture in order to predict a story's outcome.

(a) Each group of 'Analyzers' will choose one person to be the 'puzzle encoder'. This person will read aloud 'The Mystery' and silently read the solution. All others will be the 'puzzle decoders'. The decoders pose 'yes' or 'no' questions to the encoder until the solution is found.

(b) Each group of 'Synthesizers' will choose one person to be the 'prediction courier' who will read aloud the 'Story-without-an-end' and solicit a possible outcome from each of the remaining members. The group then must come to a consensus on which ending is the best.

(5) Once the Analyzers have decoded their puzzle and the Synthesizers have predicted their outcome, ask each small group to produce their own original puzzle or story-without-an-end using the one provided as a model.

(6) To 'stretch' learners' preferences, instruct 'Analyzer' groups to pass their original puzzle to 'Synthesizer' groups and vice versa. Give groups the same instructions to decode the puzzles and predict the outcomes.

(7) De-brief this activity by asking learners to share their responses to each of the tasks, discussing how their strategies and attitudes differed between 'matching' and 'stretching' phases. Share with learners your reflections on what you learned about them.

MODIFICATIONS:

Emergent learners: Write a different mystery puzzle and story-without-an-end or simplify the language of the ones provided to target learners' proficiency levels.

Technology: Rather than preparing the mystery and the story-without-an-end on paper, post them on the computer and allow students to work from their screens. To compose their original mysteries and stories, instruct learners to write them on the computer and exchange them through email attachments.

Learning Styles Activity 7: Seeker of Similarities or Discoverer of Differences

Reason respects the differences, and imagination the similitude of things. – Percy Bysshe Shelley

Level: All

Procedure:

(1) Preface this activity by explaining that this series of tasks will explore learners' preferences concerning how they memorize new language material. They will stretch and match approaches that encourage them to compare their strategies and attitudes towards seeking or reducing differences in novel vocabulary and separating or merging this new information with what they already know. 'Sharpeners' (those who look for differences and keep new material separate from the old) are usually more concerned with accuracy while the 'Levelers' (those who reduce differences and merge new material with the old), have a knack for practicality.

(2) To distinguish the 'Sharpeners' from the 'Levelers,' pose the question: In language class, what is more important to you – being correct or being fluent? In other words, when you speak, do you pay more attention to what you say or how you say it? Based upon their answers to this question, ask learners to place themselves in one of the categories.

(3) Instruct all learners for the next two weeks to write down in their language learning diaries at least 30 new vocabulary words that they have heard or read.

(4) Tell the 'Sharpeners' to write each word on a separate index card and include its phonetic spelling and definition.

(5) Tell the 'Levelers' to find similarities among the words and group them into meaningful categories. Ask them to draw upon their previous knowledge of related words and arrange the concept and its relationships to known material to create a semantic map, writing the new word in the middle of an index card and linking it via arrows and lines to other known ones.

(6) Instruct learners to memorize their lists over the next couple of days. At the same time, tell them to find at least another thirty new words in their reading and listening over the next two weeks and continue to catalogue them in their diaries.

(7) When the new lists have been constructed, reverse the instructions: Ask the 'Levelers' to create the index cards with individual words

accompanied by their phonetic spellings and definitions and the 'Sharpeners' to group their words and make semantic maps. Allow several days for both groups to attempt to memorize their lists.

(8) De-brief this activity by soliciting feedback as to whether memorizing their word lists was easier the first time, when it was supposed that their learning preference was being matched, or the second time, when theoretically their preference was being stretched.

Learning Styles Activity 8: Pattern Pursuer or Exposure Enthusiast?

The more uncompromisingly specific you are the more you end up touching the bigger universal truths. – Tom Hooper

Level: All

Preparation:

(1) Carefully select four new grammatical concepts (related or not) that are proficiency-appropriate to your group of learners.

Procedure:

(1) Preface this activity by explaining that it will encourage learners to discover their preferences concerning how they approach language rules – whether they favor going from an explanation of grammatical rules and theories and then moving on to examples and exercises or vice versa. Tell them that unlike other activities in their exploration of their individual learning styles, that you will not place them in groups before the tasks but rather the tasks will function as indicators of their preferences, and that at the end of the activity, they will have the opportunity to reflect upon whether they prefer more inductive or deductive grammar approaches.

(2) Choose two new grammatical concepts. Introduce the first one deductively, explicitly explain the rules related to its use and allow learners to practice it using the concept in a variety of different ways like fill in the blank exercises or creating new sentences.

(3) With the second grammatical concept, present learners with a variety of examples without providing any preamble concerning how it is used. Through this language contact, it is hoped that learners will notice how the form is used and inductively infer the grammar rule.

To ensure that learners understood the concept after this exposure, ask learners to explain the grammar rule.

(4)   Ask learners through a show of hands whether they preferred the deductive explanations carried out with the first concept or the inductive discovery learning encouraged with the second one. Based upon their responses, place individuals in homogeneous three- or four-member groups of 'deductive' and 'inductive' learners.

(5)   Select two more novel grammatical concepts and assign one to the groups of 'inductive' learners and the other to the 'deductive' learners. To stretch them from their favored positions, tell the inductive learners to prepare a grammar lesson that teaches their concept deductively (i.e. through explicit explanation of the rule followed by practice) and the deductive learners to prepare to teach theirs inductively (i.e. through exposure to a variety of examples followed by determination of the rule).

(6)   Once groups have prepared their lessons, pair the groups and ask them to take turns teaching their grammatical concept to 'opposite-preference' peers. This implies that although learners will be receiving the information in their more preferred mode, they will be presenting in their less preferred mode.

(7)   De-brief this activity by asking the paired groups to discuss their strategies and attitudes while matching and stretching their preferences toward deductive and inductive application of language rules by considering the following questions: Did the naturally deductive learners submitted to inductive procedures strategize by deducing the rule as quickly as possible? If so, was that helpful? Did the naturally inductive learners exposed to deductive explanations strategize by creating examples as the grammar presentation was underway? If so, what were the benefits? How did learners' attitudes change during the juxtaposition of grammar presentation modalities?

Learner Styles Activity 9: Holistically Happy or Dispersedly Delighted?

Language is not merely a set of unrelated sounds, clauses, rules, and meanings; it is a total coherent system of these integrating with each other, and with behavior, context, universe of discourse and observer perspective. – Kenneth Pike

Level: Advanced

Preparation:

(1) Reproduce the following five figures for distribution to learners.

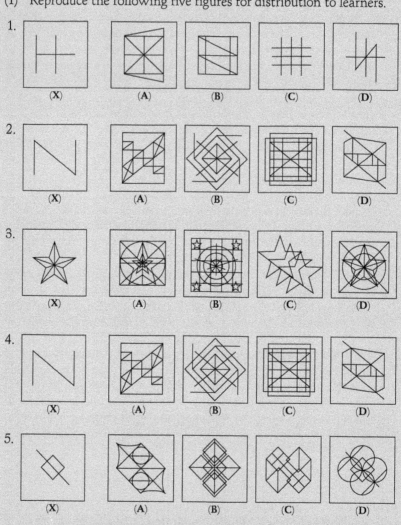

Note to teachers: These figures are included here based on the premise that field-independent individuals will be able to discern simple geometric figures from more complicated patterns more quickly than those who are field-dependent (Riding, 2000). These figures will be used to 'assess' learners' field (in)dependency – relative to each other – in your classroom.

The correct answers are: 1. (A), 2. (D), 3. (D), 4. (C), 5. (D)

(2) To maximize learning for the field independents but to challenge field dependents, provide a list of problem-solving topics for which large amounts of references and resources are available for self-directed learning tasks and which are age and proficiency appropriate for your learners. Examples might be but are not limited to topics in: Education (Academic Pressure, Cheating, Dropouts, Competency Tests, Lack Of Educational Opportunities, Parent Education), Environment (Acid Rain, Alternate Energy Sources, Climate Change), Food and Health (Dangers of Food Additives, Dental Health, Depression, Fat in Low Price Food Products, Food Labeling, Health Care, Integration Of The Disabled, Problems of the Mentally Ill, Test tube Babies, Vegetarianism) or Global issues and politics (Food Shortages, International Threats, Overpopulation)

(3) To maximize learning for the field dependents but to challenge the field independents, find a short reading on a social issue commiserate with your learners' proficiency level and interests that can be used as the basis of group work. Prepare a series of guiding questions to steer learners through its reading.

Procedure:

(1) Preface this activity by explaining that each learner will examine whether – in a 'forest and the trees' scenario – he/she has a tendency to see individual trees (inferring that he/she is able to separate information from within a larger context and is not easily distracted) or the forest as a whole (inferring that he/she sees information holistically and can be readily sidetracked). Explain that, like other learning styles continuums, there is not one 'right' preference as there are benefits to being a 'tree-seer' (aka, field independent) and a forest-seer (aka, field dependent). You may need to reiterate this after Step 3 as learners may assume that finishing faster is better, and this is not necessarily the case.

(2) Distribute the paper with the five figures shown above face down with the instructions that learners are not to look at it until you say 'go.' Instruct learners that, as quickly as possible, they are to find the alternative figure which contains figure (X) as its part and use a pencil to trace it. (If necessary, model a simple sample version on the board to ensure learners' understanding.) Tell them that when they are done they are to put their pencils down and raise their hands.

(3) Say, 'Go!' Keep track of the order in which students finish. The half who finishes first will be considered your 'field independent'

learners *relative to* the second half who will be your 'field dependent' learners. Place the halves on opposite sides of the room.

(4) Give the 'field independent' learners the following instructions, cluing them in from the start that they will be receiving minimal guidance and direction:

    (a) Working alone, choose one of the topics in the list provided. Search for and consult a variety of resources and references to define a problem and a solution to it.

    (b) Evaluate your information and select at least three information sources to defend your solution.

    (c) Using an outline or a concept map (a graphical diagram that visualizes the relationships among ideas where the concepts are represented as boxes connected with arrows) illustrate the important information you will use to solve your problem.

    (d) Create a metaphor or an analogy using a figure of speech to describe your problem/solution by asserting that it is, on some point of comparison, the same as another otherwise unrelated relationship.

    (e) Fill in the following template:

        (i) Sources consulted:

        (ii) Problem chosen:

        (iii) Three important information sources:

        (iv) Solution (presented in the form of an outline or concept map):

        (v) Metaphor:

(5) After handing out the pre-selected reading and guiding questions on a social issue and briefly reviewing its main ideas, give the 'field dependent' learners the following instructions, assuring them that you will be giving them all the guidance they need and providing extensive feedback throughout the process to completion of this activity:

    (a) Working collaboratively in small groups of three or four, and paying careful attention to your partners' social cues, create and complete the first two columns of a KWL advanced organizer (A KWL chart contains three columns and connects new information with what is already known [K], what the group would like to know [W], and upon completion of the task, what the group learned [L]. To do this, learners will need to be cued with the main ideas of the reading.

    (b) Designate one person to be the 'inquirer' whose responsibility it will be to stop and lead a discussion on the guiding questions at the appropriate time during the reading. Take turns reading the passage aloud and orally answering the questions.

(c)　At the end of the reading, fill in the last column of the KWL chart with what your group learned.

(d)　To check for understanding, distribute another copy of the guiding questions to each learner in the form that it was presented earlier and ask individuals to write the answers.

(6)　Upon completion of this series of tasks, have learners switch roles. Instruct the 'field independent people to carry out the group social issue reading tasks and the 'field dependent' people to complete the independent problem/solution research tasks.

(7)　De-brief this activity by juxtaposing the following elements from the previous tasks – all of which research suggests will stretch or match the preferences of field dependent and field independent learners (http://www.personal.psu.edu/staff/t/x/txm4/paper1.html) – and facilitate a discussion on each:

Field dependent preferences

(a)　Social environment
(b)　Deliberate structural support
(c)　Clear directions/maximum support
(d)　Extensive guidance
(e)　Embedded questions

(f)　Assess in the same form material was presented

Field independent preferences

(a)　Individual environment
(b)　Discovery learning
(c)　Independent self-instruction
(d)　Minimal feedback
(e)　Learner created outlines/concept maps
(f)　Performance-based assessment

MODIFICATIONS:

Technology:

(1)　Rather than using library research resources, ask learners to research via the internet.

(2)　Use an online resource (like http://www.eduplace.com/graphicorganizer/) for learners to fill in a KWL chart

Learning Styles Activity 10: Instinctively Impulsive or Reasonably Reflective?

There are two distinct classes of what are called thoughts: those that we produce in ourselves by reflection and the act of thinking, and those that bolt into the mind of their own accord. – Thomas Paine

Level: All

Preparation:

(1) Select a language function (i.e. apologizing, asking/giving directions, introducing oneself or others) commiserate with learners' proficiency level that allows learners to invent, exchange and spontaneously enact scenarios. (For task 1)

Procedure:

(1) Preface this activity by explaining to learners that they will embark on four different tasks, two that will cater to those learners who react quickly in acting or speaking and two that will accommodate those learners who prefer thinking things through before taking action. Explain that learners will have a chance to reflect on their impulsive/reflective preferences upon completion of the four tasks.
(2) Place learners in pairs and instruct them to take a seat next to their partners in a big circle. On a piece of paper, tell learners to reflect together and then create a scenario where the pre-selected function will be invoked. For example, if the function is 'apologizing', learners might write, 'You arrived late to your job interview. Apologize to your interviewer.' Allow plenty of time for learners to think and share their ideas.
(3) Tell learners to roll up their scenarios into a ball. Instruct the first pair of learners to throw their scenario to another dyad. Have the receiving dyad spontaneously act out the scenario without any pre-planning. The receiving dyad then tosses the scenario they created to a third pair who acts it out. Toss and role play until all of the pairs have had their turns.
(4) Divide learners into two teams and have them line up 10 feet from the board or a piece of hanging newsprint. Give a piece of chalk or a marker to the first team member and tell them that they will be competing to see which team can complete a group sentence first – with NO talking. Each learner takes a turn adding one word to the sentence by going to the board, writing it down and passing the chalk/marker to the next person in line. No words can be added

between words that have already been written. Draw learners' attention to the idea that although there is little reflection time, they must think ahead.

(5) Ask learners to take out their language diaries and individually reflect on how they usually treat their 'gut instincts' in their everyday life in general and in the language classroom in particular. Do they think and then act or act and then think? Allow plenty of time for learners to get their thoughts down on paper.

(6) De-brief this activity by asking learners how they felt about being obligated to impulsively role play and create group sentences as opposed to the reflection that was permitted in the creation of the scenarios and the journaling about 'gut instincts.' Did they learn anything about themselves?

Learning Styles Activity 11: Mad for the Metaphoric or *Loco* for the Literal?

We think we think in a very literal way, but if you really ponder it, you don't think in a literal way. You're seeing in a literal way, and you're going from point A to point B, but if you really consciously think back at what was going through your mind when you went from point A to point B, you'll find that it's a very abstract process. – John Leslie

Level: All

Preparations:

(1) Make several sets of cards (enough for one set for every four learners) with one of the following words on each card: tall, kind, fast, slow, smart, fat, sneaky, angry, beautiful, ugly, stubborn, short, thin, silly, easily scared.

Procedure:

(1) Preface this activity by explaining that learners will be experimenting with how literally they take reality. That is to say, do individuals learn better through metaphors and visualizing material using examples and stories or is their learning facilitated through a literal interpretation of concepts and working with language material as it appears on the surface.

(2) To get an initial understanding concerning where individuals are on the metaphorical/literal continuum, introduce the word, 'audacious.' Define it in two ways: (a) With its synonyms (*bold, daring, brave*; yet *risky* and *foolhardy*); and (b) By associating it with an example of a story (John was a simple, hard-working young farmer helping his father scrape by to put enough food on the table to help feed his siblings. Every animal on their farm was precious, but lately a wild and ferocious animal had been hunting down and eating their sheep. With just a sling shot and stone, John went into the woods to find and ultimately kill the savage beast.)

(3) Divide learners into groups by asking which definition, the string of synonyms ('literal' learners) or the story ('metaphoric' learners), gave them a better idea of what 'audacious' means. Sub-divide each of these two groups into small groups with four learners each. Give each small group a set of cards.

(4) To match the learning styles with the task, tell the 'literal' learners to discuss the adjective on each card and come to a consensus on a definition or a list of synonyms (for example, 'dirty' means 'not clean' or 'messy'). Tell the 'metaphoric' learners to brainstorm imaginative ways to compare somebody who embodies the adjective on the card with something else (for example, for 'dirty', learners might say, 'He is a pig.')

(5) Next, to stretch learners' styles, switch the instructions. Tell 'literal' learners to generate metaphors, and tell the 'metaphoric' learners to literally define the words or supply a list of synonyms.

(6) De-brief this activity by asking which task was easier or more comfortable. Did learners use similar strategies to carry out both assignments?

7 Willingness to Communicate

From Premise...

Exploring TL willingness to communicate (WTC) may de-mystify two enigmas that many teachers of a second language have pondered:

Paradox One: You have witnessed an animated Taeko talking incessantly in Japanese with her friends in the cafeteria. But Taeko sits silently in her FL English class. How can Taeko be so talkative when speaking Japanese but be as mute as a clam when an occasion arises to use her English? Let's call this the 'enduring influences' enigma: learners who have personality dispositions toward talking but are unwilling to tap into it by seizing TL communication moments.

    Paradox Two: John's grades on written FL German tests are outstanding, and you have heard him speaking fluent German in his small out-of-class study group, so you know he is competent! Why doesn't he speak up in class? Let's call this the 'situational influences' enigma: learners who are competent TL speakers, but for some transient, situationally dependent reason, are unwilling to snatch the TL communication opportunity.

Do these paradoxes seem familiar? In first language communication, the variables are less murky. It would be safe to predict that if Arabic-speaking Jamel, an over-the-top extrovert, tends to be talkative in his native language Arabic literature class that he would also probably contribute animatedly to a conversation with his Arabic-speaking friends in a coffee shop in downtown Cairo, like Taeko in her L1 Japanese. This is because L1 speakers develop a trait-orientation toward talking (MacIntyre *et al.*, 2003). In the case of Jamel, his willingness to communicate is observed as a regular tendency across a variety of different situations (McCroskey & Richmond, 1991). However, second language teachers know there is much more to it; they have encountered the paradoxes. Discrepancies between how L1 and TL communicators invoke volitional choice to speak or not to speak sent researchers on a mission to discover the 'what', 'why', and 'with which other variables' of TL WTC. Defined as 'the probability of initiating communication, given choice and opportunity' (MacIntyre, 2007: 567) this variable (along with all the others in this volume) is an element in a dynamic system – being worked upon and working with – other influences. In this chapter, WTC will be explored as a composite variable – a self-contained tendency that reflects the multiple interacting, sometimes conflicting influences on target language (TL) communication. Once willingness to communicate forms, it interacts with other variables to work for or against second language communication competency. Drawing directly upon the ingredients that constitute WTC in TL, guidelines and activities will be presented that create an improved recipe for developing an affective and psychological comfort zone for language learning.

Exploring WTC, Its Origin and Its Significance

What WTC Is and Where It Comes From

To expand the definition of WTC, MacIntyre *et al.* (1998) created a six-layered pyramid-shaped model of TL communication (Figure 7.1). Containing eleven factors that work as antecedents to potentially facilitate or inhibit language learners' in-the-moment decisions to speak. The variables extend on a continuum from distal, 'enduring' influences that are relatively stable and permanent (those shoring up the bottom of the pyramid) to proximal 'situational' ones that rapidly fluctuate (those crowning the apex) (MacIntyre, 2007). Language teachers are often perplexed with their learners' ping-ponging decisions to speak or not to speak, so with the goal of de-mystifying the multiple variables that contribute to WTC, we will de-construct the pyramid layer-by-layer and brick-by-brick in order to understand the complexity of TL communication choices.

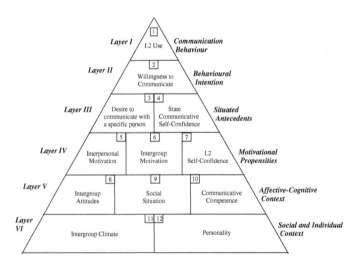

Figure 7.1 Pyramid model of WTC
Source: MacIntyre *et al.* (1998)

The base of the pyramid: Level six

Creating the foundation of the pyramid are two 'broadly interacting forces' representing the society and the individual: intergroup climate (brick 11) and personality (brick 12). Together, they set the stage for TL communication but are more tangential to learners' moment-to-moment WTC decisions. As the most distal influences, their pre-determined nature leaves learners with little to no control over them (MacIntyre, 2007). It is important to note, however, that even though learners have little control over their existence, they do have choices concerning how to deal with them (MacIntyre, 2012).

Intergroup climate is conditioned by (socioeconomic) power and (linguistic) prestige that emerge when two groups come into contact. Global societal forces create the resistant-to-change hierarchies, rivalries, animosities, and hostilities. Even while vociferous calls are made for greater cultural empathy and equality, it seems progress is painfully slow as intergroup climate passes as easily as the air itself from one generation to the next (MacIntyre, 2007). The maintenance of power and prestige tends to safeguard the favor of wealthy industrialized English-speaking countries over emerging nations. Intergroup climate also reflects Schumann's (1978) acculturation theory which predicts that immigrants adapting to a new culture must often concede to known cultural practices, including language, to reap the benefits of participation in their new home.

Accompanying intergroup climate as another distal and enduring, broadly interacting force located on the sixth level of the WTC pyramid is individual personality. Researchers caution that there is not one specific personality profile that dictates language learning success, but rather that traits work in combination with other indicators like intergroup attitudes and TL confidence, to indirectly impact learning efficacy. Personality sets the individual context in which language learning occurs and disposes learners to react positively or negatively to foreign people. As an enduring trait-like influence, it interacts with the intergroup climate to undergird TL communication (MacIntyre *et al.*, 1998). Both the intergroup climate and the genetic elements of a learner's personality exist even before she does.

The midsections: Levels four and five

Building upon the social and individual context of the sixth level of the WTC pyramid is the fifth layer's affective-cognitive context which contains the influence of intergroup attitudes (brick 8), social situation (brick 9), and communicative competence (brick 10). This layer is characterized by the motivational force found in 'the tension between a desire to approach the target language group and a sense of hesitation or fear of the implications of doing so' (MacIntyre, 2007: 567).

The influential nature of inter-group attitudes is manifest when the language learners' desire to integrate and be part of the TL community is pitted against his or her fear of assimilation – fearing that the feeling of identification with the L1 community will somehow be lost. The more salient of these opposing forces will ultimately emerge to either facilitate or disrupt language learning in the form of TL motivation. Moreover, attitudes towards the TL itself may also empower motivation as demonstrated by learners who intrinsically feel enjoyment and satisfaction in learning, who have positive experiences in the language classroom and/or have contact with positive stereotypes (MacIntyre et al., 1998).

The second WTC influence in this layer, the social situation, is characterized by five variables: participant (including age, gender, social class, relationship among interlocutors and their relative proficiencies), setting (place and time of communication), purpose (reasons for which communication is taking place), topic (familiarity with subject under discussion) and channel (medium of communication, i.e. speaking or writing). The interactions among these variables in different combinations will create significantly different communication situations. 'This implies that one's communicative experience in one situation may not be transferred automatically to another, which, in turn, increases the perceived variability in TL communication events and may generate different levels of WTC in various social situations' (MacIntyre et al., 1998: 554).

The last influence in the fifth layer of the pyramid considers the learners' communicative competencies or TL proficiency. This includes not only the ability to communicate with accurate grammaticality (linguistic competence), but also to use language in a coherent and cohesive way (discourse competence), to match communication intent with linguistic form (actional competence), to express messages with social and cultural contextual appropriateness (sociocultural competence), and to implement strategies to make up for gaps in language competence (strategic competence) (Celce-Murcia et al., 1995). It is important to note that this layer reflects self-perceived rather than actual competency. As noted in our first chapter on language anxiety, some learners systematically overestimate and others underestimate their ability. The positing of competence in the model makes it one of the contributing factors to WTC, but far from the only one. Language competence interacts with the psychology of the learner; competency is a step in the communicative process.

The fourth layer is the last of the enduring influences and is composed of motivational propensities. Factors described here are those that impact interpersonal motivation (brick 5), intergroup membership (brick 6) and TL self-confidence (brick 7). Whereas intergroup motives directly relate to membership in a specific social group, interpersonal motives arise from the social role that the learner plays within the group where affiliation and control motives are prominent. Interacting with these two motives is TL self-confidence – the learner's overall belief in being able to communicate in the TL in an adaptive and efficient manner. Cognitively, a learner self-evaluates his or her TL skills, whereas affectively a learner judges his or her degree of discomfort in the form of FL anxiety. 'The pyramid model proposes that TL self-confidence, reflected in self-perceptions of communicative competence coupled with a lack of anxiety, interact with consistent roles and motives encountered in day to day experiences' (MacIntyre *et al.*, 2011: 83).

The apex: Levels one, two and three

Focusing on the here-and-now, the third layer nearer the apex of the pyramid contains two fluctuating situated antecedents. The first is the desire to communicate with a specific person (brick 3), who 'brings unique attributes, including the role that they play (e.g. teacher vs. fellow student); attractiveness as a communication partner; and possibly a shared history' (MacIntyre *et al.*, 2011: 83). The second is state communicative self-confidence (brick 4) which 'blends the influences of prior language learning and perceived communicative skills with the motives and anxieties experienced at a particular moment in time into a state of mind broadly characterized by a tendency to approach or avoid the TL "right now."' (MacIntyre *et al.*, 2011: 84).

When these influences line up in a positive direction, second language learners will feel the behavioral intention to initiate TL discourse (the second layer of the pyramid: brick 2) on a specific occasion with a specific person and use the language (first layer of the pyramid: brick 1).

The significance of WTC

'People generally feel they are less competent in second languages than they are in their native language, and … these perceptions are substantially correlated with their willingness to communicate in those languages' (Burroughs *et al.*, 2003: 237). When considering TL communication and the importance of 'talking to learn' in order to 'learn to talk,' WTC becomes critical as both a means and as an end – as a conduit and a culmination in language learning.

First, WTC functions as a conduit to language learning as interaction in the TL during the process of language learning spurs language proficiency. Swain's Output Hypothesis (1985) proposes that through language production, learners not only test out the hypotheses of what they think they know about the TL, but they also move from a semantic level of understanding to a syntactic level of production. Receptive comprehension results in productive performance when learners demonstrate a WTC that ultimately gives rise to language use. 'Given that language development can occur through interaction, it can be assumed that more interaction leads to more language development and learning' (Kang, 2005: 278). When TL learners avoid TL communication, they will not be utilizing their opportunities to learn language by using it. Thus, to achieve greater TL communicative competence, it behooves teachers and educators to discover how WTC can be enhanced so that learners are more likely to use TL in authentic communication, function as autonomous learners who make independent efforts to seek out communication, and to extend their learning opportunities outside the classroom (Kang, 2005).

Secondly, as a culmination, WTC can be understood as a learning outcome because most people approach the task with the goal of actually using the TL outside the classroom. Only a small minority of learners will study a language for the pleasure that mastering it inside the classroom may bring. Although the contexts of use may vary, teachers and learners typically seek to develop sufficient levels of proficiency that would allow interaction with people and/or texts from other cultures. When competent TL learners restrict their WTC to the inner sanctum of the language classroom, the lofty social and political goals of language instruction – bringing cultures into contact and nations together – will not be achieved. 'By considering why a person is willing to talk at one time and not another, we can appreciate the important factors influencing classroom communication and 'real world' contact' (MacIntyre et al., 1998: 558).

Teachers often frame the ultimate goal of their language instruction in terms of attaining communicative competency; however being proficient does not necessarily guarantee that learners will use the language in communicative situations. Willing and able are two different things. MacIntyre et al. (1998) suggest that communicative competency falls a few steps short of the goal (or more aptly, a few clay bricks short of a full pyramid). The fundamental goal of language instruction should be producing students who are willing to use the language for authentic purposes. 'There is an unfortunate tendency for people in general and language learners in particular, to fail to act on their intentions' (MacIntyre & Doucette, 2010), and without the decision to act upon those behavioral intentions to communicate, learners may still not use the language, despite their ability and the opportunity to do so. Teachers who understand the many facilitating and inhibiting forces involved in TL learners' WTC will be better equipped to put into place general classroom guidelines and implement activities that will push learners to take that ultimate leap into language use.

Capitalizing on WTC: An Action Plan

Provide the greatest number of facilitating WTC factors

MacIntyre (2012) proposed the analogy of currents and waves of WTC. Currents are 'long lasting, deep-running, broad patterns of movement,' and waves, 'easy-to-see, transient, they are here and then they are gone, their action may seem random, and they are always somewhat unpredictable.'

WTC contains both long-term patterns as well as variables that fluctuate in the moment and are dependent upon a choice to communicate with a specific person at a specific time; together the enduring and situational features create a fascinating and complex process. The interplay of the situational features of WTC with the relative stability of the psychology of the individual speaker and their social milieu led MacIntyre (2007: 564) to argue: 'Methodologies must be adapted to focus upon the dynamic process of choosing to initiate or avoid second language communication when the opportunity arises.' Furthering this argument, MacIntyre and Legatto (2011), describe WTC as a dynamic system where there is variation as time progresses and where each state is somewhat reliant upon the previous one. The interconnectedness of the linguistic, social, cognitive and emotional systems that guide WTC can either function in tandem to facilitate interaction or interfere with each other and restrict the communication attempt. With this complexity in mind, we are best to heed the advice of Kang (2005). Kang found that when teachers provide the greatest number of facilitating WTC factors and discontinue spotlighting one component at the expense of others, learners will be more likely to capitalize on communication opportunities to interact in the classroom.

Concentrate on reducing restraining forces first

MacIntyre (2012) discusses both enduring and situational influences on WTC, as well as its driving vs. restraining forces. Citing Lewin (1951), MacIntyre's advice to language teachers is to focus on the momentary influences evidenced in the classroom as they will have greater impact on action than general influences, arguing that proximal factors shape individuals' specific actions in the moment more than distal ones. He also suggests that it is easier to modify a person's action in a specific situation by reducing the restraining forces than by trying to increase the driving forces. That is to say, if a learner is both motivated and anxious, to the extent that anxiety is the restraining force and motivation is the driving force, on balance, teachers will have more to gain by diminishing the anxiety before taking on motivation.

Explore learners' ambivalence and driving/restraining forces

MacIntyre et al. (2011) also comment on the moment-to-moment dynamic nature of WTC and the role that the social situation plays, in particular the key role played by the communication partner(s). The primary implication arising from their diary study was that 'the situations in which learners are most willing to communicate are not radically different from those in which they are least willing. Subtle features of the learners or the context can lead a student to speak up or to remain quiet, and the psychological situation can change rapidly. It might be helpful for teachers to approach students as if they lived in a state of ambivalence toward learning – experiencing both reasons to approach and reasons to avoid speaking the TL (p. 93).' This state of affairs might be frustrating to the teacher looking for the recipe that creates high WTC. Should error correction be avoided because it reduces WTC? – it depends. Does speaking with a friend in the TL facilitate WTC? – it depends. Does being praised by a teacher or school principal increase WTC? – it depends. Does speaking with a more capable fellow student increase WTC? – it depends. There is not a firm list of Dos and Don'ts, rather learners interpret and re-interpret the actions of teachers and peers in context. Teachers who are sensitive to the on-going fluctuations between attractor or repeller states have it within their means to capitalize on the systems that guide WTC to increase learners' desire to interact in the TL. In this chapter's Activities Section, Activities One and Two allow learners to explore both ambivalence and their driving/restraining forces.

Encourage learners to plan for hesitations

Although learners might have the intention to interact, they may still fail to act upon their intentions. To understand this phenomenon, MacIntyre and Doucette (2010), using Kuhl's Action Theory (1994), set out to discover the relationship between WTC and the three behaviors that undergird the implementation of intentions: hesitation (the ability to begin a task), preoccupation (the ability to focus on the task), and volatility (the ability to follow through to task completion). Their findings provide some important guidelines for language teachers. First, when considering learners' hesitation, where learners are unable to translate decisions into actions, MacIntyre and Doucette (2010) recommend the use of implementation intentions or 'if-then' plans which may increase the likelihood of goal attainment. For this, learners proceed with the activation of expected situational cues (if-process) or automating the response to that cue as directed by the goal (then-process). 'By making use of implementation intentions, learners might become better able to identify situational cues that provide them with the opportunity to communicate in their second language and might also be able to identify their hesitations.' (MacIntyre & Doucette, 2010: 169). Natural conversation is exquisitely well timed. Just a moment's hesitation may cause a significant blow to conversational fluency; learners who have planned methods in advance for dealing with uncomfortable conversational pauses may be better equipped to react quickly and seize the opportunity for conversation.

Another recommendation stemming from this study centered on mitigating the hindering effects of the Action Control concept of preoccupation, where learners fail to initiate or modify their behavior due to intrusive and enduring thoughts. The authors reveal that focusing on past experiences can be used to heighten learners' perceptions of language competence, even if a previously encountered TL situation did not go well. If they are framed as a temporary setback, unsuccessful moments can serve as motivation to excel in the future, and hence become an opportunity to learn. Activities Three, Four and Five in the Activities Section encourage learners to focus on past experiences to increase perceived self-competence, convert their intentions into actions through If-Then scenarios, and plan for hesitations.

Look to potential future possibilities to use the target language

While focusing on past communication experiences can encourage greater WTC, looking into the future may also be advantageous. Yashima *et al.* (2004) suggest that learners who can conceptualize when and how they could potentially use their TL are more likely to initiate communication behavior. They hypothesize that learners who see results in their daily effort to achieve their immediate goals feel a stronger sense of personal relevance because they are using language for communication and relating themselves to the world, becoming more increasingly aware of their potential and ways to contribute. Activity Six in the Activities Section provides an occasion for learners to explore potential future TL opportunities.

Increase classroom excitement and sense of security

Driven by a desire to raise language learners' situational WTC, Kang (2005) makes a variety of recommendations for language teachers to increase learners' excitement, responsibility and security. Her advice considers topic choices, interlocutors and conversational contexts. She claims that inherently interesting topics that are covered both within a lesson and across lessons that tap into learner's background knowledge and experience and which drive personal and/or intergroup motives will increase the excitement in the classroom. To find these topics of interest to both individuals and the class as a whole, Kang (2005) advocates brainstorming, surveying student opinion and permitting student topic selection. Particularly for insecure learners, those with lower proficiency, and those fearful of making mistakes, Kang (2005) recommends creating a safe environment where teacher and peers listen carefully, smile, and provide active responses. Keeping group numbers small and dividing learners by their interests, nationality and proficiency for tasks and discussion may also keep excitement and security levels high. Activity Seven taps into small group brainstorming to include learners in class topic and task selection.

Use group work to facilitate greater self-confidence, social support and WTC

Focusing specifically on WTC in group work in TL classrooms, Fushino (2010) discovered that a learners' beliefs influenced their WTC via their TL confidence in communicating. Thus, to increase WTC in group work, teachers should find ways to elevate communication confidence and beliefs about the worthiness of working in groups, thus triggering active interaction among students in the TL. In particular, Fushino (2010: 718) states: '... teachers should make extra efforts to reduce communication apprehension in TL group work by providing team-building activities with which group members can develop bonds and thus can reduce their communication apprehension. Facilitating a supportive atmosphere, where students listen to each other attentively and praise each other's effort and accomplishments and teachers' noncritical attitudes are also important.' According to Yashima (2012: 131), 'a combination of a familiar interlocutor and a dyad or a small group may lead to higher WTC.'

Along those same lines, MacIntyre *et al.* (2001) discovered that social support, especially from friends, was another cohesion-building variable that could foster greater outside-the-class WTC, higher orientations for travel, and friendship with TL counterparts. The more learners communicate inside the classroom, the greater the probability of learners communicating outside the classroom; that is why in-class communication is imperative as preparation for language use in the 'real world'. Activity Eight allows learners to reflect upon the worthiness of working in groups and provides opportunities to demonstrate support through extolling the virtues of individual group members.

Do not lose sight of important distal WTC factors: Intergroup climate

Most of our pedagogical guidelines have been targeting the more proximal, momentary WTC influences that steer language learners. The WTC concept, however, was originally defined as a 'trait-like' or stable predisposition. Later it was graphically portrayed in a heuristic pyramid model that captured the social psychological influences that converge at the moment of decision. Despite the fact that most of the recent work on WTC has moved the concept toward the more momentary, proximal influences, the creators of the original idea have not rejected the notion of long-term patterns. Any of the more enduring, stable influences could come to the forefront and become factors mitigating WTC, even personality and intergroup climate that are deemed the most distal and enduring variables (MacIntyre, 2012).

Sociolinguists have much to say about the role of intergroup climate (one of the enduring influences in the bottom layer of the WTC pyramid) in language learning. For example, Norton (1995) speculates about the variable nature of why learners will at times be willing to speak and at others they choose to remain silent. She credits this to the changing social distances between a specific group of language learners and the TL community, and to identity shifts in relation to self and the social milieu that occur every time an individual contemplates speaking. Power relations evidenced in intergroup climate result in driving and restraining forces within the language learner who is marginalized in one context, but in another, feels encouraged because he or she is highly valued. When WTC is examined through an intergroup climate lens, language learners who struggle from one intergroup position can be helped to reframe the relationship with interlocutors. That is, learners who re-evaluate their social position toward an emerging sense of power may feel more inclined to communicate in the social networks of their learning communities (Norton & Toohey, 2001: 318). For activities that permit learners to explore intergroup climate and to capitalize upon it through increased WTC, consider activities one through five in our chapter on Motivation.

Raise learners' awareness of their personalities and dispositional temperaments

Personality, another distal and enduring WTC influence, is an aspect of individuality in language learning that broadly overlaps with temperament but is distinguished from 'mood' which refers to a 'highly volatile, changing state' (Dörnyei, 2005: 11). Moods are the more common experience, with each day being shaped in subtle ways by one or more moods. More broadly, personality or temperament is a stable tendency for an individual to experience certain moods and emotions, and is often linked to physiology (MacIntyre & Gregersen, 2012a). Personality differences exist among individual learners that will influence whether they approach or avoid communication and teachers who are aware of these differences will be able to incorporate tasks and interaction opportunities that stimulate language learners to choose to initiate conversation. Activity Nine implements awareness-raising tasks where learners will explore their own dispositional temperaments particularly concerning a move toward more optimistic thinking.

Remember that anxiety is felt at all levels of proficiency

The pervasiveness of the notions of 'self' that language learners bring to any TL communicative event and their powerful effects on WTC dictate that specific guidelines for their enhancement be included. Researchers have consistently found that high FL anxiety and low TL self-confidence are the greatest predictors of a learners' unwillingness to communicate. In fact, MacIntyre et al.'s (2003: 603) investigation into talking to learn produced what they called 'possibly counter-intuitive' evidence that anxiety might be a greater problem for more advanced learners. Teachers consistently place students in learning situations beyond their comfort zone; even at advanced levels, students are expected to deal with unfamiliar material. We recommended that teachers consider anxiety reduction even among advanced learners. The anxiety guidelines and activities in Chapter 1 may also bring remediation to language learners who choose not to interact when TL opportunities arise.

Heed the significance of self-esteem in WTC

In defining self-esteem, Arnold (2007) cautions teachers against using empty praise which may lead to unreasonable expectations and unrealistic perceptions of competence. She states (p. 18), 'Confidence comes from competence. Realistic concern with learner self-esteem in the language classroom does not focus on creating false beliefs of a positive nature to replace the negative ones. Rather, it is a question of providing learners with the means to succeed in their language learning while at the same time reducing any limiting false beliefs about their worth and their abilities that keep them from reaching their potential. Learners must both *be* competent and *feel* competent.' Hence, learners must have both a constructive and true belief about themselves and their competence and also the dedication and accountability that occurs as they achieve valuable objectives.

Citing Reasoner's model of self-esteem (1982), Arnold (2007) suggests some specific applications to language classrooms using the components of security (feeling emotionally and physically safe), identity (knowing oneself), belonging (feeling accepted by others), purpose (understanding of what one wants to do and how to go about it), and competence (understanding that one can get the job done). These components work together when: (1) a secure environment is fostered that encourages risk-taking; (2) learners' interactions reaffirm positive identity construction; (3) learners know one another and feel a sense of social connection; (4) learners set manageable, short-term goals; and (5) learners use positive self-talk, develop autonomy, and focus on previous success in goal attainment. Only when the classroom climate is genuine, accepting and empathetic can learners achieve the most productive levels of self-esteem. Perhaps the word for this classroom is, optimistic. The distinction between self-esteem and optimism might help draw the focus away from strategies that make learners feel good toward strategies that give learners hope for the future. Seligman (2006) describes very clearly how optimism is learned. Teachers who can shift the focus away from permanent, pervasive, and personal explanations for difficulties toward temporary, specific and hopeful explanations may be helping students develop a sense of authentic self-esteem. Activity Ten contains a series of tasks for developing the five components of self-esteem to increase WTC and Activity Eleven looks at teacher feedback to create optimism.

To conclude the 'Premise' part of this chapter, we leave you with the words of Yashima (2012: 132–3):

> Communication is an inherently social process. It takes at least two people to communicate. This somewhat contradicts the notion of WTC as an individual tendency...WTC can only be enhanced and developed through social processes and communicating with others. It takes two to tango. Yet each person needs to be willing to dance. WTC may be created in collaborative work, yet how much an individual is willing to participate crucially affects the outcome.

... To Practice

WTC Activities

The following research-based activities, sequenced according to the order of the rationale presented in the preceding premise section, incorporate tasks that are meant to increase learners' WTC. They tap into learners' ambivalence, driving/restraining forces, past experiences, intentions, hesitations and personal preferences for tasks and topics. We also provide activities that consider learners with contrasting temperaments and self-esteem levels to target the affective needs that individuality generates.

WTC Activity 1: Flushing out Ambivalence through the Focused Essay Technique (Adapted from MacIntyre *et al.*, 2011)

How often my fear and ambivalence are rooted in what somebody else may think. But I need not present my actions, my words, myself for somebody else's approval. And basing my decisions on somebody else's approval or making my own approval contingent on somebody else's only postpones what I really want. – Jan Denise

Level: Intermediate/Advanced

Procedure:

(1) Preface this activity by explaining that its purpose is for learners to contemplate for themselves and reveal to others the subtle features of who they are and the contexts in which they find themselves that encourage them to speak up or remain silent.

(2) Instruct learners for the next six weeks to provide in their language learning journals six circumstances in which they were most willing to communicate in their TL and six in which they were least willing. In each of the entries, invite learners to define who they spoke with, where the conversation transpired, and to provide insights into how they felt about the encounter.

(3) Upon completion of the six weeks, ask learners to form groups of five and compare their responses by filling in the following template:

MOST WILLING		
Interlocutors	Contexts	Feelings
LEAST WILLING		
Interlocutors	Contexts	Feelings

(4) Ask small group participants to discuss the similarities and differences in their responses and summarize the results of the template. Invite each group to nominate a reporter.

(5) In whole group, ask the reporters from each group to share their summaries. Discuss the learners' reasons for approaching and avoiding TL communication specifically focusing on people, contexts and feelings.

(6) De-brief this activity by asking for volunteers to share ideas on how learners' WTC and desire to interact in the TL might be increased.

MODIFICATION:

Technology:

(1) Invite learners to write their entries electronically (Step 2).

(2) Put the template online as a wiki document. Divide learners into groups of five. Ask members to cut and paste their entries into the appropriate columns (Step 3).

(3) Ask small group members to summarize the results of their wiki document in a final electronic entry in their language learning diaries.

WTC Activity 2: Personal Exploration into WTC Influences: Discovering My Driving and Restraining Forces

They may forget what you said, but they will never forget how you made them feel. – Carl Buechner

Level: All

Procedure:

(1) Preface this activity by explaining that its purpose is for learners to explore the driving and restraining forces of their own WTC and whether these forces are momentarily or generally present in their communication decisions.

(2) Have learners keep a running daily list in their language diaries of the TL interaction opportunities that arise during the next two weeks, giving enough details so as to remember the incident later, and to divide them into two columns:
(A) Opportunities Seized and (B) Opportunities Lost.

(3) After two weeks of daily entries, tell learners to re-create the following table and analyze their 'opportunities' and reflect upon the 'driving forces' or 'restraining forces' that were present at the moment of their decision to engage in communication or not. Explain that there may be several influencing factors in their decision to seize or ignore the communication opportunity, so to include all of the forces that are pertinent in each instance. An example is given for each column.

Opportunities Seized	Driving forces	Opportunities Lost	Restraining forces
I initiated a conversation with a native speaker in the grocery store	1. This specific person made me want to approach. 2. I was confident I had all the vocabulary necessary to carry out the conversation.	I knew an answer in class but I did not want to volunteer	1. At that particular moment my self-confidence failed me. 2. I was not willing to expose myself to this group.

(4) Next, tell learners to look for tendencies in their responses and to finish the following two sentences on a separate piece of paper:
    (a) My three main driving forces that compelled my WTC were:
    (b) My three main restraining forces that impeded my WTC were:
(5) Collect the papers, shuffle them, and randomly pass them back to the class. Ask learners to read the sentences and write a reaction or give some feedback to the peer who wrote it. When individuals finish their written responses, tell them to exchange papers with someone who has also finished reading and reacting to the sentences they read. Have the class continue reading, writing and exchanging papers until everyone has responded to approximately five or six papers.
(6) Return the papers to their original owners and provide time for learners to read their peers' feedback.
(7) Debrief this activity by asking learners whether the sentences they read and responded to had similar driving and restraining forces as their own. Encourage learners to begin working on eliminating the restraining forces to their WTC and then concentrate on energizing their driving forces (MacIntyre, 2012).

MODIFICATIONS:

Emergent learners: Provide a list of possible driving and restraining forces written in simplified TL form, explain their significance, and allow learners to choose from among them.

Technology:

(1) To keep their two week daily list of TL interaction opportunities (Step 2):
    (a) For oral practice, learners use mobile hand-held electronic recording devices.
    (b) For written practice, learners use word processing to keep an electronic journal.
(2) To respond to the two sentence completion tasks (Step 4), post two teacher-created threads each corresponding to one of the 'driving' and 'restraining' forces on the electronic class Discussion Board.
(3) De-brief (Step 7) with learners responding to at least five of their peers' posts.

WTC Activity 3: Focusing on Past Experiences for Increased Perceived Competence

Experience tells you what to do; confidence allows you to do it. – Stan Smith

Level: All

Procedure:

(1) Preface this activity by explaining that its purpose is for learners to focus on past TL experiences so they may heighten their perceptions of their own language competence. This allows individuals to self-assess their language skill, which in turn may enhance their perceived competence (MacIntyre & Doucette, 2010).

(2) Invite learners to review their 'Opportunities Seized/Opportunities Lost' table from Activity 2 and draw their attention to the 'opportunities seized' column. Tell learners to re-write each of the seized opportunities on a separate piece of paper, leaving a space after each entry for two numbers.

(3) On a scale from 1 to 5 (1 = very low; 2 = low; 3 = neither high nor low; 4 = high; 5 = very high), tell learners to self-assess their language skill in each 'seized' TL interaction.

(4) Next, ask learners to evaluate the same 'seized' TL opportunities, but this time self-assessing perceived linguistic competence.

(5) For those opportunities self-assessed with low scores, tell learners to write a few sentences in their language diaries about how these experiences could serve as motivation to excel in the future and transform them into opportunities for learning.

(6) For those opportunities self-assessed with high scores, tell learners to write about how these confidence-boosting experiences can be kept at the forefront of their minds as they pursue future communication opportunities.

(7) De-brief this activity by asking volunteers to share some of their reflections. Remind learners that focusing on past language experiences – whether they are negative and serve as motivation to excel in the future, or they are positive and act as confidence enhancers – is an activity that will make individuals more self-aware of their WTC.

MODIFICATIONS:
Technology:

(1) To collect a class-created list of ideas of how to transform low self-assessed scores into future learning opportunities and to how to

relish confidence boosting self-assessments (Steps 5 and 6), learners tweet using two different hash tags.
(2) To de-brief (Step 7) learners access the lists via twitter and tweet two responses—one to each list.

WTC Activity 4: If-Then Scenarios: Converting Intentions into Actions

Remember, people will judge you by your actions, not your intentions. You may have a heart of gold – but so does a hard-boiled egg. – Unknown

Level: Intermediate/Advanced

Preparation:

(1) Write the following on the board: 'If situation Y is encountered, then I will initiate behavior Z in order to reach goal X.'
(2) Under that, create three columns with the following headings: 'Y' (Problems en route/bumps in the road); 'Z' (Contingency plan); and X (Desired destination)

Procedure:

(1) Preface this activity by explaining that the objective is to increase the likelihood of learners attaining their language goals by converting many of the intentions they have into actions.
(2) Divide learners into three groups of equal size and distribute 30 post-it notes in three different colors (ten of each color). Designate one color for 'Y'; one color for 'Z' and the other color for 'X.'
(3) Instruct each group to brainstorm and come to consensus on ten goals (both short term and long term) that they would like to attain in their language learning and write one on each X-colored post-it note.
(4) Tell Group 1 to go to the board and place their first X-colored post-it note with their goal written on it in the third column under 'X (Desired destination).' Then, instruct Group 2 to confer quickly and propose a possible obstacle that could arise to de-rail that goal's attainment. Tell them to write it down on the Y-colored post-it note and place it in the first column under 'Y (Problems en route/bumps in the road).' Then have Group 3 consider solutions to Group 2's problem to achieve Group 1's goal and write it down

on the Z-colored post-it note and place it in column two on the board.

(5) After this first round of if/then plans is complete, instruct Group 2 to place their X-colored post-it note with their first goal on the board; then ask Group 3 to create the obstacle and tell Group 1 to explore solutions.

(6) Continue the activity until all of the goals from the three groups have been processed.

(7) De-brief this activity by asking volunteers to share which item from each of the columns is personally most significant. Explain that setting goals, identifying potential obstacles and planning solutions in advance may help them to react more quickly and seize more communication opportunities.

MODIFICATION:

Emergent learners: Provide 30 post-it notes prepared in advance with 10 goals, 10 obstacles and 10 solutions already written. Have groups work through steps four through seven.

Large groups:

(1) Arrange for two or three sets of three groups to work simultaneously (Steps 2–6).

(2) De-brief (Step 7) by using the same small groups or invite learners to write responses to the de-briefing prompt in their language diaries.

Technology:

(1) Ask learners to collaborate and create using Electronic brainstorming or a wiki to generate their 10 goals (Step 3).

(2) The collaborative nature of the wiki and its potential to display learner contributions in a node or tree structure make it a viable technology tool with which groups, each assigned to their own computer, can collaborate and respond to other groups' postings (Steps 4–6).

(3) Because the de-briefing prompt (Step 7) demands a relatively short response, tell learners to tweet their response. Remind learners to access the complete list on Twitter to read their classmates' tweets.

WTC Activity 5: He Who Hesitates is Lost: Advanced Planning for Dealing with Uncomfortable Conversational Pauses

Upon the plains of hesitation bleach the bones of countless millions, who when on the dawn of victory paused to rest, and there resting died. – John Dretschmer

Level: All

Procedure:

(1) Preface this activity by explaining that its purpose is to have learners plan methods in advance for dealing with uncomfortable conversational pauses. Because conversation occurs at such a rapid pace, and conversational turn-taking is fraught with many regulations, a language learner who hesitates for even a second will profoundly impact the fluidity and rhythm of conversation (MacIntyre & Doucette, 2010). This in turn may lead to higher anxiety and a greater unwillingness to initiate conversation when future occasions arise.

(2) Put the following 'hesitation causes' on small slips of paper and place them in a hat:
   (a) I don't want to be wrong
   (b) I don't want to be offensive
   (c) I am searching for the right word
   (d) I got distracted from the conversation
   (e) I don't know how to respond (what is expected?)
   (f) I want to please
   (g) I don't understand what is being asked
   (h) I don't want to talk to this person
   (i) I don't want to go in the direction this conversation is going
   (j) I forgot the word
   (k) I want to plan the entire phrase in my head before I say it
   (l) I want to think twice about what I am going to say
   (m) I don't know how to pronounce the word I want to say
   (n) With what level of formality should I respond to this person?
   (o) I need more time to process what I just heard
   (p) I don't want this person to realize I am not that fluent.

(3) Pair learners and ask each dyad to draw a slip from the hat and take several minutes to prepare a role play to act out the scenario they drew. Next, invite pairs to take turns briefly role playing it in front of the group. This presents the problem of hesitations.

(4) Next, give learners a few minutes to plan three different strategies for dealing with their 'hesitation cause.' Invite each pair to take a

turn re-enacting their scenario, but this time presenting plans for dealing with it. This presents solutions to hesitations.

(5) De-brief this activity by asking learners whether they believe that planning methods in advance for dealing with uncomfortable conversational pauses will better equip them to react quickly and seize opportunities for communication. Discuss.

MODIFICATIONS:

Large groups:

(1) Assign more than one dyad to each 'hesitation cause.'
(2) For teachers wanting to exercise their creativity, dabble with inventing more hesitation causes!

Technology: Because many of the problems/solutions that learners present (Steps 3 and 4) may contain nonverbal elements, we recommend that any technology used also has a video component:

(1) Learners videotape their role plays and play them back to the class in a problem/solution format (Steps 3 and 4); or
(2) Learners use their webcams or video cameras to present their role plays through Voicethread.

WTC Activity 6: Looking to Future Communication Opportunities for Increased WTC

Communication works for those who work at it. – John Powell

Level: All

Procedure:

(1) Preface this activity by explaining that through an exploration of the future uses of their TL, the language will become more personally relevant and meaningful, thus making learners' willingness to engage in it even greater.
(2) Ask learners to close their eyes, listen to the following sentence, and complete it in their minds: '(The target language being learned) will allow me to achieve so many interpersonal goals like ....' Give them several moments to contemplate. Next, recite: 'It will also allow me

to achieve so many intercultural goals like ...' Provide several more moments for reflection. On two separate slips of paper, instruct learners to write their favorite response to each of the sentence completions.

(3) Invite learners to mingle, talking to others about their choice ending for the first phrase concerning interpersonal goals until they find others with similar responses. In small groups of individuals with like-minded answers, ask learners to imagine together future opportunities to engage in the TL where their goal is met. Create a list.

(4) Repeat the exercise, but this time ask learners to consider their responses to the second sentence completion concerning intercultural goals.

(5) De-brief this activity by asking small groups to share their lists. Ask whether it was helpful to focus on their TL as a means to an end rather than as an end in itself.

WTC Activity 7: Class Topic/Task Selection: Tapping into Small Group Brainstorming

Friends, you and me ... you brought another friend ... and then there were three ... we started our group ... our circle of friends ... and like that circle ... there is no beginning or end. – Eleanor Roosevelt

Level: All

Procedure:

(1) Preface this activity by explaining that its purpose is to increase the excitement, security and WTC in language class by: (a) tapping into their background knowledge and experience to uncover what drives their personal and group motives; and (b) having them interact with counterparts of similar interests, nationalities and proficiency levels (Kang, 2005).

(2) Tell learners that this game is about forming and reforming groups as quickly as possible, with creative brainstorming in between. Explain that a criterion will be called out by which learners must form a group as quickly as possible; once groups are formed, ask each group to brainstorm two lists: (a) Activities and tasks they would like to do in class; and (b) Topics of interest for classroom discussion.

(3) The first criterion is interest. Tell learners to find four like-minded peers who share an interest. Have them brainstorm a list of

activities and another of tasks with a recorder writing them down. Collect the papers.

(4) The second criterion is nationality. Tell learners to find four peers who share their nationality. If there are learners with no shared heritage, tell them to form groups by where they have traveled. Have them brainstorm two more lists. Collect the papers.

(5) The third criterion is proficiency. Tell learners to find four peers whose perceived linguistic self-competence is relatively similar. Have them brainstorm two more lists. Collect the papers.

(6) De-brief this activity by asking learners what changes they noticed in the way different groups interacted. Were the exchanges different when combined with learners based upon interests, nationalities or proficiencies? Explain that their input is integral to planning future lessons where their selected topics and tasks will encourage an exciting, secure classroom where language learners are willing to communicate.

MODIFICATIONS:

Emergent learners: Make an exhaustive list of activities and topics available to the class, and clarify any vocabulary confusion. When groups form, have each choose their top five from each list.

Technology: When groups are formed according to the criterion, rather than a recorder writing the answers on paper to be collected, each group tweets their responses with a hash tag that defines their unifying feature (Steps 3–5). This permits teachers to easily access the lists and also to disseminate it later for further learner feedback.

WTC Activity 8: Group Groupies: Building Bonds

Individually we are one drop; together we are an ocean. – Ryunosuke Satoro

Level: All

Procedure:

(1) Preface this activity by explaining that when group members believe that working in groups is a worthy endeavor and when individual members feel valued through praise, they will more than likely increase their WTC.

(2) Place learners in groups of five with others they know well. Tell groups to brainstorm a list of things that they can accomplish in groups that cannot be done alone. Ask small groups to share their responses with the whole class.

(3) Have members of the small groups write their names on a slip of paper and put them in a hat or bag. Pass the hat or bag around the group asking each member to extract one name. Tell learners to think about one characteristic of the person whose name they drew that they appreciate. Using material both inside and outside the classroom, ask individuals to find a gift for their selected person. For example, 'Here is a stick of glue. It represents your ability to help us stick together as a group.'

(4) When learners have had enough time to scavenge for their gift, ask the small groups to hold gift-giving ceremonies where learners bestow their gifts upon one another.

(5) De-brief this activity by reinforcing the idea that supporting one another and giving praise when it is due is an important part of positive group dynamics in the language classroom, and when learners value the work they do in groups and feel valued as a member of the group, then individuals will be more likely to engage in TL communication.

MODIFICATIONS:

Technology: Allow learners to bestow 'virtual' gifts rather than the 'real' thing. For example, 'I would like to give you this glue stick that I found online at the office supply store ...' (Step 4).

WTC Activity 9: Capitalizing on 'Optimism'

The principle of all successful effort is to try to do not what is absolutely the best, but what is easily within our power, and suited for our temperament and condition. – John Ruskin

Level: Intermediate/Advanced

Procedure:

(1) Preface this activity by explaining that its objective is to improve learners' WTC by providing opportunities for learners to explore their optimism.

(2) To discover learners' temperament disposition, ask learners to complete the 'Language Classroom Temperament Scale' found at the end of this activity and to self-score using the subsequent scoring key.

(3) Introduce what Seligman (2006) calls the 'ABCDE model' (A = Adversity; B = Belief; C = Consequences; D = Disputation; and E = Energization)

- **Adversity** is a situation that happens (e.g. your teacher gave you a failing grade on your last grammar test).
- **Belief** is how one interprets it (You think: 'the teacher has it in for me!).
- **Consequences** are feelings and actions stemming from the beliefs (You become upset and your anxiety increases as you think about your language class). In order to learn optimism, learners must first understand their dispositional reaction and interpretation of adversity.

(4) Tell learners to keep track of any adverse experiences they have with the language and the beliefs and consequences that followed for two days in their language diaries. This is the 'A' in the model.

(5) Ask learners to highlight instances of pessimism they find in their written descriptions of events. This is the 'D' (for Disputation) in the model: Look for counter-evidence to negative beliefs, the causes of the event, or the implications.

(6) For 'Disputation', tell learners to silently read their highlighted 'Adversity' events followed by their 'Beliefs' about the event and their 'Consequences.' Invite learners to individually brainstorm a list of potential counter-evidence to: (a) the negative beliefs in general; (b) the causes of the event; or (c) the implications. Using the above example of the failing grade on the grammar test, 'Disputation' might sound like this: 'I am over-reacting. Truth is, I was watching tv the night before instead of studying. I have gotten good grades before and when I put in a greater effort, I have done well. I will try harder next time.'

(7) De-brief this activity in dyads, asking one learner to read his/her new scripts aloud to the other and come up with three reasons why it would be beneficial to move on from adversity in each situation.

Language classroom dispositional temperament scale

(Items adapted from Seligman's 'Learned Optimism Scale' [Seligman, 2006]).

(1) Your language teacher corrects a classmate's error a bit harshly. You think:
      (a) My teacher is so insensitive!
      (b) *My teacher must be having a bad day.*
(2) Your best friend just got the top score in your language class on the oral exam. You think:
      (a) Wow! My friend is really a hard worker
      (b) *Wow! My friend is really lucky to get this honor!*
(3) You get hired to tutor someone to learn your TL even though other applicants were extremely qualified. You think:
      (a) I must have been more qualified than I gave myself credit for!
      (b) *I must have interviewed really well!*
(4) You meet a new conversation partner at a party who will be a great help in gaining more language proficiency. You think:
      (a) Lucky me! I was in the right place at the right time.
      (b) *I was smart to come to this party tonight*
(5) You are the first one in your class to find the answer to your teacher's comprehension question in a reading passage. You think:
      (a) Hey! How lucky!
      (b) *Hey! I'm pretty observant!*
(6) Your teacher just announced a pop quiz and you had forgotten your book in the classroom the day before so you did not study. You think:
      (a) This must not be my day!
      (b) *I am so unlucky!*
(7) You get the highest score on a grammar test. You think:
      (a) Wow! I got lucky with those questions! They were all ones I knew!
      (b) *Wow! I sure must know my grammar! I guess I have a good memory!*
(8) You find you don't have the money at the end of the month to buy the language book you wanted. You think:
      (a) It's been a financially heavy month for me. It will be better next month.
      (b) *I'm not very good at managing my money. This is a serious problem.*
(9) You miss your bus that you wanted to take to arrive early to your class and have to wait for another one. You think:
      (a) There's lots of traffic. I guess I'll make the next one that comes.
      (b) *I should have planned better. I'm always late and I knew this would happen.*
(10) You have been studying hard to get pass your language class with high scores, and you just got top marks on your public presentation. You think:
      (a) My studying strategies really work! I hope I can continue!

(b) *My hard work is paying off! I'll be speaking my target language in no time!*

(11) You're trying to complete some computer assisted language learning tasks that were assigned for independent study, and after hours of trying, you still cannot get it. You think:
(a) Wow! Technology is so complex! It will take me a bit longer to finally get this.
(b) *I am just not good at computers. I will fall behind, but there's nothing I can do.*

(12) You stay up half the night preparing for an exam, and you are thoroughly exhausted the next morning. You think:
(a) Wow! I am not as young as I used to be!
(b) *Wow! I worked hard last night!*

SCORING: 1) a = 0; b = 1; 2) a = 1; b = 0; 3) a = 1; b = 0; 4) a = 0; b = 1; 5) a = 0; b = 1; 6) a = 0; b = 1; 7) a = 0; b = 1; 8) a = 1; b = 0; 9) a = 1; b = 0; 10) a = 0; b = 1; 11) a = 1; b = 0; 12) a = 0; b = 0.

MODIFICATION:

Technology:

(1) Journals entries (Step 5) can be written electronically on a computer or orally recorded through a mobile, hand-held device.
(2) Electronic brainstorming or a wiki where learners collaborate and create are both options for generating counter-evidence (Step 7) and for reflecting upon reasons for moving on from diversity (Step 8).

WTC Activity 10: Developing Five Components of Self-Esteem for Increased WTC (Adapted from Arnold, 2007)

Risk more than others think is safe. Care more than others think is wise. Dream more than others think is practical. Expect more than others think is possible. – Claude Bissell

Level: Intermediate/Advanced

Procedure:

(1) Preface this activity by explaining that its purpose is to enhance learners' WTC through exploring five components of self-esteem. Explain that while becoming acquainted with each other and

working in groups, learners foster their sense of **belonging**; that as they set short-term group goals for risk-taking they promote their feelings of **security** and **purpose**; and that as they become 'mirrors' and 'inner voices' for each other, they nurture their **identity and competence.**

(2) Place learners in teams of five and designate a recorder for each. Give a roll of toilet paper to each group. Explain they are going camping and need to take as much toilet paper as they need for a two day trip. Once everyone has an ample supply, explain that for every square in their possession, they must share something that they perceive would be risk-taking in using the TL. (Define risk as the tendency to engage in behaviors that have the potential to be harmful or dangerous, yet at the same time provide the opportunity for some kind of outcome that can be perceived as positive.) Tell the designated recorder to list everyone's contribution.

(3) Tell team members to use the lists to come to a consensus on five risk-taking activities and then create a goal plan for achieving it. For example, if Team 1 reaches consensus that Learner A's risk-taking idea to volunteer to speak in class at least three times during every class period is one that they want to adopt, their next step is to outline a short-term goal plan so that all team members work together to accomplish it. Use the following template:

	Action Steps	Timeline (by when?)	Potential obstacles	Evidence of success
Risk-taking Goal #1:	1. 2. 3.			
Risk-taking Goal #2	1. 2. 3.			
Risk-taking Goal #3	1. 2. 3.			

(4) Once teams formulate their risk-taking actions plans, explain that the 'positive self-talk' strategies from previous activities will be expanded as group members strive to be positive 'inner voices' for each other. To do this, provide regularly scheduled class time for learners to meet and discuss whether their 'potential obstacles' have become realities and what 'evidence of success' is available.

(5) Explain that once the timeline for the Risk-taking Goal plan has run its complete course, the five team members will become mirrors for each other. Place the five team members' names in a hat. Each member extracts one name. Tell learners that for the following class period, the drawer of the name will find two gifts for the person whose name he/she drew. The gifts should represent one positive and one constructively critical message given in response to the Risk-taking process the group completed. For example, 'Here is a paintbrush that represents your artistic creativity, something that all members of our team admire' ... and, 'Here is a blindfold to cover your eyes so that you are less easily distracted by peripheral class-room activity.' If team members cannot find the appropriate object, he/she can mime the gift, which allows any object to be gifted.

(6) De-brief this activity by soliciting learner feedback on how this series of tasks impacted their self-esteem, risk-taking success, and ultimately their WTC.

MODIFICATIONS:

Technology:

(1) Team members use electronic brainstorming to create their initial risk-taking lists (Step 2).
(2) The template for the Goal Plans can be created as a separate wiki which each group can collaboratively fill in (Step 3).
(3) The 'inner voices' sessions can be done through synchronous chats (Step 4).
(4) Team members use 'Google images' to select visual representations of the gifts they would like to give each other (Step 5).

Epilogue

For every complex problem there is an answer that is clear,
simple, and wrong.
– H.L. Mencken

After reviewing the ideas, theories, suggestions and activities in this text, we are left with a pressing question: what is the recipe for success in language learning? Throughout the book we have tried to offer the reader state of the art knowledge about individuality among learners and how a variety of factors work in the language classroom, choosing to let this section tackle the issue of how these different variables work together.

Putting together a plan for capitalizing on the differences among learners is an ongoing process. Much of the literature on this topic can be likened to a kind of recipe. Creating that recipe for success involves considering a variety of individual factors. First we identify the ingredients, and the quantities, then the process of putting them together, like baking cookies. Take a cup of butter, ¾ cup of sugar, 2½ cups of flour and a hint of vanilla. Combine, roll, cut and bake at 350 degrees and you have shortbread cookies.

By analogy, the pedagogical research literature suggests that if we take a language classroom with students who have high levels of motivation, a talkative learning style, strongly imagined future success with TL speakers, and a hint of anxiety, we will have successful learning. The research consistently shows that higher levels of motivation predict success. Research also shows that students who talk in order to learn tend to be more willing to communicate in the long run. Recent research on the self-system shows a very promising connection between the imagination and future success. It has been observed for some time that high levels of anxiety are distracting and debilitating, but students who care about their language performance often do report low-to-moderate levels of anxiety. There is no reason to doubt that this combination of factors will lead to success in most cases.

For teachers, the question remains: how do we begin putting these factors together? How much motivation, willingness to communicate, hoped-for self, and anxiety is the right amount? Research has not taken this more global approach, so it is not possible to offer a single recipe. It probably is not advisable to approach the question of capitalizing on individuality with the recipe metaphor. A teacher will never have the same classroom twice because the learning situation changes on a day-to-day basis. Even if we could identify all of the relevant ingredients, it is not possible to measure them with enough precision to predict how the specific combination will work as the different pieces interact with each other. If we follow a recipe correctly we will get pretty much the same cookies every time. This approach seems implausible when applied to a language classroom, so perhaps a different guiding metaphor is in order.

We would suggest that readers approach the individuals in their classroom much as we approach a weather forecast. In any area where weather systems converge, the local forecaster has a difficult job. For example, on the east coast of Canada where the weather changes quickly, the ingredients of a sunny day are well known: high temperatures, high barometric pressure, low humidity, a southwest breeze and so on. Most of the time the local weather forecaster does a pretty good job of predicting what will happen in a short time (in the next few hours). Weather forecasters generally also do a good job of predicting broad trends in the weather, changes that accompany seasons such as hot summers and cold winters in the Midwestern United States. But in all of these predictions, there is an accepted element of randomness. As we write this, the temperature in both Cape Breton and Iowa is just around the freezing point, so the weather today might feature snow, rain and/or freezing rain. In the bigger picture, a small variation in wind direction or ocean temperature might be enough to turn a hurricane away from land, or toward a city. Under such conditions, it makes sense that the weather forecast explicitly presents some margin of error. We might expect 5 to 10 cm of snow tonight, winds of up to 50 km per hour, and a 30% chance of rain tomorrow. Even though meteorologists know that factors that contribute to the weather, they are not able to measure them precisely enough to give an exact, fool-proof prediction of how those variables will interact.

Returning to the language classroom, the research literature certainly suggests that if we take a student with high levels of motivation, a talkative learning style, strongly imagined future success, and a hint of anxiety, we likely will have successful learning, most of the time. This combination of factors often does predict success; over a long period of time these are positive conditions for a classroom. But the local situation will change on a day-to-day basis. Classrooms are more like dynamic and somewhat unpredictable weather systems than they are like recipes. Although much of this book has been dedicated to reviewing the types of factors most relevant to language learning, we have been hinting at incorporating these constituent parts into a dynamic whole.

Dynamic Systems

There is a growing movement to examine language learning in terms of dynamic systems theory (see Larsen-Freeman & Cameron, 2008; de Bot *et al.*, 2007; Dörnyei & MacIntyre, 2013). The variables that we have addressed throughout this book can be seen as interacting components of the system. Dynamic systems approach the study of language learning more like the meteorologists approach predicting the weather than a baker approaches using a recipe. Dynamic systems take the moment-by-moment changes in behavior, cognition and affect occurring in a classroom as being inherently somewhat unpredictable. Systems will tend to settle into comfortable, relatively stable states, as when a swinging pendulum comes to rest or a beach ball settles for some time as it is blown around on the sand by the wind. These are called attractor states. Even a settled system can be disturbed and will tend to move out of an attractor state because there are always multiple forces acting on it, including at a minimum the inevitable effects of the passage of time. Change is to be expected, even from attractor states. With dynamic systems, each new state of the system is a function of its preceding state combined with the effect of forces acting on that state (Howe & Lewis, 2005). The weather tonight will be what it is partially because of the type of afternoon it was (cool vs. hot, humid vs. dry). Each new state of the system emerges from the previous state of the system. This is where our recipe metaphor really breaks down. A new cookie is a combination of ingredients put together in a specific way. Each cookie is created from its ingredients – it does not emerge from a previous state of the cookie. The weather forecast metaphor recognizes that weather systems are always in motion by describing increasing clouds or diminishing wind. We think about the weather as changing from one state to another, infused with some degree of randomness.

The strength of using Dynamic Systems Theory (DST) to think about capitalizing on individuality in the language classroom lies in the description of how systems change. Disturbances of the system lead to personal development and change over time. Perturbations (disturbances) of an attractor state exert pressure on the system to settle into a new attractor state. In the introduction, we mentioned that tugging on a net in one place will change the shape of the whole net. In a sense, the activities provided on the preceding pages tug on the network of learners that make up a language classroom. In some cases, these activities might produce a temporary bulge in the net, but other activities might produce a greater shift in the shape of the system.

Phase shifts describe a period of high variability, as the system moves from one attractor state to another. For a time, the system might show a 'soft assembly' or combination of incompatible states (for example: high anxiety + high willingness to communicate). Soft assembly might be an especially useful concept for understanding the ambivalence of affect in language learning. Changes such as shifting identity can be thought of in non-linear terms. Sometimes called 'the butterfly effect,' non-linearity means that small changes in initial conditions can have a major impact on the rest of the system. Conversely, a major change in a system might have few longer term effects. DST specifically recognizes that the degree of change in the overall system is not proportional to the change in the input variable(s). For example, a small error in grammar might be catastrophic for a form-focussed, perfectionist learner with high anxiety, bringing his communication to an abrupt halt. That same error might be completely ignored by the same high anxious learner who is focused in a particular moment on meaning rather than form because he is helping a stranger find the airport.

Thinking in terms of dynamic systems highlights the importance of timescales. One of the more powerful ideas in DST is the idea of multiple timescales. In language learning, we can identify several ways of looking at the timing of an event. For example, a specific utterance lasts only a few seconds, a meeting might last a few minutes, a language course might take a few months, language acquisition itself often is measured in years. It is important to understand that all of these time scales are in play at once. Accounting for multiple, interacting timescales allows for a more detailed understanding of the many factors that affect learning, in a highly contextualized way. Language learning is embedded in both a social system and within the individual.

The idea of embedded systems has been influential in theories of human development. Thelen (2000) notes that embedded systems tend to have multiple causes and are self-organizing. There are redundancies built into the learning process: positive attitudes, future goals and an encouraging teacher all pull the learner toward the target language (TL). At the same time, negative redundant processes such as hurtful stereotypes, self-doubt, and anxiety push the same learner away. The trajectory of an individual learner is an emergent pattern, a convergence of several moving parts, including the systems of the physical body (e.g. skeletal–muscular, neurological systems), the social system (native language groups, TL groups), and learning context (relationships with teachers and peers). All of these components interact to give learning its meaning, order and pattern. There is not a master plan or pre-set script for where the learning is going, but neither are these examples of completely random, disconnected factors. As with a game of chess, there is purpose to the activity (see Corning, 2002).

Research is beginning to tackle individual differences from a dynamic perspective. MacIntrye and Legatto (2011) used a dynamic systems approach to examine personality traits, communication-related traits, and dynamic changes during an eight-question second language interview, akin to an oral examination. They reported data for a group of learners, all with different patterns of reactions. For example, one learner was extroverted, low-anxious and highly willing to speak in the TL. She excelled at the language tasks and her WTC was high throughout the interview. A second learner had a problem with vocabulary retrieval (specifically, she could not recall the number 80) but persisted in trying to figure out the missing item long after others faced with a similar issue simply abandoned the task. There was no data available to predict her exceptional degree of dogged persistence. Overall, the study showed that no two patterns were exactly the same for the different learners. Yet all of the patterns made sense from a dynamic systems perspective, and each one led to questions that can be followed up in future research.

So how do we capitalize on individuality in language learning? The various activities that are available in each chapter will help teachers and students get to know each other. As their regular patterns emerge, exceptions to the general rule will become noticeable. If we begin with an openness to the process, encourage variety wherever possible, and carefully observe the results, we can facilitate the learning process on the learner's terms. By looking into the kaleidoscope of people in the classroom, taking note of the patterns that are forming and the forces that cause those patterns to change, teachers and learners each can use the information emerging from emotion, cognition and behavior to understand and influence the ongoing stream of activity in the classroom. We wish you much success!

References

Abraham, R.G. and Vann, R.J. (1987) Strategies of two language learners: A case study. In A. L. Wenden and J. Rubin (eds) *Learner Strategies in Language Learning* (pp. 85–102) Englewood Cliffs, NJ: Prentice-Hall.

Aida, Y. (1994) Examination of Horwitz, Horwitz, and Cope's construct of foreign language anxiety: The case of students of Japanese. *The Modern Language Journal* 78, 155–168.

Anstey, M. (1988) Helping children learn how to learn. *Australian Journal of Reading* 11, 269–277.

Armstrong, T. (1994) *Multiple Intelligences in the Classroom*. Alexandria, VA: Association for Supervision and Curriculum Development.

Armstrong, T. (1999) *Seven Kinds of Smart: Identifying and Developing your Multiple Intelligences*. New York: Penguin Putnam, Inc.

Arnold, J. (1999) *Affect in Language Learning*. Cambridge: Cambridge University Press.

Arnold, J. (2007) Self-concept and the affective domain in language learning. In F. Rubio (ed.) *Self-esteem and Foreign Language Learning* (pp. 13–27). New Castle: Cambridge Scholars Publishing.

Arnold, J. and Fonseca, M.C. (2004) Multiple intelligence theory and foreign language learning: A brain-based perspective. *International Journal of English Studies* 4, 119–136.

Baddeley, A.D. (2000) The episodic buffer: A new component of working memory? *Trends in Cognitive Science* 4, 417–423.

Baddeley, A.D. and Hitch, G. (1974) Working memory. In G. H. Bower (ed.) *Recent advances in learning and motivation* (pp. 47–89). New York: Academic Press.

Bailey, K. (1983) Competitiveness and anxiety in adult second language learning: Looking at and through the diary studies. In W. Welinger and M. Long (eds) *Classroom oriented research in second language acquisition* (pp. 67–102). Rowley, MA: Newbury House.

Bailey, P., Daley, C. and Onweugbuzie, A. (1999) Foreign language anxiety and learning style. *Foreign Language Annals* 32, 63–76.

Bailey, P., Onwuegbuzie, A. and Daley, C. (2000) Correlates of anxiety at three stages of the foreign language learning process. *Journal of Language and Social Psychology* 19, 474–490.

Baker, S. and MacIntyre, P.D. (2000) The role of gender and immersion in communication and second language orientations. *Language Learning* 50, 311–341.

Bandura, A. and Schunk, D. (1981) Cultivating competence, self-efficacy, and intrinsic interest through proximal self-motivation. *Journal of Personality and Social Pathology* 41, 586–598.

Baumgartner, H., Pieters, R. and Bagozzi, R. (2008) Future-oriented emotions: Conceptualization and behavioral effects. *European Journal of Social Psychology* 38, 685–696.

Benson, P. and Lor, W. (1999) Conceptions of language and language learning. *System* 27, 459–472.

Bernat, E. and Gvozdenko, I. (2005) Beliefs about language learning: Current knowledge, pedagogical implications, and new research directions. *Teaching English as a Second or Foreign Language* 9. Retrived from http://www.tesl.ej.org/ej33ia1.pdf. Accessed 21 August 2012.

Bourdieu, P. (1977) The economics of linguistic exchanges. *Social Science Information* 16, 645–668.

Breen, M.P. (1991) Understanding the language teacher. In R. Philipson, E. Kellerman, L. Selinker, M. Sharwood Smith and M. Swain (eds) *Foreign/Second Language Pedagogy Research* (pp. 213–233). Clevedon: Multilingual Matters.

Brown, H.D. (2000) *Principles of Language Learning and Teaching* (4th edn). New York: Longman.

Burroughs, N.F., Marie, V. and McCroskey, J.C. (2003) Relationships of self-perceived communication competence and communication apprehension with willingness to communicate: A comparison with first and second languages in Micronesia. *Communication Research Reports* 20, 230–239.

Campbell, L. (1997) Variations on a theme: How teachers interpret MI theory. *Educational Leadership* 55, 14–19.

Carroll, J.B. (1962) The predition of success in intensive foreign language training. In R. Glaser (ed.) *Training Research and Education* (pp. 87–136). Pittsburgh, PA: University of Pittsburgh Press.

Carroll, J.B. (1973) Implications of aptitude test research and psycholinguistic theory for foreign language teaching. *International Journal of Psycholinguistics* 2, 5–14.

Carroll, J.B. (1981) Twenty-five years of research in foreign language aptitude. In K.C. Diller (ed.) *Individual Differences and Universals in Language Learning Aptitude* (pp. 83–113). Rowley, MA: Newbury House.

Carroll, J.B. and Sapon, S.M. (1959) *Modern Language Aptitude Test (MLAT)*. San Antonio, TX: Psychological Corporation.

Cavanaugh, T. and Cavanaugh, B. (2004) *The Sower's Seeds: One Hundred and Twenty Inspiring Stories for Preaching, Teaching and Public Speaking*. Mahwah, NJ: Paulist Press.

Celce-Murcia, M., Dörnyei, Z. and Thurrell, S. (1995) A pedagogically motivated model with content specifications. *Issues in Applied Linguistics* 6, 5–35.

Chamot, A. (2004) Issues in language learning strategy research and teaching. *Electronic Journal of Foreign Language Teaching*. Retrieved from http://www.e_flt.nus.edu.sg/fv1n12004/chot.pdf

Chamot, A.U. (2005) Language learning strategy instruction: Current issues and research. *Annual Review of Applied Linguistics* 25, 112–130.

Chamot, A.U., Barhardt, S., El-Dinary, P.B. and Robbins, J. (1999) *The Learning Strategies Handbook*. New York: Longman.

Cheng, Y. (2002) Factors associated with foreign language writing anxiety. *Foreign Language Annals* 35, 647–656.

Cheng, M.H. and Banya, K. (1998) Bridging the gap between teaching style and learning styles. In Reid, J. (ed.) *Understanding Learning Styles in the Second Language Classroom*. (pp. 80–85). Upper Saddle River, NJ: Prentice-Hall Regents.

Cheng, Y., Horwitz, E. and Schallert, D. (1999) Language anxiety: Differentiating writing and speaking components. *Language Learning* 49, 417–446.

Christison, M.A. (1996) Teaching and learning through multiple intelligences. *TESOL Journal* 46 (9), 10–14.

Clement, R. and Noels, K. (1992) Toward a situated approach to ethnolinguistic identity: The effects of status on individuals and groups. *Journal of Language and Social Psychology* 11, 203–232.

Clement, R., Baker, S. and Macintyre, P.D. (2003) Willingness to communicate in second languages: The effects of context, norms, and vitality. *Journal of Language and Social Psychology* 22, 190–209.

Cohen, A.D. (1996) *Second Language Learning and Uses Strategies: Clarifying the issues*. Minneapolis, MN: National Language Resource Center, University of Minnesota.

Cohen, A.D. (1998) *Strategies in Learning and Using a Second Language*. London: Longman.

Cohen, A.D. (2003) The learner's side of foreign language learning: Where do styles, strategies and tasks meet? *IRAL* 41, 279–291.

Cohen, A.D. (2007) Coming to terms with language learner strategies: Surveying the experts. In A. Cohen and E. Macaro (eds) *Language Learner Strategies* (pp. 29–46). Oxford: Oxford University Press.

Cohen, A.D. (2009) Focus on the language learner: Styles, strategies and motivation. In R. Schmidt (ed.) *An Introduction to Applied Linguistics* (pp. 161–178). London: Hodder Education.

Cohen, A.D. (2012) Strategies: The Interface of Styles, Strategies, and Motivation on Tasks. In S. Mercer, S. Ryan and M. Williams (eds) *Language Learning Psychology: Research, Theory and Pedagogy* (pp. 136–150). Basingstoke, Hampshire: Palgrave.

Cohen, A.D., Weaver, S.J. and Li, T.Y. (1996) *The Impact of Strategies-Based Instruction on Speaking a Foreign Language*. Minneapolis, MN: National Language Resource Center, University of Minnesota.

Cohen, A.D. and Dörnyei, Z. (2002) Focus on the language learner: Motivation, styles, and strategies. In N. Schmitt (ed.) *An Introduction to Applied Linguistics* (pp. 170–190). London: Arnold.

Cohen, A.D., Oxford, R.L. and Chi, J.C. (2001) *Learning Style Survey*. Retrieved from http://carla.acad.umn.edu/profiles/Cohen-profile.html. Accessed 21 August 2012.

Cook, V.J. (2001) *Second Language Learning and Language Teaching* (3rd edn). London: Edward Arnold.

Corning, P.A. (2002) The re-emergence of 'emergence': A venerable concept in search of a theory. *Complexity* 7, 6, 18–30.

Costigan Lederman, L. (2009) Assessing educational effectiveness: The focus group interview as a technique for data collection. *Communication Education* 39, 117–127.

Cotterall, S. (1995) Readiness for autonomy: Investigating learner beliefs. *System* 23, 195–205.

Cotterall, S. (1999) Key variables in language learning: What do learners believe about them? *System* 27, 493–513.

Covey, S. (2004) *7 Habits of Highly Effective People*. Detroit, MI: Free Press.

de Bot, K., Lowie, W. and Verspoor, M. (2007) A dynamic systems theory approach to second language acquisition. *Bilingualism: Language and Cognition* 10, 7–21.

Dewaele, J. (2002) Psychologoical and sociodemographic correlates of communicative anxiety in L2 and L3 production. *International Journal of Bilingualism* 6, 23–39.

Dewaele, J., Petrides, K. and Furnham, A. (2008) Effects of trait emotional intelligence and sociobiographical variables on communicative anxiety and foreign language anxiety among adult multilinguals: A review and empirical investigation. *Language Learning* 58, 911–960.

Dörnyei, Z. (2001) *Motivational Strategies in the Language Classroom*. Cambridge: Cambridge University Press.

Dörnyei, Z. (2005) *The Psychology of the Language Learner: Individual Differences in Second Language Acquisition*. Mahwah, NJ: Lawrence Erlbaum Associates, Inc.

Dörnyei, Z. and Otto, I. (1998) Motivation in action: A process model of L2 motivation. *Working Papers in Applied Linguistics* 4, 43–69.

Dörnyei, Z. and Skehan, P. (2003) Individual differences in second language learning. In C.J. Doughty and M.H. Long (eds) *The Handbook of Second Language Acquisition* (pp. 589–630). Oxford: Blackwell.

Dörnyei, Z. and Ushioda, E. (eds) (2009) *Motivation, Language Identity and the L2 Self.* Bristol: Multilingual Matters.

Dörnyei, Z. and MacIntyre, P.D. (2013) Motivational dynamics in second language acquisition. Symposium at the American Association of Applied Linguistics, Dallas, TX: March, 2013.

Dweck, C. (1999) *Self-theories: Their Role in Motivation, Personality and Development.* Philadelphia: Psychology Press.

Ehrman, M.E. (1996) *Understanding Second Language Difficulties.* Thousand Oaks, CA: Sage Publication.

Ehrman, M.E. and Oxford, R. L. (1995) Cognition plus: Correlates of language learning success. *Modern Language Journal 79* (1), 67–89.

Ehrman, M.E. and Leaver, B.L. (2003) Cognitive styles in the service of language learning. *System* 31, 391–415.

Ehrman, M.E., Leaver, B.S. and Oxford, R.L. (2003) A brief overview of individual differences in second language learning. *System* 31, 313–330.

Ellis, R. (1994) *The Study of Second Language Acquisition.* Oxford: Oxford University Press.

Ellis, R. (2008) Learner beliefs and language learning. *Asian EFL Journal* 10 (4), 7–25.

Elkhafaifi, H. (2005) Listening comprehension and anxiety in the Arabic language classroom. *The Modern Language Journal* 89, 206–220.

Ely, C.M. (1986) An analysis of discomfort, risktaking, sociability, and motivation in the L2 classroom. *Language Learning* 36, 1–25.

Ely, C. and Pease-Alvarez, L. (eds) (1996) Learning styles and strategies (Special Issue Introduction) *TESOL Journal* 6, 1–5.

Engle, R.W. (2007) Working memory: The mind is richer than the models. In H.L. Roediger, Y. Dudai and S.M. Fitzpatrick (eds) *Science of memory: Concepts* (pp. 159–164). Oxford: Oxford University Press.

Ewald, J.D. (2007) Foreign language learning anxiety in upper-level classes: Involving students as researchers. *Foreign Language Annals* 40, 122–142.

Felder, R.M. and Henriques, E.R. (1995) Learning and teaching styles in foreign and second language education. *Foreign Language Annals* 28, 21–31.

Flavell, J.H. (1979) Metacognition and cognitive monitoring: A new era of cognitive-developmental inquiry. *American Psychologist* 34, 906–911.

Fredrickson, B.L. (2001) The role of positive emotions in positive psychology: The broaden and build theory of positive emotions. *American Psychologist* 56, 218–226.

Fushino, K. (2010) Causal relationships between communication confidence, beliefs about group work, and willingness to communicate in foreign language group work. *TESOL Quarterly* 44, 700–724.

Gardner, H. (1983) *Frames of Mind: The Theory of Multiple Intelligences.* New York: Basic Books.

Gardner, H. (1991) *The Unschooled Mind: How Children Think, and How Schools Should Teach.* New York: Basic Books.

Gardner, H. (1993) *Frames of the Mind: The Theory of Multiple Intelligences 10th Anniversary Edition.* New York: Basic Books.

Gardner, R.C. (1985) *Social Psychology and Second Language Learning: The Role of Attitudes and Motivation.* London: Edward Arnold.

Gardner, R.C. (2010) *Motivation and Second Language Acquisition: The Socio-educational Model.* New York: Peter Lang.

Gardner, R.C. and Lambert, W.E. (1959) Motivational variables in second-language acquisition. *Canadian Journal of Psychology* 13, 266–272.

Gardner, R.C. and Lambert, W.E. (1972) *Attitudes and Motivation in Second Language Learning.* Rowley, MA: Newbury House.

Gardner, R.C. and MacIntyre, P.D. (1993) A student's contributions to second language learning: Part II. Affective variables. *Language Teaching* 26, 1–11.

Gardner, R.C. and Clément, R. (1990) Social psychological perspectives on second language acquisition. In H. Giles and W.P. Robinson (eds) *Handbook of language and social psychology* (pp. 495–517). Chichester: John Wiley and Sons.

Gathercole, S. and Alloway, T. (2008) *Working Memory and Learning: A Practical Guide for teachers.* Los Angeles: Sage Publications.

Gregersen, T.S. (2003) To err is human: A reminder to teachers of language-anxious students. *Foreign Language Annals* 36, 25–32.

Gregersen, T.S. (2005) Non-verbal cues: Clues to the detection of foreign language anxiety. *Foreign Language Annals* 38, 388–397.

Gregersen, T.S. (2006) The despair of disparity: The connection between foreign language anxiety and the recognition of proficiency differences in L2 skills. *Lenguas Modernas* 31, 7–20.

Gregersen, T.S. (2007) Breaking the code of silence: A study of teachers' nonverbal decoding accuracy of foreign language anxiety. *Language Teaching Research* 11, 209–221.

Gregersen, T.S. (2009) Recognizing visual and auditory cues in the detection of foreign-language anxiety. *TESL Canada Journal/Revue TESL Du Canada* 26, 46–64.

Gregersen, T. and Horwitz, E. (2002) Language learning and perfectionism: Anxious and non-anxious language learners' reactions to their own oral performance. *The Modern Language Journal* 86, 562–570.

Gregersen, T., Olivares-Cuhat, G. and Storm, J. (2009) An examination of L1 and L2 gesture use: What role does proficiency play? *The Modern Language Journal* 75, 195–208.

Grenfell, M. and Harris, V. (1999) *Modern Languages and Learning Strategies: In Theory and Practice.* London: Routledge.

Griffiths, C. (2008) Strategies and good language learners. In C. Griffiths (ed.) *Lessons from Good Language Learners* (pp. 83–98). Cambridge: Cambridge University Press.

Griffiths, C. (2012) Learning styles: Traversing the quagmire. In S. Mercer, S. Ryan and M. Williams (eds) *Psychology for Language Learning* (pp. 151–168). New York: Palgrave MacMillan.

Griggs, R.E. (1985) A storm of ideas. *Training* 22, 66.

Gu, Y. (2010) *Advance review: A new book on Teaching and Researching Language Learning Strategies.* Unpublished review, New Zeland: Wellington University.

Gu, P.Y. (2007) Foreword. In A. Cohenand and E. Macaro (eds) *Language Learner Strategies* (pp. vii–viii). Oxford: Oxford University Press.

Haley, M.G. (2004) Learner-centered instruction and the theory of multiple intelligences with second language learners. *Teachers College Record* 1, 163–180.

Horwitz, E.K. (1985) Using student beliefs about language learning and teaching in the foreign language methods course. *Foreign Language Annals* 18, 333–340.

Horwitz, E.K. (1988) The beliefs about language learning of beginning university foreign language students. *The Modern Language Journal* 72, 283–294.

Horwitz, E. (1996) Even teachers get the blues: Recognizing and alleviating language teachers' feelings of foreign language anxiety. *Foreign Language Annals* 29, 365–372.

Horwitz, E. (1997a) Some suggestions for decreasing foreign language anxiety: Part II. *Forum* 8, 48–53.

Horwitz, E.K. (1997b) Student beliefs about language learning and the implementation of instructional change, *Forum* 9, 41–46.

Horwitz, E.K. (1999) Cultural and situational influences on foreign language learners' beliefs about language learning: A review of BALLI studies. *System* 27, 557–576.

Horwitz, E. (2001) Language anxiety and achievement. *Annual Review of Applied Linguistics* 21, 112–126.

Horwitz, E. (2010) Foreign and second language anxiety. *Language Teaching* 43, 154–167.

Horwitz, E., Horwitz, M. and Cope, J. (1986) Foreign language classroom anxiety. *The Modern Language Journal* 70, 125–132.

Hosenfeld, C. (1978) Learning about learning: Discovering our students' strategies. *Foreign Language Annals* 9, 117–129.

Howe, M.L. and Lewis, M.D. (2005) The importance of dynamic systems approaches for understanding development. *Developmental Review* 25, 247–251. doi:10.1016/j. dr.2005.09.002.

Hummel, K.M. (2002) Second language acquisition and working memory. In F. Fabbro (ed.) *Advances in the Neurolinguistics of Bilingualism* (pp. 95–117). Udine, Italy: Forum.

Hummel, K.M. and French, L.M. (2010) Phonological memory and implications for the second language classroom. *Canadian Modern Language Review* 66, 371–391.

James, W.B. and Gardner, D.L. (1995) Learning styles: Implications for distance learning. *New Directions for Adult and Continuing Education* 67, 19–32.

Juffs, A. and Harrington, M. (2011) Aspects of working memory in L2 learning. *Language Teaching* 44, 137–166.

Julkunen, K. (2001) Situation- and task-specific motivation in foreign language learning. In Z. Dörnyei and R. Schmidt (eds) *Motivation and Second Language Acquisition* (pp. 29–42). Honolulu: University of Hawaii Press.

Kang, C. (2000) Nonverbal communication skills in the EFL curriculum. *The Korea TESOL Journal* 3, 13–28.

Kang, S. (2005) Dynamic emergence of situational willingness to communicate in a second language. *System* 33, 277–292.

Kanno, Y. and Norton, B. (2003) Imagined communities and educational possibilities: Introduction. *Journal of Language, Identity, and Education* 2, 241–249.

Kennedy, J. (1996) The role of teacher beliefs and attitudes in teacher behavior. In G.T. Sachs, M. Brock and R. Lo (eds) *Directions in Second Language Teacher Education* (pp. 107–122). Hong Kong: City University of Hong Kong.

Kern, R. (1995) Students' and teachers' beliefs about language learning. *Foreign Language Annals* 28, 71–92.

Kim, S. (2009) Questioning the stability of foreign language classroom anxiety and motivation across different classroom contexts. *Foreign Language Annals* 42, 138–157.

Knapp, M. and Hall, J. (2010) *Nonverbal Communication in Human Interaction* (7th edn). Boston, MA: Wadsworth Cengage Learning.

Koch, A.S. and Terrell, T.D. (1991) Affective reaction and foreign language students to natural approach activities and teaching techniques. In E.K. Horwitz and D.J. Young (eds) *Language Anxiety: From Theory and Research to Classroom Implications* (pp. 109–126). Englewood Cliffs, NJ: Prentice Hall.

Kubanyiova, M. (2009) Possible selves in language teacher development. In Z. Dörnyei and E. Ushioda (eds) *Motivation, Language Identity and the L2 Self.* (pp. 144–163). Bristol: Multilingual Matters.

Kuhl, J. (1994) A theory of action and state orientations. In J. Kuhl and J. Beckmann (eds) *Volition and Personality* (pp. 9–46). Gottingen, Germany: Hogrefe and Huber Publishers.

Kukulska-Hulme, A. and Bull, S. (2009) Theory-based support for mobile language learning: Noticing and recording. *iJIM* 3, 2, 12–18.

Lamb, M. (2004) Integrative motivation in a globalizing world. *System* 32, 3–19.

Lantolf, J. and Pavlenko, A. (2001) Second language activity theory: Understanding second language learners as people. In M. Breed (ed.) *Learner Contributions to Language Learning: New Directions in Research.* (pp. 141–158) London: Longman.

Lewin, K. (1951) *Field Theory in the Social Sciences: Selected Theoretical Papers*. New York: Harper.

Lewis, M. (1993) *The Lexical Approach: The State of ELT a New Way Forward*. Boston: Thompson Publishing.

Lightbown, P.M. and Spada, N. (2006) *How Languages Are Learned*. Oxford: Oxford University Press.

Liu, M. and Jackson, J. (2008) An exploration of Chinese EFL learners' unwillingness to communicate and foreign language anxiety. *The Modern Language Journal* 92, 71–86.

Macaro, E. (2001) *Learning Strategies in Foreign and Second Language Classrooms*. London: Continuum.

Macaro, E. (2006) Strategies for language learning and for language use: Revising the theoretical framework. *The Modern Language Journal* 90, 320–337.

Macaro, E. and Cohen, A. (2007) Introduction. In A. Cohen and E. Macaro (eds) *Language Learner Strategies* (pp. 1–5). Oxford: Oxford University Press.

MacIntyre, P.D. (2007) Willingness to communicate in the second language: Understanding the decision to speak as a volitional process. *The Modern Language Journal* 91, 4, 564–576.

MacIntyre, P.D. (2012) Currents and waves: Examining willingness to communicate on multiple timescales. *Contact: Research Symposium Special Issue* 38, 2, 12–22.

MacIntyre, P.D. and Gardner, R. (1989) Anxiety and second-language learning: Toward a theoretical clarification. *Language Learning* 39, 251–275.

MacIntyre, P.D. and Gardner, R. (1991a) Investigating language class anxiety using the focused essay technique. *The Modern Language Journal* 75, 296–304.

MacIntyre, P.D. and Gardner, R. (1991b) Language anxiety: Its relationship to other anxieties and to processing in native and second languages. *Language Learning* 41, 513–534.

MacIntyre, P.D. and Gardner, R.C. (1991c) Methods and results in the study of anxiety in language learning: A review of the literature. *Language Learning* 41, 85–117.

MacIntyre, P.D. and Gardner, R. (1994) The subtle effects of languae anxiety on cognitive processing in the second language. *Language Learning* 44, 283–305.

MacIntyre, P.D. and Doucette, J. (2010) Willingness to communicate and action control. *System* 38, 161–171.

MacIntyre, P.D. and Legatto, J. (2011) A synamic system approach to willingness to communicate: Developing an idiodynamic method to capture rapidly changing affect. *Applied Linguistics* 32, 149–171.

MacIntyre, P.D. and Gregersen, T. (2012a) The Positive-broadening emotional power of the imagination in language learning. *Studies of Second Language Learning and Teaching* 2, 193–213.

MacIntyre, P.D. and Gregersen, T. (2012b) Affective responses to language learning. In S. Mercer, S. Ryan and M. Williams (eds) *Language Learning Psychology: Research, Theory and Pedagogy* (pp. 103–118). Basingstoke, Hampshire: Palgrave.

MacIntyre, P.D., Noels, K.A. and Clément, R. (1997) Biases in self-rating of second language proficiency: The role of language anxiety. *Language Learning* 47, 265–287.

MacIntyre, P.D., Clément, R., Dörnyei, Z. and Noels, K.A. (1998) Conceptualizing willingness to communicate in a L2: A situational model of L2 confidence and affiliation. *The Modern Language Journal* 82, 545–562.

MacIntyre, P.D., Baker, S. C., Clement, R. and Conrod, S. (2001) Willingness to communicate, social support, and language-learning orientations of immersion students. *Studies in Second Language Acquisition* 23, 369–388.

MacIntyre, P.D., MacKinnon, S. and Clement, R. (2009) Toward the development of a scale to assess possible selves as a source of language learning. In Z. Dörnyei and E.

Ushioda (eds) *Motivation, Language Identity and the L2 Self* (pp. 193–163). Bristol: Multilingual Matters.

MacIntyre, P.D., Burns, C. and Jessome, A. (2011) A dynamic system for approach to willingness to communicate: Developing an idiodynamic method to capture rapidly changing affect. *Applied Linguistics* 32, 149–171.

Mantle-Bromley, C. (1995) Positive attitudes and realistic beliefs: Links to proficiency. *The Modern Language Journal* 79, 372–386.

Markus, H. and Nurius, P. (1986) Possible selves. *American Psychologist* 41, 954–969.

Markus, H. and Ruvolo, A. (1989) Possible selves: Personalized representations of goals. In L.A. Pervin (ed.) *Goal Concepts in Personality and Social Psychology* (pp. 211–241). Hillsdale, NJ: Lawrence Erlbaum Associates.

McCroskey, J.C. and Richmond, V.P. (1991) Willingness to communicate: A cognitive view. In M. Booth-Butterfield (ed.) *Communication, Cognition and Anxiety* (pp. 19–37). Newbury Park, CA: Sage.

McDonough, S. (1999) Learner strategies. *Language Teaching Research* 32, 1–18.

Mori, Y. (1999) Epistemological beliefs and language learning beliefs: What do language learners believe about their learning? *Language Learning* 49, 377–415.

Murphey, T. (2001) Reported belief changes through near peer role modeling. *TESL-EJ Teaching English as a Second or Foreign Language* 5, 3.

Nation, P. (1989) Improving speaking fluency. *System* 17, 377–384.

Nel, C. (2008) Learning style and good language learners. In C. Griffiths (ed.) *Lessons from Good Language Learners* (pp. 49–60). Cambridge: Cambridge University Press.

Newell, G.E. (1996) Reader-based and teacher-centered tasks: Writing and learning about a short story in middle-track classrooms. *Journal of Literacy Research* 28, 147–172.

Norton, B. (1995) Social identity, investment, and language learning. *TESOL Quarterly* 29, 9–31.

Norton, B. (1997) Language, identity, and the ownership of English. *TESOL Quarterly* 31, 409–429.

Norton, B. (2001) Non-participation, imagined communities and the language classroom. In M. Breen (ed.) *Learner Contributions to Language Learning: New Directions in Research Applied Linguistics and Language Study* (pp. 159–171). Glenview, IL: Pearson Education.

Norton, B. (2010) Language and identity. In N. Hornberger and S. McKay (eds) *Sociolinguistics and Language Education* (pp. 349–369). Bristol: Multilingual Matters.

Norton, B. and Toohey, K. (2001) Changing perspectives on good language learners. *TESOL Quarterly* 35, 307–322.

Oh, J. (1992) The effects of L2 reading assessment methods on anxiety level. *TESOL Quarterly* 26, 172–176.

O'Malley, J.M. and Chamot, A.U (1990) *Learning Strategies in Second Language Acquisition.* NY: Cambridge University Press.

O'Malley, J.M. and Chamot, A.U. (1994) Learning strategies in second language learning. In *The International Encyclopedia of Education* (vol. 6, pp. 3329–3335) Oxford: Pergamon Press.

Omaggio, A.C. (1978) Successful language learners: What do we know about them? *ERIC/CLL News Bulletin* May, 2–3.

Onwuegbuzie, A., Bailey, P. and Daley, C. (2000) The validation in three scales measuring anxiety at different stages of the foreign language learning process: The input anxiety scale, the processing anxiety scale, and the output anxiety scale. *Language Learning* 50, 87–117.

Oxford, R. (1990a) *Language Learning Strategies: What Every Teacher Should Know.* Boston, MA: Heinle and Heinle Publishers.

Oxford, R. (1990b) Styles, strategies, and aptitude: Connections for language learning. In T.S. Parry and C.W. Stansfield (eds) *Language Aptitude Reconsidered* (pp. 67–125). Englewood Cliffs, NJ: Prentice Hall.

Oxford, R. (1999) Style wars as a source of anxiety in language classrooms. In D.J. Young (ed.) *Affect in Second Language Learning: A Practical Guide to Dealing with Learning Anxiety* (pp. 216–237). Boston: McGraw-Hill.

Oxford, R.L. (2003) Language learning styles and strategies: An overview. *Gala,* 1–25.

Oxford, R. (2012) *Teaching and Researching Language Learning Strategies.* Harlow: Longman.

Oxford, R. and Anderson, J.J. (1995) A crosscultural view of learning styles. *Language Teaching* 28, 201–215.

Oxford, R. and Schramm, K. (2007) Bridging the gap between psychological and socio-cultural perspectives on L2 learner strategies. In A. Cohenand and E. Macaro (eds) *Language Learner Strategies* (pp. 47–68). Oxford: Oxford University Press.

Pavlenko, A. (2001) 'In the world of the tradition I was unimagined': Negotiation of identities in cross-cultural autobiographies. *The International Journal of Bilingualism* 5, 317–344.

Pavlenko, A. and Norton, B. (2007) Imagined communities, identity, and English language learning. In J. Cummins and C. Davison (eds) *International Handbook of English* (pp. 669–680). NY: Springer.

Peacock, M. (2001a) Pre-service ESL teachers' beliefs about second language learning: A longitudinal study. *System* 29, 177–195.

Peacock, M. (2001b) Match or mismatch? Learning styles and teaching styles in EFL. *International Journal of Applied Linguistics* 11, 1–20.

Peyton, J.K. (2000) Dialogue journals: Interactive writing to develop language and literacy. Eric Q and A National Center for ESL Literacy Education. ERIC #ED450614.

Phillips, E.M. (1992) The effects of language anxiety on students' oral test performance and attitudes. *The Modern Language Journal* 76, 14–26.

Price, M. (1991) The subjective experience of foreign language anxiety: Interviews with highly anxious students. In E.K. Horwitz and D.J. Young (eds) *Language Anxiety: From Theory and Research to Classroom Implications* (pp. 101–108). Englewood Cliffs, NJ: Prentice Hall.

Rai, M., Loschky, L., Harris, R., Peck, N. and Cook, L. (2010) Effects of stress and working memory capacity on foreign language readers' inferential processing during comprehension. *Language Learning* 61, 1–32.

Ranta, L. (2008) Aptitude and good language learners. In C. Griffiths (ed.) *Lessons from Good Language Learners* (pp. 142–155). Cambridge: Cambridge University Press.

Reasoner, R. (1982) *Building Self-esteem in Secondary Schools.* Palo Alto, CA: Consulting Psychologists Press, Inc.

Reeve, J. (2005) *Understanding Motivation and Emotion* (5th edn). Toronto, Canada: JohnWiley and Sons.

Reid, J. (1987) The learning style preferences of ESL students. *TESOL Quarterly* 21, 87–111.

Reid, J. (ed.) (1998) *Understanding Learning Styles in the Second Language Classroom.* Upper Saddle River, NJ: Prentice-Hall Regents.

Reid, D.K. and Hresko, W.P. (1982) *Metacognition and Learning Disabilities: Topics in Learning and Learning Disabilities* 2, 1. Bethesda, Maryland: Aspen Systems Corporation.

Riding, R. (2000) Cognitive style: A review. In R. Riding and S.G. Rayner (eds) *Interpersonal Perspectives on Individual Differences* (vol. 1, Cognitive styles, pp. 315–344). Stamford, CT: Ablex.

Riding, R. and Rayner, S.G. (1998) *Cognitive Styles and Learning Strategies: Understanding Style Differences in Language and Behavior.* London: David Fulton.

Riley, P. (1980) Mud and stars: Personal constructs sensitization and learning. (ERIC Document Reproduction Service, No. ED 20198).

Rivers, W. (1981) *Teaching Foreign Language Skills.* Chicago: The University of Chicago Press.

Robinson, P. (2001) Individual differences, cognitive abilities, aptitude complexes and learning conditions in second language acquisition. *Second Language Research* 17, 368–392.

Robinson, P. (2002) Learning conditions, aptitude complexes and SLA: A framework for research and pedagogy. In P. Robinson (ed.) *Individual Differences and Instructed Language Learning* (pp. 113–133). Amsterdam: John Benjamins.

Robinson, P. (2005) Aptitude and second language acquisition. *Annual Review of Applied Linguistics* 25, 46–73.

Robinson, P. (2007) Aptitudes, abilities, contexts, and practice. In R.M. DeKeyser (ed.) *Practice in a Second Language: Perspectives from applied linguistics and cognitive psychology* (pp. 256–286). Cambridge: Cambridge University Press.

Rubin, J. (1975) What the 'good language learner' can teach us. *TESOL Quarterly 9*, 41–51.

Rubin, J., Chamot, A., Harris, V. and Anderson, N. (2007) Intervening in the use of strategies. In A. Cohen and E. Macaro (eds) *Language Learner Strategies* (pp. 47–68). Oxford: Oxford University Press.

Saito, Y., Garza, T. and Horwitz, E. (1999) Foreign language reading anxiety. *The Modern Language Journal* 83, 202–218.

Scarcella, R.C. and Oxford, R.L. (1992) *The Tapestry of Language Learning: The Individual in the Communicative Classroom*. Boston, MA: Heinle and Heinle.

Schlenker, B.R. and Leary, M.R. (1982) Social anxiety. In L. Wheeler (ed.) *Review of Personality and Social Psychology* (pp. 641–669). Beverly Hills, CA: Sage Publication.

Schumann, J.H. (1976) Social distance as a factor in second language acquisition. *Language Learning* 26, 135–143.

Seligman, M. (2006) *Learned Optimism: How To Change Your Mind And Your Life*. NY: Simon and Schuster.

Selinker, L. (1972) Interlanguage. *International Review of Applied Linguistics* 10, 209–231.

Sellers, V. (2000) Anxiety and reading comprehension in Spanish as a foreign language. *Foreign Language Annals* 33, 512–520.

Sharkey, J., Shi, L., Thompson, B. and Norton, B. (2003) Dialogues around 'social identity, investment, and language learning,' by Bonny Norton Peirce (1995) In J. Sharkey and K. Johnson (eds) *Dialogues: Rethinking Issues of Language, Culture, and Power* (pp. 55–74). Alexandria, VA: Teaching English to Speakers of Other Languages, Inc.

Singelis, T. (1994) Nonverbal communication in intercultural interactions. In R. Brislin and T. Yoshida (eds) *Improving Intercultural Interactions* (pp. 268–294) Thousand Oaks, CA: Sage Publications, Inc.

Skehan, P. (1991) Individual differences in second language learning. *Studies in Second Language Acquisition* 13, 275–298.

Skehan, P. (1998) *A Cognitive Approach to Language Learning*. Oxford: Oxford University Press.

Skehan, P. (2002) Theorising and updating aptitude. In P. Robingson (ed.) *Individual Differences and Instructed Language Learning* (pp. 69–93). Amsterdam: John Benjamins.

Smith, L.H. and Renzulli, J.S. (1984) Learning style preferences: A practical approach for classroom teachers. *Theory into Practice* 23, 44–50.

Steinberg, F.S. and Horwitz, E.K. (1986) The effect of induced anxiety on the denotative and interpretative content of second language speech. *TESOL Quarterly* 20, 131–136.

Stevick, E.W. (1980) *Teaching Languages: A Way and Ways*. Rowley, MA: Newbury House.

Sukui, K. and Gaies, S.J. (1999) Investigating Japanese learners' beliefs about language learning. *System* 27, 473–492.

Sunderman, G. and Kroll, J.F. (2009) When study abroad fails to deliver: The internal resources threshold effect. *Applied Psycholinguistics* 30, 79–99.

Thelen, E. (2000) Grounded in the world: developmental origins of the embodied mind. *Infancy* 1, 3–28. doi:10.1207/S15327078IN0101_02.

Tight, D.G. (2010) Perceptual learning style matching and L2 vocabulary acquisition. *Language Learning* 60, 792–833.

Tudor, I. (1996) *Learner Centredness as Language Education*. Cambridge: Cambridge University Press.

Tyacke, M. (1998) Learning style diversity and the reading class: Curriculum design and assessment. In J. Reid (ed.) *Understanding Learning Styles in the Second Language Classroom*. Upper Saddle River, NJ: Prentice-Hall Regents.

Victori, M. and Lockhart, W. (1995) Enhancing metacognition in self-directed language learning. *System* 23, 223–234.

Vogely, A.J. (1998) Listening comprehension anxiety: Students' reported sources and solutions. *Foreign Language Annals* 31, 67–80.

Vygotsky, L. S. (1962) *Language and Thought*. Cambridge, MA: Massachusetts Institute of Technology Press.

Wallace, C. (2003) *Critical Reading in Language education*. Basingstoke: Palgrave Macmillan.

Weiner, B. (1976) Attribution theory, achievement motivation and the education process. *Review of Educational Research* 42, 201–215.

Weinstein, C.E., Husman, J. and Dierkind, D.R. (2000) Self-regulation interventions with a focus on learning strategies. In M. Boekaerts, P.R. Pintrich and M. Zeidner (eds) *Handbook of Self-regulation* (pp. 727–747). San Diego, CA: Academic Press.

Wen, Z. and Skehan, P. (2011) A new perspective on foreign language aptitude research: Building and supporting a case for 'working memory as language aptitude'. *Ilha Do Desterro: A Journal of English Language, Literature and Cultural Studies* 60, 15–44.

Wenden, A. (1986) What do second language learners know about their language learning? A second look at retrospective accounts. *Applied Linguistics* 7 (2), 186–205.

Wenden, A. (1999) An introduction to metacognitive knowledge and beliefs in language learning: Beyond the basics. *System* 27, 435–441.

White, C. (1999) Expectations and emergent beliefs of self-instructed language learners. *System* 27, 443–457.

Willis, P. (2003) Foot soldiers of modernity: The dialectics of cultural consumption and the 21st-century school. *Harvard Educational Review* 73, 390–415.

Wolpe, J. (1958) *Psychotherapy by Reciprical Inhibition*. Stanford, CA: Stanford University Press.

Yang, N. (1999) The relationship between EFL learners' beliefs and learning strategy use. *System* 27, 515–535.

Yang, J. and Horwitz, E. (2008) Learners' perceptions on how anxiety interacts with personal and instructional factors to influence their achievement in English: A qualitative analysis of EFL learners in China. *Language Learning* 58, 151–183.

Yashima, T., Zenuk-Nishide, L. and Shimizu, K. (2004) The influence of attitudes and affect on willingness to communicate and second language communication. *Language Learning* 54, 119–152.

Yashima, T. (2009) International Posture and the Ideal L2 Self in the Japanese EFL Context. In Z. Dörnyei and E. Ushioda (eds) *Motivation, Language Identity and the L2 Self* (pp. 144–163). Bristol: Multilingual Matters.

Yashima, T. (2012) Willingness to communicate: Momentary volition that results in L2 behavior. In S. Mercer, S. Ryanand and M. Williams (eds) *Language Learning Psychology: Research, Theory and Pedagogy* (pp. 119–135). Basingstoke, Hampshire: Palgrave.

Young, D.J. (1991) Creating a low-anxiety classroom environment: What does language anxiety research suggest? *The Modern Language Journal* 75, 426–439.

Young, D. (1992) Language anxiety from the foreign language specialist's perspective: Interviews with Krashen, Omaggio, Hadley, Terrell, and Rardin. *Foreign Language Annals* 25, 157–172.

Young, T. (2010) How valid and useful is the notion of learning style? A multicultural investigation. *Procedia Social and Behavioral Sciences* 2, 427–433.

Index

visualization, xviii, xx–xxii, 16–17, 73, 79,
117. *see also* working memory (WM)
    activities, 16–17, 91, 96, 138–39,
    140–43, 159–160
Voicethread, xx–xxii, 231
    activity modifications, 45, 48, 84, 168
Vygotsky, Lev, 86, 155

wikis, xviii–xx
    activity modifications, 24, 51, 85, 94,
    224, 229, 237
willingness to communicate (WTC),
    xii–xiii, 211–223
    activities, 223–239
    definition, 212
    factors affecting, 212–15, 219–222
    and learner awareness, 221
    and learner confidence, 215, 220
    and motivation, 213–14
    significance of, 215–16

and social milieu of classroom, 213–15,
217–220
working memory (WM), 71–74. *see also*
    SRVS Working Memory Enhance-
    ment
    action plan for, 72–74
    activities, 79–80, 88–97
    and aptitude, 73
    avoiding overload, 73
    and contingent speech, 69
    definition, 71
    preconditions for, 65–66
    significance of, 72
writing skills, 9

YouTube, xx–xxii
    activity modifications, 44, 57, 58, 92,
    94, 102, 124, 138, 139

Zone of Proximal Development (ZPD),
86–88